**Front cover:**
*Great Mosque, Domes, 1400, Bayezid I, Bursa.*

**TURKEY**    **Museum With No Frontiers International Exhibition Cycle**

ISLAMIC ART IN THE MEDITERRANEAN

# EARLY OTTOMAN ART
## THE LEGACY OF THE EMIRATES

**MUSEUM
WITH NO**    **TURKEY**
**FRONTIERS**    **WESTERN ANATOLIA AND THRACE**

**EUROPEAN UNION**
Euromed Heritage
Programme

The realisation of the Museum With No Frontiers Exhibition "EARLY OTTOMAN ART: The Legacy of the Emirates" has been inaugurated as an activity of the celebration of the 700th anniversary of the Foundation of the Ottoman State and has been co-financed by the European Union within the framework of the MEDA-Euromed Heritage Programme and received the support of the following Turkish and international institutions:

Ministry of Culture,
Republic of Turkey, İstanbul

Ministry of Culture, Republic of Turkey, İstanbul

Ege University, İzmir

Ege University, İzmir

Celebration Committee for the 700th anniversary of the Foundation of the Ottoman State

Spanish Ministry of Education, Culture and Sports which has financed the scientific co-ordination of the international cycles "Islamic Art in the Mediterranean" and has contributed in the scientific process of different exhibitions, in collaboration with:

© 2002 Ege University, İzmir & Museum With No Frontiers, Vienna, Austria (Texts and illustrations).

© 2002 Electa (Grupo Editorial Random House Mondadori, S.L.) & Museum With No Frontiers, Vienna, Austria.

© 2002 Archaeology and Art Publications, İstanbul, Turkey

ISBN: 1-874044-45-7
ISBN: 975-6899-68-9 (Turkey)
D.L.: B-29087-02

Federal Ministry of Foreign Affairs, Austria Ministry of Cultural and Environmental Heritage (National Museum for Oriental Arts, Rome), Italy Secretary of State for Tourism, Portugal Museum of Mediterranean and Near-Eastern Antiquities, Stockholm, Sweden

Information
www.mwnf.org

**Local contact**
Sınırlar Ötesi Müze
Ege Üniversitesi Edebiyat Fakültesi
Sanat Tarihi Bolümü
Bornova -İzmir
Tel: +90 532 4254896
(Mehmet Kahyaoğlu, PM)
Fax: + 90 232 3881102,
+90.232.4632804
msfturk@bornova.ege.edu.tr

**International Secretariat**
Museo Sin Fronteras
Barquillo 15 B - 4º G
28004 Madrid
Tel: + 34 91 5312824
Fax: + 34 91 5235775
msf.madrid@teleline.es

**Idea and overall concept of Museum With No Frontiers Programme**
*Eva Schubert*

**Head of the project**
Prof. Dr. Gönül Öney
*EGE University, Izmir*

**Scientific Committee**
Lale Bulut, Ege University, İzmir
Şakir Çakmak, Ege University, İzmir
Ertan Daş, Ege University, İzmir
Aydoğan Demir, Ege University, İzmir
Yekta Demiralp, Ege University, İzmir
İnci Kuyulu, Ege University, İzmir
Gönül Öney, Ege University, İzmir
Rahmi H. Ünal, Ege University, İzmir

**Catalogue**

*Introductions*
Gönül Öney
Aydoğan Demir

*Presentation of itineraries*
Scientific Committee

*Scientific Editors*
Gönül Öney
Rahmi H. Ünal

*Revision of the Itineraries*
Inci Türkoglu

*Technical Advisor*
Pier Paolo Racioppi

*Technical Editing*
Mehmet Kahyaoğlu
Yavuz Tuna

*Photographs*
Ertan Daş, İzmir
Österreichische Nationalbibliothek, Vienna
İş Bank Collection, İstanbul
Library of Topkapı Palace, İstanbul

*General map*
Yekta Demiralp, İzmir

*Monuments plans and Sketches*
Şakir Çakmak, İzmir
Yekta Demiralp, İzmir

*General introduction*
*"Islamic Art in the Mediterranean"*

*Text*
Jamila Binous, Tunis
Mahmoud Hawari, East Jerusalem
Manuela Marín, Madrid
Gönül Öney, İzmir

*Maps*
Şakir Çakmak, İzmir
Ertan Daş, İzmir
Yekta Demiralp, İzmir

*Translation*
Sarah Walker, Madrid

*Copy editors*
Mandi Gomez, London
Sarah Walker, Madrid

*Lay-out and design*
Agustina Fernández, Madrid

*Production*
Electa (Grupo Editorial Random House Mondadori, S. L.), Madrid

**Technical co-ordination**

*Production Managers*
Mehmet Kahyaoğlu, İzmir
Yavuz Tuna, İzmir

**International co-ordination**
of the exhibition cycle "Islamic Art in the Mediterranean"

*General co-ordination*
Eva Schubert, Vienna-Madrid-Rome

*Scientific committees, translations, editing and catalogue production*
Sakina Missoum, Madrid

# Acknowledgements

We thank the following institutions and people for their support in our project:

Republic of Turkey, Ministry of Culture
Republic of Turkey, Prime Ministry General Directorate of the Foundations
Republic of Turkey, Prime Ministry Department of Religious Affairs
Republic of Turkey, Prime Ministry Promotion Fund Celebration Committee for the 700th Anniversary of the Foundation of the Ottoman State
Austrian Culture Office, İstanbul
Topkapı Palace Museum Directorate, İstanbul
Türkiye İş Bankası, İstanbul
Österreichisches National Bibliothek, Vienna
Kıymet Giray
Üstün Erek

## Photographic references

See page 5, as well as
Österreichesches National Bibliothek, Vienna (pages 84, 156, 159, 178, 190, 205 & 206)
Library of Topkapı Palace, İstanbul (page 40, 41, 42, 153, 157, 158, 177, 228 & 230)

*General introduction "Islamic Art in the Mediterranean"*
Ann & Peter Jousiffe, London, page 20 (Aleppo)
Archives of Oronoz Photographs, Madrid, page 23 (Alhambra, Granada)

## Plan references

Ayverdi, E. H. (İstanbul, 1989), page 53 (Bedesten, Edirne), page 54 (Issız Han, Ulubat)

Çakmak, Ş. (İzmir, 1999), page 43 (Decoration on portal of Great Mosque, Bursa), page 68 (Decoration on portal of Yeşil Mosque, İznik), page 135 (Decoration on portal of Yeşil Mosque, Bursa)
Daş, E. (İzmir, 1998), page 52 (Saadet Hatun Hamamı, Selçuk)
Demiralp, Y. (Ankara, 1999), page 147 (Decoration on the *iwan* facade of Muradiye Madrasa, Bursa), page 50 (Yıldırım Madrasa, Bursa)
Demiriz, Y. (İstanbul, 1979), page 165 (Nilüfer Hatun İmaret, İznik)
Durukan, A. (Ankara, 1988), page 44 (İlyas Bey Mosque, Balat)
Emir, S. (İzmir, 1994), page 184 (Postinpuş Baba Zawiya, Yenişehir)
Sönmez, Z. (Ankara, 1995), page 45 (Eski Mosque, Edirne), page 47 (İsa Bey Mosque, Selçuk), page 48 (Firuz Bey Mosque, Milas), page 49 (Üç Şerefeli Mosque, Edirne), page 51 (Yeşil Türbe, Bursa), page 119 (Great Mosque, Manisa), page 136 (Yeşil Mosque, Bursa)
Ünal, R. H., page 46 (Great Mosque, Birgi), page 105 (Aydınoğlu Mehmed Bey Türbesi, Birgi)

*General introduction "Islamic Art in the Mediterranean"*
Ettinghaussen, R. and Grabar, O. (Madrid, I, 1997), page 26 (Damascus Mosque) and page 30 (Qasr al-Khayr al-Sharqi)
Blair, S. S. and Bloom, J. M. (Madrid, II, 1999), Page 29 (Sultan Hassan Madrasa)
Kuran, A. (İstanbul, 1986), page 31 (Sultan Khan Aksaray)
Sönmez, Z. (Ankara, 1995), page 27 (Mosques of Divriği & İstanbul) and page 28 (Mosque of Sivas)
Viguera, S. (Madrid), page 28 (Minaret types)

The opinions expressed in this work do not necessarily reflect the opinion either of the European Union or of its Member States.

# Preface

Great art exhibitions represent far-reaching scientific and cultural events which over the years have turned Art, in all its forms and manifestations, into an essential element in the creation of the image of a country. In this way, cultural events have come to be the privileged stage of important civic accomplishments and large companies invest in art in order to give their products a better position in the global market place.

The objective of the Museum With No Frontiers program and of its exhibition cycle "Islamic Art in the Mediterranean" is to gain the active participation of the Mediterranean countries in this process of political and economic enhancement of their cultural heritage.

This program, based on a new exhibition format where the works of art remain in place to be exhibited in their true context, combines research on specific topics with raising awareness about artistic heritage and aims to promote investment in the fields of restoration and preservation.

The Museum With No Frontiers Exhibition has been conceived around a special theme and for a particular geographic area (the space of the exhibition) and is organised along specific itineraries (exhibition sites) each one dealing with a particular aspect of the general theme. The visitor no longer moves within an enclosed space, but travels to find the artistic objects, monuments, archaeological sites, urban centres, landscapes and places that have been the theatre of transcendental historical events. The visitor follows an exhibition guide and signposting system created by the Museum With No Frontiers to facilitate the identification of the works displayed.

The financial support of the European Union, under the auspices of the MEDA-Euromed Heritage Programme (the regional program supporting the enhancement of Euro-Mediterranean cultural heritage), has made possible the creation of the exhibition cycle "Islamic Art in the Mediterranean" and the exhibitions carried out in Algeria, Palestine, Egypt, Israel, Jordan, Morocco, Tunisia and Turkey; Spain, Italy and Portugal, providing their own finance for the project, have joined the effort. Other European Union Community finance authorised through the Community's policies covering tourism, heritage (RAPHAEL program) and inter-regional co-operation (a pilot project involving the co-operation of Spain, Portugal and Morocco) has enabled specific activities to be carried out at different stages of the project.

On behalf of the Museum With No Frontiers, I would like to express my sincerest gratitude to those who, personally or as representatives of numerous institutions support our organisation and this project, and have participated in the creation of this museum with no frontiers on Islamic Art in the Mediterranean.

Eva Schubert
*President*
*Museum With No Frontier*

## Some preliminary words

**EARLY OTTOMAN ART: The legacy of the Emirates** Exhibition has been realised by the joint work of the European Commission, Republic of Turkey Ministry of Culture and Ege University. For Turkey, this is the first time this kind of a work has been realised. We believe that similar exhibitions covering different periods will be very helpful for the presentation of a common Mediterranean heritage.

I hereby take the opportunity to thank members of the Scientific Committee, Production Managers, our Rector Prof Dr. Refet Saygılı, who has provided us with the help and facilities of the University, and Mr. İstemihan Talay, Minister of Culture of the Republic of Turkey who has supported us in many ways.

I would like to thank the head of the Celebration Committee of the 700th anniversary of the foundation of the Ottoman State, Mr. Fikret Ünlü, Minister of State of the Republic of Turkey and Mrs. Füsun Koroğlu, the assistant under-secretary for the Prime Ministry of the Republic of Turkey.

I would also like to thank the following people who have helped us overcome all kinds of difficulties: Mr. Fikret Üçcan, under-secretary of the Ministry of Culture, Mr. Tekin Aybaş the ex-undersecretary of the Ministry of Culture, Mr. Alpay Pasinli General Director of Monuments and Antiquities, Mr. Kenan Yurttagül Acting General Director of Monuments and Antiquities, and the Ministry of Culture, Mrs. Nilüfer Ertan Director of the Cultural Activities Department in the Ministry of Culture.

The extraordinary efforts of Eva Schubert have been key to overcoming the problems we encountered and for the final realisation of the exhibition. On behalf of the Turkish team I congratulate her and give her my special thanks.

Prof. Dr. Gönül ÖNEY
*Head of the Turkish Exhibition*

The MWNF Exhibition in Turkey "Early Ottoman Art. The Legacy of the Emirates" contains eight itineraries, which take nine days to visit. The itineraries in the catalogue are given Roman numbers, whereas the cities/centres within each itinerary are given cardinal numbers and the monuments are given letters. Before each itinerary there is a sketch in which the location and the types of monuments are shown. The aim of these sketches is to orient the visitor. The visitor will need a more detailed map and city plan to travel from one place to the another. Turkey has a very practical public transport system of "*dolmush*" minibuses and intercity buses, yet it is always necessary to inquire about the timings beforehand.

A signposting system has been established along the itineraries consisting of various elements. These signs lead visitors to the monuments and the Info-towers in the town centres, while brief information is given about each place. Besides the signposting elements, each monument included in the exhibition has a panel at the entrance for easier identification. Moreover, on the main roads there are brown signs for the major venues.

On the sketches the main route is indicated with a black line. Some monuments within the itineraries, which are indicated by grey circles, are optional; hence the grey routes are the way to these optional monuments. There are two types of icons in the sketches: the bigger ones are for the primary monuments and the smaller ones are for the optionalones. Right after the name of the monuments some technical information is given (for example the address, the opening/closing hours, etc.). Museum With No Frontiers is not responsible for any changes that may occur after publication of this catalogue.

In the catalogue some additional information on the other attractions of the region/town is given in a frame with a beige background.

Some sites are not open to the public; Museum With No Frontiers continues to negotiate with the authorities to have these sites opened.

The religious monuments included in the exhibition should not be visited during religious services. Since some mosques are open only for prayer, they can be visited shortly before or after prayers. Visitors should be appropriately dressed. For these visits please make sure you do not wear shorts and you have your shoulders covered. Women visitors are asked to wear a scarf to cover their hair.

Generally speaking Turkish museums to not allow photographs to be taken with a flash, and they do not allow tripods. Taking photographs or filming on or around military areas is strictly prohibited.

We have retained standard spelling for Turkish words in common use and included in the English dictionary. We have used spellings for the names as provided by the authors themselves, as well as the Turkish spelling of the localities. Words in italic in the text without an accompanying translation or explanation can be found in the glossary.

Museum With No Frontiers is not responsible for any accident, theft, etc. that may occur during your visit.

Mehmet Kahyaoğlu
Yavuz Tuna
*Production Managers*

# ISLAMIC DYNASTIES IN THE MEDITERRANEAN

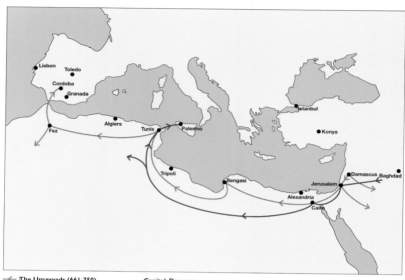

—← The Umayyads (661-750)      Capital: Damascus
—← The Abbasids (750-1258)      Capital: Baghdad

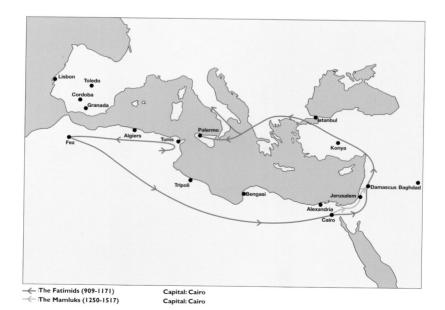

—← The Fatimids (909-1171)      Capital: Cairo
—← The Mamluks (1250-1517)      Capital: Cairo

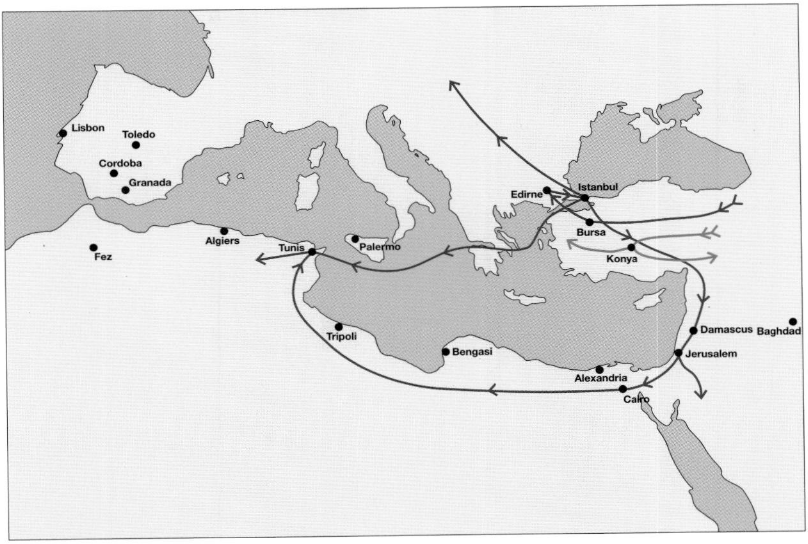


The Seljuqs (1075-1318) Capital: Konya
The Ottomans (1299-1922) Capital: Istanbul

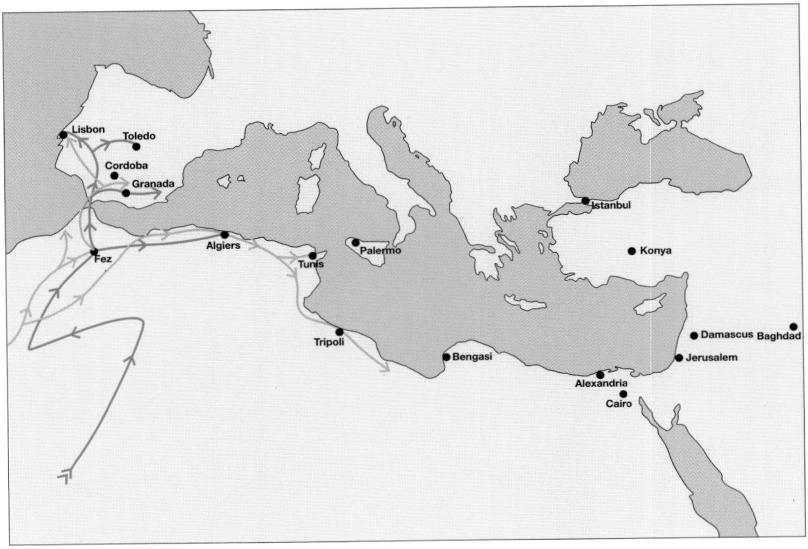


The Almoravids (1036-1147) Capital: Marrakesh
The Almohads (1121–1269) Capital: Marrakesh

*Qusayr 'Amra, mural in the Audience Hall, Badiya of Jordan.*

# ISLAMIC ART IN THE MEDITERRANEAN

Jamila Binous
Mahmoud Hawari
Manuela Marín
Gönül Öney

## The Legacy of Islam in the Mediterranean

Since the first half of the 7th century, the history of the Mediterranean Basin has belonged, in remarkably similar proportion, to two cultures, Islam and the Christian West. This extensive history of conflict and contact has created a mythology that is widely diffused in the collective imagination, a mythology based on the image of the other as the unyielding enemy, strange and alien, and as such, incomprehensible. It is of course true that battles punctuated those centuries from the time when the Muslims spilled forth from the Arabian Peninsula and took possession of the Fertile Crescent, Egypt, and later, North Africa, Sicily, and the Iberian Peninsula, penetrating into Western Europe as far as the south of France. At the beginning of the 8th century, the Mediterranean came under Islamic control.

This drive to expand, of an intensity seldom equalled in human history, was carried out in the name of a religion that considered itself then heir to its two immediate antecedents: Judaism and Christianity. It would be a gross over-simplification to explain the Islamic expansion exclusively in religious terms. One widespread image in the West presents Islam as a religion of simple dog-mas adapted to the needs of the common people, spread by vulgar warriors who poured out from the desert bearing the *Koran* on the blades of their swords. This coarse image does away with the intellectual complexity of a re-ligious message that transformed the world from the moment of its inception. It identifies this message with a military threat, and thus justifies a response on the same terms. Finally, it reduces an entire culture to only one of its ele-ments, religion, and in doing so, deprives it of the potential for evolution and change.

The Mediterranean countries that were progressively incorporated into the Muslim world began their journeys from very different starting points. Forms of Islamic life that began to develop in each were quite logically different with-in the unity that resulted from their shared adhesion to the new religious dog-ma. It is precisely the capacity to assimilate elements of previous cultures (Hellenistic, Roman, etc.), which has been one of the defining characteristics of Islamic societies. If one restricts his observations to the geographical area of the Mediterranean, which was extremely diverse culturally at the time of the emergence of Islam, one will discern quickly that this initial moment does not represent a break with previous history in the least. One comes to realise that it is impossible to imagine a monolithic and immutable Islamic world, blindl following an inalterable religious message.

If anything can be singled out as the *leitmotiv* running through the area o the Mediterranean, it is diversity of expression combined with harmony o sentiment, a sentiment more cultural than religious. In the Iberian Peninsul —to begin with the western perimeter of the Mediterranean— the presenc of Islam, initially brought about by military conquest, produced a societ clearly differentiated from, but in permanent contact with Christian society The importance of the cultural expression of this Islamic society was felt eve after it ceased to exist as such, and gave rise to perhaps one of the mos original components of Spanish culture, Mudejar art. Portugal maintaine strong Mozarab traditions throughout the Islamic period and there are man imprints from this time that are still clearly visible today. In Morocco an Tunisia, the legacy of al-Andalus was assimilated into the local forms an continues to be evident to this day. The western Mediterranean produce original forms of expression that reflected its conflicting and plural historica evolution.

Lodged between East and West, the Mediterranean Sea is endowed with ter restrial enclaves, such as Sicily, that represent centuries-old key historical lo cations. Conquered by the Arabs established in Tunisia, Sicily has continued t perpetuate the cultural and historical memory of Islam long after the Muslim ceased to have any political presence on the island. The presence of Sicilian Norman aesthetic forms preserved in architectural monuments clearly demon strates that the history of these regions cannot be explained without an un derstanding of the diversity of social, economic and cultural experiences tha flourished on their soil.

In sharp contrast, then, to the immutable and constant image alluded to at th outset, the history of Mediterranean Islam is characterised by surprising di versity. It is made up of a mixture of peoples and ethnicities, deserts and fer tile lands. As the major religion has been Islam since the early Middle Ages it is also true that religious minorities have maintained a presence historically The Classical Arabic language of the *Koran,* has coexisted side-by-sid with other languages, as well as with other dialects of Arabic. Within a setting of undeniable unity (Muslim religion, Arabic language and culture), each so ciety has evolved and responded to the challenges of history in its ow characteristic manner.

# The Emergence and Development of Islamic Art

Throughout these countries, with ancient and diverse civilisations, a new art permeated with images from the Islamic faith emerged at the end of the 8th century and which successfully imposed itself in a period of less than 100 years. This art, in its own particular manner, gave rise to creations and innovations based on unifying regional formulas and architectural and decorative processes, and was simultaneously inspired by the artistic traditions that proceeded it: Greco-Roman and Byzantine, Sasanian, Visigothic, Berber or even Central Asian.

The initial aim of Islamic art was to serve the needs of religion and various aspects of socio-economic life. New buildings appeared for religious purposes such as mosques and sanctuaries. For this reason, architecture played a central role in Islamic art because a whole series of other arts are dependent on it. Apart from architecture a whole range of complimentary minor arts found their artistic expressions in a variety of materials, such as wood, pottery, metal, glass, textiles and paper. In pottery, a great variety of glaze techniques were employed and among these distinguished groups are the lustre and polychrome painted wares. Glass of great beauty was manufactured, reaching excellence with the type adorned with gold and bright enamel colours. In metal work, the most sophisticated technique is inlaying bronze with silver or copper. High quality textiles and carpets, with geometric, animal and human designs, were made. Illuminated manuscripts with miniature painting represent a spectacular achievement in the arts of the book. These types of minor arts serve to attest the brilliance of Islamic art.

Figurative art, however, is excluded from the Islamic liturgical domain, which means it is ostracised from the central core of Islamic civilisation and that it is tolerated only at its periphery. Relief work is rare in the decoration of monuments and sculptures are almost flat. This deficit is compensated with a richness in ornamentation on the lavish carved plaster panelling, sculpted wooden panelling, wall tiling and glazed mosaics, as well as on the stalactite friezes, or *muqarnas*. Decorative elements taken from nature, such as leaves, flowers and branches, are generally stylised to the extreme and are so complicated that they rarely call to mind their sources of origin. The intertwining and combining of geometric motifs such as rhombus and etiolated polygons, form interlacing networks that completely cover the surface, resulting in shapes often called arabesques. One innovation within the decorative repertoire is the introduction of epigraphic elements

*Dome of the Rock, Jerusalem.*

in the ornamentation of monuments, furniture and various objects. Muslim craftsmen made use of the beauty of Arabic calligraphy, the language of the sacred book, the *Koran,* not only for the transcription of the Qur'anic verses but in all of its variations simply as a decorative motif for the ornamentation of stucco panelling and the edges of panels.

Art was also at the service of rulers. It was for patrons that architects built palaces, mosques, schools, hospitals, bathhouses, *caravanserais* and mausoleums, which would sometimes bear their names. Islamic art is, above all, dynastic art. Each one contributed tendencies that would bring about a partial or complete renewal of artistic forms, depending on historical conditions, the prosperity enjoyed by their states, and the traditions of each society. Islamic art, in spite of its relative unity, allowed for a diversity that gave rise to different styles, each one identified with a dynasty.

The Umayyad dynasty (661–750), which transferred the capital of the caliphate to Damascus, represents a singular achievement in the history of Islam. It absorbed and incorporated the Hellenistic and Byzantine legacy in such a way that the classical tradition of the Mediterranean was recast in a new and innovative mould. Islamic art, thus, was formed in Syria, and the architecture, unmistakably Islamic due to the personality of the founders, would continue to bear a relation to Hellenistic and Byzantine art as well. The most important of these monuments are the Dome of the Rock in Jerusalem, the earliest existing monumental Islamic sanctuary, the Great Mosque of Damascus, which served as a model for later mosques, and the desert palaces of Syria, Jordan and Palestine.

When the Abbasid caliphate (750–1258) succeeded the Umayyads, the political centre of Islam was moved from the Mediterranean to Baghdad in Mesopotamia. This factor would influence the development of Islamic civilisation and the entire range of culture, and art would bear the mark of that change. Abbasid art and architecture were influenced by three major traditions: Sassanian, Central Asian and Seljuq. Central Asian influence was already present in Sassanian architecture, but at Samarra this influence is represented by the stucco style with its arabesque ornamentation that would rapidly spread throughout the Islamic world. The influence of the Abbasid monuments can be observed in the buildings constructed during this period in the other regions of the empire, particularly Egypt and Ifriqiya. In Cairo, the Mosque of Ibn Tulun (876–879) is a masterpiece, remarkable for its plan and unity of conception. It was modelled after the Abbasid Great Mosque of Samarra, particularly its spiral minaret. In Kairouan, the capital of Ifriqiya, vassals of the Abbasid caliphs, the Aghlabids (800–909) expanded the Great Mosque of Kairouan, one of the most venerable congregational mosques in the Maghreb. Its *mihrab* was covered by ceramic tiles from Mesopotamia.

*Kairouan Mosque, mihrab, Tunisia.*

*Kairouan Mosque, minaret, Tunisia.*

19

*Citadel of Aleppo, view
of the entrance, Syria.*

*Complex of Qaluwun,
Cairo, Egypt.*

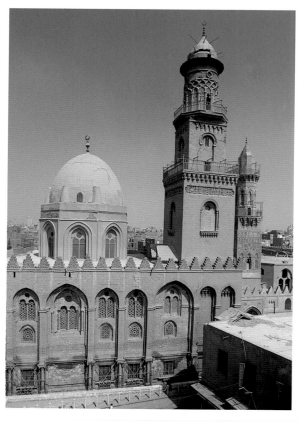

The reign of the Fatimids (909–1171) represents a remarkable period in the history of the Islamic countries of the Mediterranean: North Africa, Sicily, Egypt and Syria. Of their architectural constructions, a few examples remain that bear witness to their past glory. In the central Maghreb the Qal'a of the Banu Hammad and the Mosque of Mahdiya; in Sicily, the Cuba (*Qubba*) and the Zisa (*al-'Aziza*) in Palermo, constructed by Fatimid craftsmen under the Norman king William II; in Cairo, the Azhar Mosque is the most prominent example of Fatimid architecture in Egypt.

The Ayyubids (1171–1250), who overthrew the Fatimid dynasty in Cairo, were important patrons of architecture. They established religious institutions (*madrasas, khanqas*) for the propagation of *Sunni* Islam, mausoleums and welfare projects, as well as awesome fortifications pertaining to the military conflict with the Crusaders. The Citadel of Aleppo in Syria is a remarkable example of their military architecture.

The Mamluks (1250–1517) successors to the Ayyubids who had successfully resisted the Crusades and the Mongols, achieved the unity of Syria and Egypt and created a formidable empire. The wealth and luxury of the Mamluk sultan's court in Cairo motivated artists and architects to achieve an extraordinarily elegant style of architecture.

For the world of Islam, the Mamluk period marked a rebirth and renaissance. The enthusiasm for establishing religious foundations and reconstructing existing ones place the Mamluks among the greatest patrons of art and architecture in the history of Islam. The Mosque of Hassan (1356), a funerary mosque built with a cruciform plan in which the four arms of the cross were formed by four *iwans* of the building around a central courtyard, was typical of the era.

*Selimiye Mosque, general view, Edirne, Turkey.*

Anatolia was the birthplace of two great Islamic dynasties: the Seljuqs (1075–1318), who introduced Islam to the region; and the Ottomans (1299–1922), who brought about the end of the Byzantine Empire upon capturing Constantinople, and asserted their hegemony throughout the region.

A distinctive style of Seljuq art and architecture flourished with influences from Central Asia, Iran, Mesopotamia and Syria, which merged with elements deriving from Anatolian Christian and antiquity heritage. Konya, the new capital in Central Anatolia, but other cities as well, were enriched with buildings in the newly developed Seljuq style. Numerous mosques, *madrasas*, *turbes* and *caravanserais*, which were richly decorated by stucco and tiling with diverse figural representations, have survived to our day.

*Tile of Kubadabad Palace, Karatay Museum, Konya, Turkey.*

As the Seljuq emirates disintegrated and Byzantium declined, the Ottomans expanded their territory swiftly changing their capital from Iznik to Bursa and then again to Edirne. The conquest of Constantinople in 1453 by Sultan Mehmet II provided the necessary impetus for the transition of an emerging state into a great empire. A superpower that extended its boundaries to Vienna including the Balkans in the West and to Iran in the East, as well as

*Great Mosque of Cordoba, mihrab, Spain.*

*Madinat al-Zahra', Dar al-Yund, Spain.*

North Africa from Egypt to Algeria, turning the Eastern Mediterranean into an Ottoman sea. The race to surpass the grandeur of the inherited Byzantine churches, exemplified by the Hagia Sophia, culminated in the construction of great mosques in Istanbul. The most significant one is the Mosque of Süleymaniye. Built in the 16th century by the famous Ottoman architect Sinan, it epitomises the climax in architectural harmony in domed buildings. Most major Ottoman mosques were part of a large building complex called *kulliye* that also consisted several *madrasas*, a *Koran* school, a library, a hospital (*darüşşifa*), a hostel (*tabhane*), a public kitchen, a *caravanserai* and mausoleums (*turbes*). From the beginning of the 18th century, during the so-called Tulip Period, Ottoman architecture and decorative style reflected the influence of French Baroque and Rococo, heralding the Westernisation period in arts and architecture.

Al-Andalus at the western part of the Islamic world became the cradle of a brilliant artistic and cultural expression. 'Abd al-Rahman I established an independent Umayyad caliphate (750–1031) with Cordoba as its capital. The Great Mosque of Cordoba would pioneer innovative artistic tendencies such as the double tiered arches with two alternating colours nd panels with vegetal ornamentation which would become part of he repertoire of Andalusian artistic orms.

n the 11<sup>th</sup> century, the caliphate of Cordoba broke up into a score of principalities incapable of preventng the progressive advance of the reconquest initiated by the Christian tates of the Northwestern Iberian Peninsula. These petty kings, or Taifa Kings, called the Almoravids in 1086 and the Almohads in 1145, repelled the Christians and reestablished partial unity in al-Andalus.

*Tinmal Mosque, aerial view, Morocco.*

Through their intervention in the Iberian Peninsula, the Almoravids (1036–1147) came into contact with a new civilisation and were captivated quickly by the refinement of Andalusian art as reflected in their capital, Marrakesh, where they built a grand mosque and palaces. The influence of the architecture of Cordoba and other capitals such as Seville would be felt in all of the Almoravid monuments from Tlemcen, Algiers to Fez.

Under the rule of the Almohads (1121–1269), who expanded their hegemony as far as Tunisia, western Islamic art reached its climax. During this period, artistic creativity that originated with the Almoravid rulers was renewed and masterpieces of Islamic art were created. The Great Mosque of

*Ladies Tower and Gardens, Alhambra, Granada, Spain.*

Seville with its minaret the Giralda, the Kutubiya in Marrakesh, the Mosque of Hassan in Rabat and the Mosque of Tinmal high in the Atlas Mountains in Morocco are notable examples.

Upon the dissolution of the Almohad Empire, the Nasrid dynasty (1232–1492) installed itself in Granada and was to experience a period of splendour in the 14<sup>th</sup> century. The civilisation of Granada would become a cultural model in

*Mertola, general view, Portugal.*

future centuries in Spain (Mudejar art) and particularly in Morocco, where this artistic tradition enjoyed great popularity and would be preserved until the present day in the areas of architecture and decoration, music and cuisine. The famous palace and fort of *al-Hamra'* (the Alhambra) in Granada marks the crowning achievement of Andalusian art, with all features of its artistic repertoire.

*Decoration detail, Abu Inan Madrasa, Meknes, Morocco.*

At the same time in Morocco, the Merinids (1243–1471) replaced the Almohads, while in Algeria the 'Abd al-Wadid's reigned (1235–1516), as did the Hafsids (1228–1534) in Tunisia. The Merinids perpetuated al-Andalus art, enriching it with new features. They embellished their capital Fez with an abundance of mosques, palaces and *madrasa*s, with their clay mosaic and *zellij* panelling in the wall decorations, considered to be the most perfect works of

*Qal'a of the Bani Hammad, minaret, Algeria.*

*Sa'adian Tomb Marrakesh, Morocco.*

Islamic art. The later Moroccan dynasties, the Sa'adians (1527–1659) and the 'Alawite (1659 – until the present day), carried on the artistic tradition of al-Andalus that was exiled from its native soil in 1492. They continued to build and decorate their monuments using the same formulas and the same decorative themes as had the preceding dynasties, adding innovative touches characteristic of their creative genius. In the early 17th century, emigrants from al-Andalus (the *Moriscos*), who took up residence in the northern cities of Morocco, introduced numerous features of Andalusian art. Today, Morocco is one of the few countries that has kept traditions of Andalusian alive in its architecture and furniture, using innovative designs incorporating the architectural techniques and styles of the 20th century.

## ARCHITECTURAL SUMMARY

In general terms, Islamic architecture can be classified into two categories: re
ligious, such as mosques, *madrasas*, mausoleums, and secular, such as palaces
*caravanserais*, fortifications, etc.

### Religious Architecture

### Mosques

The mosque for obvious reasons lies at the very heart of Islamic architec
ture. It is an apt symbol of the faith that it serves. That symbolic role was
understood by Muslims at a very early stage, and played an important part
in the creation of suitable visual markers for the building: minaret, dome,
*mihrab*, *minbar*, etc.

The first mosque in Islam was the courtyard of the Prophet's house in Medina,
with no architectural refinements. Early mosques built by the Muslims as their
empire was expanding were simple. From these buildings developed the congregational or Friday mosque (*jami'*), essential features of which remain today
unchanged for nearly 1400 years. The general plan consists of a large courtyard
surrounded by arched porticoes, with more aisles or arcades on the side facing Mecca (*qibla*) than the other sides. The Great Umayyad Mosque in Damascus,
which followed the plan of the Prophet's mosque, became the prototype for
many mosques built in various parts of the Islamic world.

*Umayyad Mosque of
Damascus, Syria.*

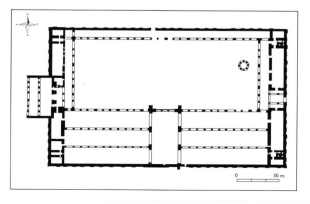

Two other types of mosques developed in Anatolia and afterwards in
the Ottoman domains: the basilical
and the dome types. The first type is
a simple pillared hall or basilica that
follows late Roman and Byzantine
Syrian tradition, introduced with
some modifications in the 11th century. The second type, which developed during the Ottoman period,
has its organisation of interior space
under a single dome. The Ottoman

chitects in great imperial mosques eated a new style of domed conruction by merging the Islamic osque tradition with that of dome uilding in Anatolia. The main dome sts on hexagonal support system, hile lateral bays are covered by naller domes. This emphasis on interior space dominated by a ngle dome became the starting pint of a style that was to be inoduced in the 16th century. uring this period, mosques beme multipurpose social com-

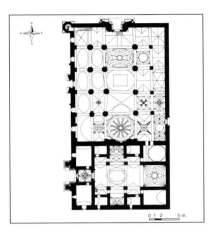

*Great Mosque, Divriği, Turkey.*

exes consisting of a *zawiya*, a *madrasa*, a public kitchen, a bath, a *caranserai* and a mausoleum of the founder. The supreme monument of this yle is the Sülaymeniye Mosque in Istanbul built in 1557 by the great chitect Sinan.

he minaret from the top of which the *muezzin* calls Muslims to prayer, is the lost prominent marker of the mosque. In Syria the traditional minaret consts of a square-plan tower built of stone. In Mamluk Egypt minarets are each vided into three distinct zones: a square section at the bottom, an octagonal liddle section and a circular section with a small dome on the top. Its shaft is

chly decorated and the transition beveen each section is covered with a nd of *muqarnas* decoration. Minarets North Africa and Spain, that share le square—tower form with Syria, are ecorated with panels of motifs around aired sets of windows. During the )ttoman period the octagonal or cylinrical minarets replaced the square )wer. Often these are tall pointed iinarets and although mosques genrally have only one minaret, in major cities there are two, four or even six iinarets.

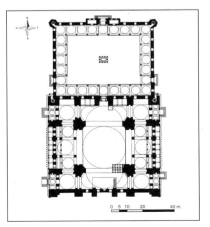

*Sülaymeniye Mosque, Istanbul, Turkey.*

27

## Madrasas

It seems likely that the Seljuqs bu the first *madrasa*s in Persia in the ear 11ᵗʰ century when they were sm structures with a domed courtya and two lateral *iwan*s. A later type develop has an open courtyard wi a central *iwan* and surrounded l arcades. During the 12ᵗʰ century Anatolia, the *madrasa* becan multifunctional and was intended serve as a medical school, ment hospital, a hospice with a public kitchen (*imaret*) and a mausoleum.

The promotion of *Sunni* (orthodox) Islam reached a new zenith in Syr and Egypt under the Zengids and the Ayyubids (12ᵗʰ–13ᵗʰ centuries This era witnessed the introduction of the *madrasa* established by a civ or political leader for the advancement of Islamic jurisprudence. Tl foundation was funded by an endowment in perpetuity (*waqf*), usual. the revenues of land or property in the form of an orchard, shops in market (*suq*), or a bathhouse (*hammam*). The *madrasa* traditionally fo

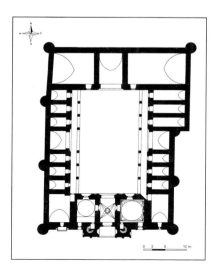

lowed a cruciform plan with a cer tral court surrounded by fou *iwan*s. Soon the *madrasa* became dominant architectural form wit mosques adopting a four-*iwan* plar The *madrasa* gradually lost its so religious and political function a propaganda tool and tended t have a broader civic function, serv ing as a congregational mosque an a mausoleum for the benefactor. The construction of *madrasa*s i Egypt and particularly in Cair gathered new momentum with th coming of the Mamluks. The typic Cairene *madrasa* of this era was ultifunctional gigantic four-*iwan* structure with a stalactite (*muqarnas*) portal and splendid facades. With the advent of the Ottomans in the 5th century, the joint foundation, typically a mosque-*madrasa*, became a widespread large complex that enjoyed imperial patronage. The *iwan* disappeared gradually and was replaced by a dominant dome chamber. A substantial increase in the number of domed cells used by students is a characteristic of Ottoman madrasas.

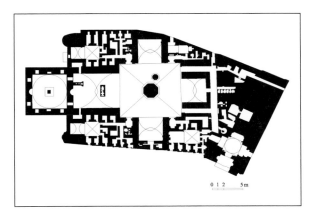

*Mosque and madrasa Sultan Hassan, Cairo, Egypt.*

One of the various building types that by virtue of their function and of their form can be related to the *madrasa* is the *khanqa*. The term indicates an institution, rather than a particular kind of building, that houses members of a Muslim mystical (*sufi*) order. Several other words used by Muslim historians as synonyms for *khanqa* include: in the Maghreb, *zawiya*; in Ottoman domain, *tekke*; and in general, *ribat*. *Sufism* permanently dominated the *khanqa*, which originated in eastern Persia during the 4th/10th century. In its simplest form the *khanqa* was a house where a group of pupils gathered around a master (*shaykh*), and it had the facilities for assembly, prayer and communal living. The establishment of khanqas flourished under the Seljuqs during the 11th and the 12th centuries and benefited from the close association between *Sufism* and the *Shafi'i madhhab* (doctrine) favoured by the ruling elite.

## Mausoleums

The terminology of the building type of the mausoleum used in Islamic Sources varied. The standard descriptive term *turbe* refers to the function of the building as for burial. Another term is *qubba* that refers to the most identifiable, the dome, and often marks a structure commemorating Biblical prophets, companions of the Prophet Muhammad and religious or military notables. The function of mausoleums is not limited simply to a place of burial and commemo-

29

*Qasr al-Khayr
al-Sharqi, Syria.*

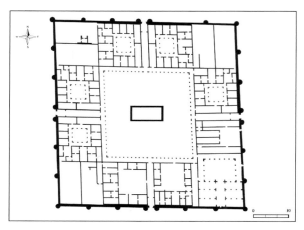

ration, but also plays an importa
role in "popular" religion. They a
venerated as tombs of local saints a
became places of pilgrimage. Oft
the structure of a mausoleum is er
bellished with Qur'anic quotatio
and contains a *mihrab* within it to re
der it a place of prayer. In some ca
es the mausoleum became part of
joint foundation. Forms of Mediev
Islamic mausoleums are varied, b
the traditional one has a domed squa
plan.

## Secular Architecture

### Palaces

The Umayyad period is characte
ised by sumptuous palaces an
bathhouses in remote dese
regions. Their basic plan is large
derived from Roman militai
models. Although the decoration
these structures is eclectic, the
constitute the best examples of th
budding Islamic decorative styl

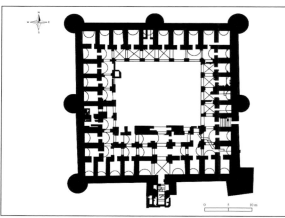

*Ribat of Sousse,
Tunisia.*

Mosaics, mural paintings, stone or stucco sculpture were used for
remarkable variety of decorations and themes. Abbasid palaces in Irac
such as those at Samarra and Ukhaidir, follow the same plan as the
Umayyad forerunners, but are marked by an increase in size, the use
the great *iwan*, dome and courtyard, and the extensive use of stucc
decorations. Palaces in the later Islamic period developed a distinctive sty
that was more decorative and less monumental. The most remarkab
example of royal or princely palaces is the Alhambra. The vast area
the palace is broken up into a series of separate units: gardens, pavilior

nd courts. The most striking
eature of Alhambra, however, is
he decoration that provides an
xtraordinary effect in the interior
f the building.

*Aksaray Sultan Khan,
Turkey.*

## aravanserais

caravanserai generally refers to a
arge structure that provides a lodg-
ag place for travellers and mer-
hants. Normally, it is a square or
ectangular floor plan, with a sin-
le projecting monumental entrance
nd towers in the exterior walls. A central courtyard is surrounded by por-
coes and rooms for lodging travellers, storing merchandise and for the
tabling of animals.

'he characteristic type of building has a wide range of functions since it has
een described as *khan*, *han*, *funduq*, *ribat*. These terms may imply no more
han differences in regional vocabularies rather than being distinctive func-
ons or types. The architectural sources of the various types of *caravanserais*
re difficult to identify. Some are perhaps derived from the Roman *castrum*
r military camp to which the Umayyad desert palaces are related. Other types,
a Mesopotamia and Persia, are associated with domestic architecture.

## Irban organisation

rom about the 10th century every town of any significance acquired fortified
alls and towers, elaborate gates and a mighty citadel (*qal'a* or *qasba*) as seat
f power. These are massive constructions built in materials characteristic of
ae region in which they are found; stone in Syria, Palestine and Egypt, or
rick, stone and rammed earth in the Iberian Peninsula and North Africa. A
nique example of military architecture is the *ribat*. Technically, this is a fortified
alace designated for the temporary or permanent warriors of Islam who
ommitted themselves to the defence of frontiers. The *ribat* of Sousse in Tunisia

bears resemblance to early Islamic palaces, but with a different interior arrangement of large halls, mosque and a minaret.

The division of the majority of Islamic cities into neighbourhoods is based on ethnic and religious affinity and it is also a system of urban organisation that facilitates the administration of the population. In the neighbourhood there is always a mosque. A bathhouse, a fountain, an oven and a group of stores are located either within or nearby. Its structure is formed by a network of streets, alleys and a collection of houses. Depending on the region and era, the home takes on diverse features governed by the historical and cultural traditions, climate and construction materials available.

The market (*suq*), which functions as the nerve-centre for local businesses would be the most relevant characteristic of Islamic cities. Its distance from the mosque determines the spatial organisation of the markets by specialised guilds. For instance, the professions considered clean and honourable (bookmakers, perfume makers, tailors) are located in the mosque's immediate environs, and the noisy and foul-smelling crafts (blacksmiths, tanning, cloth dying) are situated  progressively further from it. This geographic distribution responds to imperatives that rank on strictly technical grounds.

*Türbes of Osman Gazi
and Orhan Gazi, oil
painting by Mineli
Muhip, 19th century,
İş Bank Collection,
Istanbul.*

# EARLY OTTOMAN ART: THE LEGACY OF THE EMIRATES

### Gönül Öney

The 14th and 15th centuries in West Anatolia marked the beginning of a new era with respect to the art and culture of Turkish communities. It was at this time, approximately 200 years after the conquest of Central Anatolia that the shores of the Aegean and Marmara Seas came under Turkish control. With the many ruins of ancient cities and the presence of Venetian and Genoese merchants in the region, many new horizons opened up to Turkish culture and architecture. The art that developed in West Anatolia under the administration of the ruling emirates, including the Ottomans, was heavily influenced by the present local art. Turkish art of the 14th-15th century had its roots in the Central Asian, Great Seljuq, and Anatolian Seljuq periods and reached its zenith during the 16th century.

The buildings and works recommended for viewing on the eight itineraries suggested in this Museum With No Frontiers Exhibition are ones that are believed will contribute to the perception of Turkish culture in the Ottoman period. These routes, which run from southern to northern West Anatolia, were not brought together coincidentally, but were chosen with this aim in mind.

In almost every period of Anatolia's rich history that stretches back 9000 years, cultures that were essentially different from one another developed alongside each other. As a result of Anatolia's unique geographical location between Europe and Asia, the peninsula acted as a bridge between East and West. Various communities that immigrated to Anatolia preserved the cultural bonds with their original homelands.

Classical period West Anatolia civilisation (1050-323 BC) lasted until the foundation of the Ionian city-states. In the Hellenistic period (323-30 BC) the cities of Miletus (today Milet or Balat), Ephesus (today Efes and Selçuk), and Pergamum (today Bergama) were adorned with monumental buildings and statues. The Romans who took over this rich culture and art raised it to the highest level, especially in the West Anatolian cities of Aphrodisias, Tralles, Ephesus, and Pergamum. The remains of colonnaded roads, market areas, gymnasiums, theatres, palaces, baths, stadiums, aqueducts, and

*Bafa Han, view from the west, Bafa (Çamiçi).*

35

*Great Mosque, re-used lion statue on the southeast corner, 1312-13, Aydınoğlu Mehmed Bey, Birgi.*

together with Anatolia's own cultura and artistic accumulation of many cen turies. While the heterogeneity of seed from Byzantium, Central Asia, Persia Arabian and the Antique world are clear ly recognisable here and there approaches and modes of research unique to the Seljuqs are especially evi dent. The Emirates period that followe the Seljuq rule did not merely absorb th evident Seljuq legacy, but was incline towards new experiments and modes o inquiry. The Menteşe Emirate ruled ove Halicarnassus (today Bodrum), th famous city of Classical civilisation Miletus along with Milas, Muğla, an Beçin; the Aydın Emirate contained th cities of ancient Tralles (Aydın), Ephesu (Efes, Selçuk), and Teos (Seferihisar) along with Tire, Birgi, and İzmir; th Saruhan Emirate comprised a region stretching from ancient Magnesia a Spilum (Manisa) to Pergamum (Berga ma); the Karasi Emirate was situated i the Balıkesir region; and as for th Ottoman Emirate, it first occupied th region between the famous Byzantin city of Nicea (İznik) and Bursa, and late ruled over a broad area that stretched a far as Edirne. The re-used materials, lik columns, column capitals and bases, o the Antique or Byzantine periods tha one often comes across in monumenta portals, and walls of the edifices of thi period serve as reminders of the region' centuries-long heritage.

During the Ottoman period, wherea *Sufi* beliefs and old Turkish tradition such as *Ahi* organisations and Islamic tra ditions gained strength, a simultaneou movement began towards a cosmopoli tan culture and social life, under th influence of the Islamic countries sur-

statues that we see in the Hellenistic and Roman cities are among the period's most dazzling works. After the fall of the Roman Empire, especially during the Early Christian and Early Byzantine periods between the 4th and 6th centuries AD, West Anatolia in particular reached a new cultural peak. Ancient cities like Pergamum, Sardis, Ephesus, Priene, Miletus, and Hierapolis maintained their importance during the period of the Byzantine Empire whose architectural legacy and road system in West Anatolia assisted the rapid development of cultural and commercial life in the 14th and 15th centuries.

Turkish art was first produced in Anatolia during the Seljuq era (1077-1318). During the high times of the Anatolian Seljuq State, the influences of Persia, Syria, and Iraq, through which the Turks had passed during their migration from Central Asia to Anatolia, were kneaded

ounding the Mediterranean, the Balka-
as, Byzantium and especially Constan-
inople. The presence of poets, itinerant
haykhs, *dervishe*s, and artisans made the
Ottoman Palace more colourful. The
Turkish language was the uniting factor
or the Anatolian mosaic. Strong Islamic
raditions could not stop many Byzantine
tructures from being assigned new func-
ions. For example, Orhan Gazi converted the famous Hagia Sophia (Ayasofya)
Church in İznik into a mosque and had an
adjoining *madrasa* added to it. Osman
Gazi, Orhan Gazi, Murad I, and Bayezid
I adorned the important Ottoman cities
of İznik, Bursa, Yenisehir, and Edirne in
particular with mosques, *madrasas*,
*imaret*s, *tabhane*s, *zawiya*s, *hammam*s,
*bedesten*s, *han*s, *türbe*s, bridges, and
fortresses. Despite the rich architectural heritage that they passed down from
the 14th-15th centuries to the present, no
traces of their palaces and houses have
survived. These buildings, which were
probably constructed with non-durable
materials like wood and sun-dried bricks,
became one with the earth and disappeared as a result of fires and the harsh
natural environment.

We believe people who are inquisitive,
and interested in learning about the 14th-
and 15th-century works of West Anatolia, will be inspired by this exhibition
and catalogue to become more familiar
with Classical Ottoman Art, as well as
Turkish Art in a more general sense.

*Osman Gazi,
Illumination from
Kıyafetü'l-İnsâniyye fi
Şemâili'l'-Osmâniyye
by Seyyid Lokman
Çelebi, 1579,
H.1563, 24b, Library
of Topkapı Palace,
Istanbul.*

*Orhan Gazi,
Illumination from
Kıyafetü'l-İnsâniyye fi
Şemâili'l'-Osmâniyye
by Seyyid Lokman
Çelebi, 1579,
H.1563, 29a, Library
of Topkapı Palace,
Istanbul.*

# 14<sup>th</sup>- and 15<sup>th</sup>-CENTURY WEST ANATOLIAN HISTORY

## Aydoğan Demir

Anatolia, a land to which many ethnic groups have migrated and which was destroyed by various invasions, met with the Turks as a group in ancient times. The Turks began to play an especially important military role during the Middle Ages in the time of the Abbasid Caliphate (750-1258) centred in Baghdad. In order to protect their boundaries against the Byzantine Empire (395-1453) and to raid Byzantine-controlled Anatolia, the Abbasids set up military bases in the cities of Tarsus, Adana, Misis, Maraş and Malatya in eastern and southern Anatolia. There were many Turks among the soldiers the Abbasids settled at these bases and an extremely large part of the Abbasid Caliph al-Mu'tasim's (833-842) army, which advanced as far as the shores of the Sakarya River in Anatolia, was also made up of Turks.

During the second half of the 11<sup>th</sup> century, the Great Seljuq Empire (1040-1157) directed the waves of immigrants flooding into Khorasan (a historical region located within the boundaries of today's Iran and the Republic of Turkmenistan) to the West, and to Anatolia in particular. As a result, Anatolia, except for the coasts, came under the administration of the Turks.

At the end of the 11<sup>th</sup> century (1096-1097), members of the First Crusaders who were trying to get to Jerusalem via Anatolia, spoke of places called "Romania" that were under Turkish sovereignty. One century later, the Third Crusaders, who were trying to cross Anatolia under the command of Friedrich I Barbarossa (r. 1152-1190), called the same places "Turcia/ Turchia/ Türkiye". Anatolia, with its unchanging ethnic structure consisting of Turks, Kurds, Rums, Armenians, Jews, and Christian Syrians was witnessing the formation of Turkish Islamic culture, a new culture formed under the inspiration of the monumental architecture constructed by the Seljuqs, Danishmendids, Mengücekids, Saltukids and Artukids.

Anatolian Seljuq Sultan Alaeddin Keykubad I (1220-1237), who ruled over the cities of Alanya and Antalya on the Mediterranean coast, the cities of Sinop and Samsun on the Black Sea coast, and a large part of Anatolia, took a series of measures to promote the development of trade in his country. In order to ensure safe travel on the Silk and Spice Routes that passed through Anatolia, Alaeddin Keykubad I encouraged the construction of fortress-like *caravanserais* begun by his forefathers. *Caravanserais* were buildings offering shelter, food, and sanitation provisions to merchants and other travellers, and care and food for their pack animals as well.

The other way in which trade was developed and made safe during this period was by special agreements entered into with interested states. In 1213 a commercial agreement was signed between the Anatolian Seljuqs and the Cypriots. Legal works that started before Alaeddin Keykubad I were examined in the finest detail during the reign of this sultan; on 8 March 1220, a pact was signed with the Venetians in order to insure protection of the lives and goods of Venetian merchants trading in Turkey. The ease with which Venetians and their allies could trade paved the way for the formation of Latin colonies in Turkey's most important cities.

The Italian communes, led by the Venetians, organised the Fourth Crusade in

204; the Fourth-Crusader Army occu-
ied Istanbul instead of going to
rusalem, opening the way for the divi-
on of the Byzantine Empire, that was
ever again able to reach its previous
rength. The Nicean Emperor Michael
III Palaeologus (1259-1282) captured
stanbul back from the Latins in the year
261 and he and his successors had to
ruggle with the Latins and the problems
a the Balkans. Michael VIII Palaeologus
ould not, however, afford to take the
ecessary interest in West Anatolia; when
e could not pay the guardsmen (*akritoi*)
heir wages, they left their posts along the
orders. The borderland *Bey*s, who had
een waiting for such an opportunity,
egan occupying West Anatolia along the
outes leading to the seas. Consequently,
y the end of the 13th century, the
Menteşe, Aydın, Saruhan, Karasi, and
Ottoman Emirates were founded in West
Anatolia.

t is necessary to treat in careful detail
he subject of the relationship between
he Turkish community, the Rums, and
he other ethnic groups that came
ogether in the areas governed by the
West Anatolian Emirates, where truly
mportant civilisations began to develop.
The heterodox Islamic beliefs by which
. large part of the Turks that settled in
West Anatolia, especially those living in
ural areas, led their lives, must have
played an important role in relationships
mongst these peoples. These beliefs,
which we can call "People's Islam", con-
ain traces of Shamanism, nature cults,
Buddhism, Manichaeanism, Zoroastri-
nism, Christianity and Judaism.
Approaching people with tolerance, par-
icipating in religious ceremonies with
to segregation between the sexes, and

imbibing alcoholic drinks at ceremonies
were common to their way of life. Different ethnic groups mingled at the markets, the bazaar, and even in the administration of the emirates, which
occasionally led to love affairs and even
marriages. The following lines taken
from a Turkish folk song are proof of
how these people, who, far from ethni-
cal discrimination, also approached each
other lovingly:

How you wait on the rooftop, beam-
ing like the moon,
Your cheeks like an apple, like a pomegranate.
Come, let us embrace, both of us
entwined into one being
I have only learned, you are Armenian,
what if you are Armenian
You are my heart's desire, my succour,
my succour.

More important than the date and origin
of this folk song is its inspiration from
centuries-old, deeply held sentiments.
When in the mid-13th century, tradesmen
from all lines of work gave up hope on
the Anatolian Seljuq Sultanate, which was
at this time under intense pressure from
the Mongols, they began to organise
themselves and founded a union that
called its members by the name *Ahi*. It is
generally accepted that this word is
derived from the Turkish word "akı"
meaning "munificent, generous young
man" or the Arabic word "Akhi" meaning
"my brother." The *Ahi* organisation
founded on the concepts of "bravery"
(chivalry), "morality" and "art," determined its own rules by which the unions
had to abide, and permission to do work
would not be granted to those who did

not abide by their rules. In times of political chaos, the *Ahis* defended the city they lived in and even administered it. *Ahi* leaders were experts in law, science, literature, and art.

According to the traveller Ibn Battuta (1304-1369), the *Ahis* organised themselves by founding small *zawiyas* in cities, towns, and villages. Besides masters, assistant masters, and apprentices, *müderrises*, *kadıs*, poets, calligraphers, and regional administrators also attended the meetings held at the small *zawiyas*. High-level administrators, governors, commanders, teachers, judges, and doctors were educated among the *Ahis*. Together with the people they educated, the *Ahis* took on important roles

in institutions of the emirates, especially in the Ottoman Emirate. They did not interfere in the rights of the Armenian and Rum masters working in Anatolia but instead allowed them to freely continue working in their various occupations.

Religious men, *Ahis*, and travellers wandering from one city to the next also stayed in the *Ahi's zawiyas*, which were sometimes built in a mosque structure and sometimes as independent units. The *zawiyas* fulfilled a social need by offering free food and lodging to their overnight guests in cities, towns, and even in the villages during times when travelling by road was not safe.

The Menteşe and Aydın Emirates also tried to assume control over the islands in the Aegean. The Papacy even organised crusade and took back the coastal city of İzmir (1344) when Gazi Umur Bey (1334-1348) of Aydın Emirate became too powerful in the Aegean.

Not only wars but great alliances, too, took place in the Aegean. After boundaries became definite, trade relations were set up between the West Anatolian Emirates and the Latins and commercial agreements were signed. The cities of Balat (Miletus), Selçuk (Ayasuluğ, Ephesus) and Foça (Phocea) were important trade centres during this period. The capital of the Ottoman State, at the time Bursa, was also among the cities that placed an emphasis on trade.

Although internal peace was eventually achieved among the people, the emirates were not slow to war with one another. One of Anatolia's strongest emirates, the Karamanids (1256-1483), maintained that it was the heir to the Anatolian Seljuq State. For this reason, the Kara nanids and the other Anatolian Emirates, with the Ottomans leading, experienced heavy wars that caused great suffering. In order to prevent these wars full of resentment and hate, the Ottomans took as their ultimate goal the achievement of Anatolian unity and, by taking advantage of their opportunities, they took the other emirates under their sovereignty. But even if the West Anatolian Emirates had been re-established after Ottoman Sultan Bayezid I was defeated by Tamerlane in the Battle of Ankara (1402), in reality, all of the emirates were erased from the stage of history in the time of Sultans Mehmed I (r. 1413-1421) and Murad II (r. 1421-1451). The Anatolian *Beys* considered the

development of the regions under their rule extremely important: scientific work was supported; they opened up their palaces to men of learning from various places; many works were translated from what may be considered that era's language of science: Arabic, into Turkish. In addition, original works written in the fields of medicine, astronomy, history, *fiqh*, Sufism, etc., were presented to the *Beys*.

Though the Ottoman Emirate founded by Osman Gazi in 1299 in the Marmara region was the smallest of the Anatolian Emirates, by intelligently using the advantages of their location, in a short time they became one of the most powerful. The Byzantine Empire (395-

*Mehmed I,*
*Illumination from*
*Kıyafetü'l-İnsâniyye fî*
*Şemâili'l'-Osmâniyye*
*by Seyyid Lokman*
*Çelebi, 1579,*
*H.1563, 40b, Library*
*of Topkapı Palace,*
*İstanbul.*

*Murad II,*
*Illumination from*
*Kıyafetü'l-İnsâniyye fî*
*Şemâili'l'-Osmâniyye*
*by Seyyid Lokman*
*Çelebi, 1579,*
*H.1563, 44a, Library*
*of Topkapı Palace,*
*İstanbul.*

*Portrait of Süleyman the Magnificent by Nigari, 1560-65, Topkapı Palace, H.2134, fol.16.*

1453), which had acquired a feudal structure in the Marmara region, could not protect their land against the Ottoman State. As a result of disputes over the throne and the matter of protecting the Balkans against the Serbs, they were left with no choice but to ask Orhan Gazi (r. 1324-1362) for help. The Ottoman soldiers brought about Cantacuzenus' ascent to the position of emperor and achieved the withdrawal of the Serbs, and thus got acquainted with Rumelia.

In return for their help, the Byzantines gave the Çimpe (Tzympe) Fortress in Gelibolu (Gallipoli) to the Ottoman military units for use as a military base. From this point on, in 1354, the Ottomans began their conquests in Thrace. After the taking of Edirne during the reign of Sultan Murad I (1362-1389), the Ottoman troops looked for areas to rule over in Bulgaria, Macedonia, and Serbia. During the time of Sultan Bayezid I (r. 1389-1402), the boundaries of the Ottoman State reached the Danube and the Walachia Principality was brought under vassalage. When Sultan Bayezid I lost the Battle of Ankara in 1402, disputes over the throne broke out among his sons and the Interregnum was concluded finally in 1413 with the victory of Sultan Mehmed I.

Sultan Murad II caused the Crusaders, gathered with the aim of breaking the Ottoman State's superiority in the Balkans, to suffer a harsh defeat in Varna (1444) and Kosovo (1448).

Sultan Mehmed II (r. 1451-1481), who twice served as sultan while his father was still alive, had great ideals when he ascended the throne aged 19. Bringing history's longest rooted empire to an end by conquering Istanbul at the age of 21, he was saluted as the Roman Emperor by the Rum advisers who gathered around him. Sultan of an empire that stretched from the Danube to the Euphrates, Sultan Mehmed II, also known as Mehmed the Conqueror, in addition to the country's political developments, also considered public and scientific works to be a top priority. It is known that he personally oversaw the *madrasas*, that he listened to lectures by the *müderrises*, and that the ones he commended were awarded. Sultan Mehmed II knew Latin and Greek in addition to Turkish, Arabic, and Persian; of the books from his library that have survived to the present, 50 of them are about Western culture. He decorated the palace walls with Renaissance-style frescos, and in the year 1479, the Venetian painter Gentile Bellini painted a portrait of Sultan Mehmed II.

me historians have raised doubts about ultan Mehmed II falling off his horse uring a campaign on 3 May 1481, and s consequent death at the age of 49. Sultan Mehmed II had reduced the living area of the Venetians on the Aegean and Black eas and had led a campaign to southern aly in 1480; therefore, in order to do way with Sultan Mehmed II, the Venetians arranged 12 assassination plots, as ne well-known historian F. Babinger suggests.

Until the year 1495, Cem Sultan was a angerous nuisance to his brother, Sultan ayezid II, who ascended the throne in 481. After losing two wars in an attempt o overtake the throne, Cem Sultan took efuge with the Knights of St. John who rst took him to France, and then to Italy. Until the death of his brother in 1495,

Sultan Bayezid II lived in fear that the release of Cem Sultan would cause another dispute for the throne and, for this reason, followed a passive political policy towards the West.

Sultan Bayezid II (r. 1481-1512), the last sultan of the 15th century, was succeeded by Sultans Selim I (r. 1512-1520) and Süleyman I, also known as Süleyman the Magnificent or the Lawgiver (r. 1520-1566), who brought the Ottoman State up to the status of World Empire and dominated the Mediterranean, Black Sea, and Indian Ocean.

The boundlessly tolerant Ottoman Sultans improved the land and protected scholars; the peaceful life they provided for their people has been named Pax Ottomana (Ottoman Peace) by some scholars.

# ART AND SOCIAL LIFE IN THE EMIRATES AND EARLY OTTOMAN PERIODS

**Gönül Öney**

The Emirates and Early Ottoman periods are striking from an art historical point of view because of their extreme colourfulness, and their new experiments and influences. The Emirates, which declared their independence in various regions of Anatolia and whose strength increased as time went on, began intense public improvements as if they wanted to leave their mark on the regions they ruled. New works produced in various areas of Anatolia reflected traces of the vicinity former architectural, cultural, and artistic traditions.

Our itineraries are located in West Anatolia where new modes of search and experimentation in architecture and art are more obvious since it was the first time this region had encountered Turkish-Islamic culture. The buildings and art works that first appeared during the Emirates and Early Ottoman period deeply influenced Classical Ottoman art. After the 14th and 15th centuries – period characterised by its constant search for and exploration of new and different artistic, cultural, and social modes– a settled, mature period was finally reached. Parallel to the growth in political strength during the 16th century, the mature style and design in every area of art left its mark on Anatolia and in all the Empire's activities.

Despite new experiments in Emirates and Early Ottoman Art, differences between the regions are not very clear-cut. An innovation tried in one area could also be seen in the neighbouring emirates. Like seeds thrown before the blowing wind, new experiments took root and blossomed in various regions.

We are going to try to introduce the art works briefly by separating them into various typological groups; works similar to those introduced here are found in Anatolia's other emirates as well. The Architecture, Architectural Ornamental, and Handicrafts are presented under separate headings and with general features in the belief that this is the easiest approach. The visitor/reader will find various examples from each group in the Itineraries.

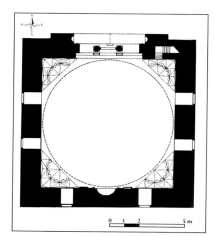

*Plan of the İlyas Bey Mosque, 1404, İlyas Bey, Balat (from A. Durukan).*

*İlyas Bey Complex, north façade of the mosque, 1404, İlyas Bey, Balat.*

# rchitecture

he presentation of a brief overview of mirates and Early Ottoman architecture, t which each of the building types is ealt with separately, will make the comrehension of architectural development onsiderably easier.

## Iosques and Masjids

Iosques (*Cami* in Turkish) and *masjids* *nescit* in Turkish) are the most impornt buildings of the 14th and 15th cenuries. The differences and innovations hat appear in mosques and *masjids* over ime are easier to comprehend if they re categorised according to their plan ypes.

## ingle-Domed Cubical Mosques nd Masjids

Represented by plain examples, mosques nd *masjids* from this group are often ncountered in the Emirates and Early Ottoman period and the roots of this plan ype extend back to the mosques and *nasjids* of the Great Seljuq and Anatolian ieljuq periods. In addition to simple, lain examples without a minaret and a ortico, there are also more magnificent xamples of monumental dimensions vith multi-bayed porticoes. There are oth simple and complex examples of ubic single-domed mosques and *masjids* on our Itineraries.
The Beçin Yelli Mosque (beginning of the 15th century), İznik Yeşil Mosque (1392) and Balat İlyas Bey Mosque (1404) are a ew examples in this group. As in Tire

Yavukluoğlu Mosque Complex (15th century) and Edirne Bayezid II Mosque Complex (1488), a monumental courtyard surrounded with porticoes was added to the front of some single-domed cubical mosques and in the Tire example, the mosque and *madrasa* share the same courtyard. In these buildings of symmetrical design and monumental character, ornamentation is seen especially on the main facade.

*Yıldırım Mosque, fireplace and shelves in the tabhane, 1389-99, Bayezid I, Bursa.*

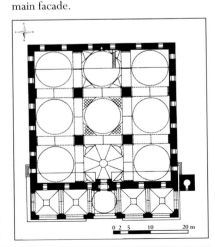

0 2 5   10     20 m

*Plan of Eski Mosque, 1414, Mehmed I, Edirne (from Z. Sönmez).*

45

*Great Mosque, prayer hall, 1312-13, Aydınoğlu Mehmed Bey, Birgi.*

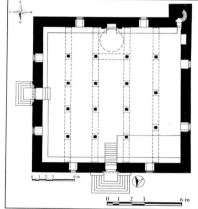

*Plan of Great Mosque, 1312-13, Aydınoğlu Mehmed Bey, Birgi.*

## Mosques of Equal-Size Multiple Bays

These mosques, an altered application of the Seljuq mosques in the Kufa type with pillars at equal intervals, appeared during the Early Ottoman period. As we see in the examples of both the Bursa Great Mosque (1400) and Edirne Eski Mosque (1414), in this plan, the prayer hall is divided into bays of equal size each of which is covered by a dome.

These mosques without courtyards are usually a square or a lateral rectangle in shape.

## Basilical Mosques

The Basilical plan inspired by the many examples of Armenian and Byzantine basilicas in Anatolia, was also applied to mosques with a new synthesis. The prayer hall of basilical mosques is divided into three or five aisles, set off from one another with rows of pillars or columns extending perpendicularly to the *qibla* wall. Many examples have domes, especially over the central aisle, which is broader and higher. The Basilical plan frequently seen in Anatolian mosques during the Seljuq period, is also encountered during the Emirates period although less often: for example, Birgi Great Mosque (1312/13) and Milas Great Mosque (1378).

## Mosques with Transept Aisles

In such a building the aisle parallel to the *qibla* wall is intersected by a perpendicular one; this intersection is centrally located in front of the *mihrab* and usually covered by a dome.

Continuing the influence of Syrian Umayyad-period mosques (e.g. Great [Umayyad] Mosque in Damascus), mosques with transept aisles were common in the Southeast Anatolian region during the Artukid period. However, this design was also applied to the Aydın Emirate's İsa Bey Mosque (1375) in Selçuk as a result of the Umayyad-,

*İsa Bey Mosque, view
from the northeast,
1375, İsa Bey, Selçuk.*

Fatimid-, Ayyubid-, and Mamluk-periods' particular architectural and ornamental characteristics reaching West Anatolia from Syria via the Mediterranean and the Aegean. The obvious Syrian characteristics in the buildings' plan and ornamentation must be related to the architect's Damascan origins; work similar to the colourful marble workmanship in the portal and facades are frequently encountered in medieval Syrian architecture.

The domes that crown the transept aisle of İsa Bey Mosque assume the status of a more developed central dome in Saruhan Emirate's Great Mosque in Manisa (1367). The re-used Byzantine columns in the courtyard reflect the region's synthesis of artistic periods and styles.

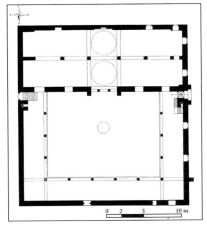

*Plan of İsa Bey
Mosque, 1375, İsa
Bey, Selçuk (from Z.
Sönmez).*

## Mosques with Tabhanes (Zawiyas)

These buildings are examples of a new mosque plan developed in the Emirates

47

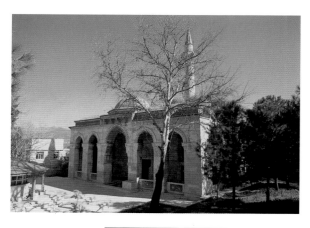

*Firuz Bey Mosque, view from the northwest, 1396, Hoca Firuz, Milas.*

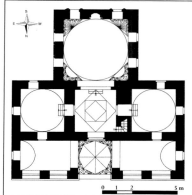

*Plan of Firuz Bey Mosque, 1396, Hoca Firuz, Milas (from Z. Sönmez).*

and Early Ottoman periods. The plan layout, which was applied at Bursa Orhan Gazi Mosque (1339/40) and Milas Firuz Bey Mosque (1396), reminds one of an upside down letter "T". Facing the direction of the *qibla* is a domed or vaulted *iwan* in which the prayer ritual is performed. In front of the prayer hall is a central area generally covered with a dome and flanked with *tabhanes* and in some examples *iwans* on both sides. These side rooms called *tabhanes* were

used in order to shelter the itinerant dervishes.

There is a fireplace in each *tabhane* of the İznik Nilüfer Hatun İmaret (1388), which was commissioned by Sultan Murad I. We are familiar with examples of *tekke*s and *hanikah*s, in which itinerant *dervishes* and *shaykh*s were hosted from the Seljuq period, but we do not have much knowledge about them in the Emirates period. In the 14th and 15th centuries, the *Ahi* organisation's activities were conducted in the mosques with *tabhanes*. The Ottoman sultans, considered members of the organisation, owned a private loge. Itinerant *Ahi* *dervishes* were also sheltered in these *tabhanes*. In addition to religious authority, these people also influenced the social and cultural arenas. We know that various mosques with *tabhanes* were commissioned for itinerant *dervishes* during the time of the first Ottoman Sultan Osman Gazi (r. 1281–1324).

## Complexes with Tabhane (Zawiya)

Most mosques with *Tabhane (zawiya)* or, by its other name, mosques with T-plans or multi-functional mosques, are the centres of large complexes, the construction of which was accelerated during the Early Ottoman period. Within the scope of the Ottoman sultans' urbanisation efforts, monumental complexes, including structures such as a mosque, *madrasa*, *darüşşifa*, *hammam*, *imaret*, *han*, and *türbe* were constructed in the city centres. These structures symbolised the power of the palace elite and the high-ranking government officials who commissioned them. The well-organised social and religious *waqf* system provided for the maintenance

nd orderly administration of the com-
lexes. In addition to being a place of
orship, this group of buildings served as
place where education was given, where
ne poor were fed free of charge, and
here *dervishes* were entertained. The
videspread tradition of mosque-complex
onstruction in Syria and Egypt certainly
ifluenced the spread of this tradition in
natolia.

structure with two floors and three
vans, the Bursa Hüdavendigar Mosque
1385) is an interesting mosque complex
vith its *madrasa, imaret* and spas. The
icade arrangement reflecting the influen-
e of 13th-century Byzantine buildings can
e considered as a trace of the syntheses
f different cultures, visible in most of the
4th- and 15th-century structures. The
3ursa Yıldırım Complex (1389-1399)
lso consists of buildings of monumental
limensions. The Bursa Yeşil Mosque
1419-1424) commissioned by Sultan
Mehmed I and the Muradiye Mosques
hat Sultan Murad II had built in Bursa
1426) and Edirne (1426/27), are mosques with *tabhanes* (*zawiyas*) located in
arge mosque complexes of the period.

## Mosques with a Central Dome

Developed with the aim of gathering a
congregation in one large unified space,
structures with a central dome of an ever-
increasing diameter underwent rapid
development in the 14th and 15th centuries. The majority of these monumental mosques were the centres of large
complexes.
As with the Edirne Üç Şerefeli Mosque
(1445) commissioned by Sultan Murad II,
the silhouettes of these mosques are

*Üç Şerefeli Mosque, prayer hall, 1445, Murad II, Edirne.*

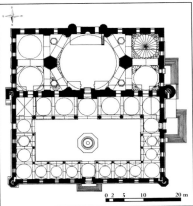

*Plan of Üç Şerefeli Mosque, 1445, Murad II, Edirne (from Z. Sönmez).*

arranged in a vertical line. It is possible to
follow the development of the central-
dome mosque type step by step in the
Selçuk İsa Bey Mosque (1375), Manisa
Great Mosque (1367), and Manisa Hatuniye Mosque (1491) respectively.

## Madrasas and Darüşşifas

In the Islamic world, mosques were
used outside of worshipping hours to

49

*Yıldırım Madrasa, east and south fronts, 1389-99, Bayezid I, Bursa.*

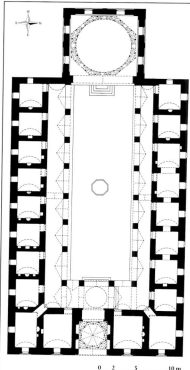

*Plan of Yıldırım Madrasa, 1389-1399, Bayezid I, Bursa (from Y. Demiralp).*

educate the religious community. Cons tructed very close to the mosque o adjoining it, *madrasas* were envisione purely as educational institutions wher advanced education would be given The sultan, a high level administrato or a wealthy person could commissio a *madrasa*. The pious foundations calle *waqfs* covered the maintenance an management expenses of the *madras* buildings as well as the costs of feedin the students, for the *madrasa* did no charge for education. In addition t Islamic sciences, lessons like philoso phy, medicine, mathematics, and astro nomy were also taught at the *madrasa* the first examples of which were cons tructed in Persia during the time of th Great Seljuq *vizier* Nizam al-Mulk. Th layout of the *madrasa* was applied i *şifahanes*, too, the institutions in whicl medical education was given. In th *madrasas* and *darüşşifas*, the chamber surrounded a large courtyard and a dome usually covered the main *iwan* located across from the entrance *iwan* Although we do not know the exact function of the vaulted or domed rooms located on either side of the main *iwan,* it is thought that these areas, which are of greater dimensions than the student cells, were used as *dershanes* for the lectures and in most of the *madrasas* there are porticoes on at least two sides of the courtyard. This layout is the same in the Anatolian Seljuq *madrasas*.

Constructed in Beçin during the Menteşe Emirate period, Ahmet Gazi Madrasa (1375) is one of the earliest examples of a *madrasa* with two *iwans* and the tomb of its founder Ahmet Gazi is in the main *iwan* covered by a single dome. Bursa

*Türbe of Şehzade Mustafa and Cem Sultan, mihrab and sarcophagi, 1479, Bursa.*

Yeşil Madrasa (1419-1424), Bursa Yıldırım Madrasa (1399), and İznik Süleyman Pasha Madrasa (mid-14th century) are monumental examples of Early Ottoman *madrasa*s that we introduce on our Itineraries.

## Türbes

Emirates- and Early Ottoman-period tombs exhibit great variety in appearance and design. With their polygonal or cylindrical shaped main body, *türbes* —the monumental tombs— are almost always covered with a dome. The conical or pyramidal spire of the Seljuq *türbes* is not encountered very often during the Emirates and Early Ottoman periods. The number of examples with crypts also decreased considerably during these periods. Osman Gazi, the first Ottoman Sultan, was buried in Bursa in an old Byzantine church. This is an indication of the Ottoman sultans' positive approach to architectural and cultural heritage.

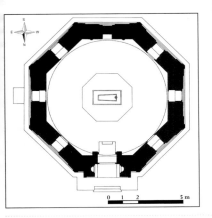

Although usually plain structures, some *türbes* are richly decorated. For example, the polygonal body of the Yeşil Türbe (1419-1424) in Bursa is decorated inside and out with tiles. Some Early Ottoman *türbes* such as the Bursa Hatuniye Türbe (1449) possess a monumental *iwan*-shaped portal that dominates the facade. There are also examples of *türbes* with square bodies covered by conical spires, such as the *türbes* of Bursa Gülşah Hatun

*Plan of Yeşil Türbe, 1419-1424, Mehmed I, Bursa (from Z. Sönmez).*

51

*Saadet Hatun Hammam, Soyunmalık, 14ᵗʰ-15ᵗʰ century, Selçuk.*

(1486) and Bursa Devlet Hatun (1413-1414). The roots of the 14ᵗʰ- and 15ᵗʰ-century *türbe* style stretch beyond the Anatolian Seljuqs and Great Seljuqs all the way to Central Asia. Interesting and dazzling examples like the Bursa Yeşil Türbe are rare amongst them, which generally do not differ much from one another in regard to exterior appearance and plan.

## Hammams

Cleanliness is a matter of great importance in the Islamic religion. For example, every Muslim man or woman must wash their entire body with water after sexual intercourse. A Muslim must also wash his or her hands, face, and feet in a specific manner in order to be able to perform *namaz*, the ritual prayer. According to a Muslim expression, "cleanliness is the condition of religious faith". It is because of the importance of cleanliness that so many *hammam*s were constructed in the Emirates- and Early Ottoman-period cities. In addition to small scale *hammam*s like the İznik İsmail Bey Hammam (late 14ᵗʰ-early 15ᵗʰ century), there are also large, double *hammam*s made up of separate areas for men and women. *Hammam*s were usually built on spas or in near proximity to mosques and were an important source of income for the *waqf*s. The Turkish baths followed Roman baths as an example when it came to a heating system and units: *hammam*s are heated with smoky hot air that circulates through the hypocaust under the floor and is released to the outside via ducts inside the walls; the

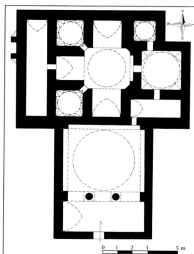

*Plan of Saadet Hatun Hammam, 14ᵗʰ-15ᵗʰ Century, Selçuk (from E. Daş).*

*Bedesten, View from south, 1413-21, Mehmed I, Edirne.*

*lıklık* (tepidarium) set aside for resting follows the domed *soyunmalık* (apoditerium) at the entrance for disrobing; and the actual bathing area called *sıcaklık* (calidarium) is the hottest section. In most *hammam*s, the *sıcaklık* plan resembles a cross, such as in Selçuk Saadet Hatun Hammam with its three *iwan*s or İznik Murad II Hammam with its four *iwan*s. Bathers lie down for a massage and scrub with a *kese* on a hot platform in the centre of the sıcaklık. *Halvet*s located in the corners of the hot-bath area are used as private bathing areas. Unlike the Roman baths, the Turkish baths do not have cold-bath areas with pools (*frigidarium*).

Ottoman *hammam*s were an important part of social life and tradition that met the needs for entertainment, rest, and cleanliness and held a special place in the social life of women.

## Bedestens and Hans (Caravanserais)

Located on important trade routes, most of the *han*s, or by the other name —*caravanserais*—, that sheltered caravans and merchants were plain structures with a rectangular plan, a single entrance, and a fortress-like appearance. Travellers ate their meals and slept on benches in the courtyards and covered sections of these vaulted *han*s, in which *tandır*s were used for cooking and heating purposes. Typical structures of the Seljuq period, *menzil han*s, literally *han*s at a day's journey, on the roads between cities, were slowly overtaken by "city *han*s" during the Emirates and Early

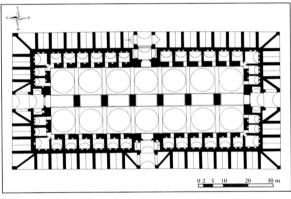

Ottoman periods. In the Ottoman *han*s, the stone benches usually adjoin the walls of the covered section; the fireplaces, used to cook food and provide heat when necessary, were constructed side by side on the walls and pack animals were tied to the edges of the stone benches and their fodder put in the feed trough that stretched along the stone bench. An Early Ottoman *han*, the Ulubat Issız Han (1394-95) on the edge of Apolyont (Ulubat) Lake, with its two fireplaces together with their chimneys resting upon short columns placed on

*Plan of Edirne Bedesten (from E. H. Ayverdi).*

53

*Issız Han, view from the north, 1394, İne (Eyne) Bey, Ulubat.*

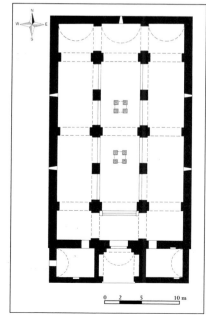

*Plan of Issız Han, Ulubat (from E. H. Ayverdi).*

the bench in the centre, is an example of the transition from Seljuq *han* to the Ottoman *han*.

Each city *han*, where caravans and merchants spent the night, was an important trade centre. Each city might have one or more *hans* depending upon the size of the city and the dimensions of trade therein. In the city *hans*, which were usually two-storied, there were rooms behind porticoes surrounding the open courtyard in the middle. For security reasons, a single door was used as both the entrance and the exit. There is a *masjid* and/or *şadırvan* in the centre of the courtyard of most of the *hans*, as in Bursa Koza Han (1492) for example. Shops were constructed adjoining the outer walls of some of the *hans*, and the *bedestens* as well. The Bursa Emir Han (14th century) is another typical example of a city *han*. Most of these *hans*, built with wood and mud brick, have not survived to the present day.

Bedestens, hans, and bazaars are special structures that adorned the trade centres of large Ottoman cities. In the early Ottoman period trade with the Mediterranean and the Balkan countries was quite healthy, and so the cities of Bursa and Edirne were famous for their bedestens, hans, and bazaars. The interior of the rectangular *bedesten*s was divided by a row of stone piers into two distinct aisles the tops of whose bays were covered by domes of equal size. A door placed in the centre of each side provided access to the outside. There are also shops adjoining the outside walls in most of the *bedesten*s. The Bursa Bedesten, which was commissioned by Bayezid I, as well as the Edirne Bedesten commissioned by Mehmed I, are still important trade centres today.

*Bedesten*s are monumental buildings where merchants gathered and valuable goods were stored, protected, bought and sold. Valuable belongings like jewels and silk cloth, and the money deposited by the merchants for safe-keeping would be kept in *bedesten*s, which were secure, sound buildings. The *bedesten* merchants performed price and quality control and acted as experts in trade lawsuits; therefore, care was taken to ensure that the people who traded in the *bedesten*s could be trusted. Employees working in the *bedesten*s received their wages from the *waqf*. *Bedesten*s, which were the centre of gravity for trade in the city, played an important role in the relationship between the state and guilds.

Bursa was an important textile- and silk-production centre of West Anatolia in the 15th century and the textiles for

*Orhan Mosque, west side of the portico, 1339-40, Orhan Gazi, Bursa.*

*Yeşil Mosque, A window on the north facade, 1419-24, Mehmed I, Bursa.*

*Bedesten, view from the southwest, 1413-21, Mehmed I, Edirne.*

the palace were woven in Bursa, where at that time there were more than 10,000 weaving looms. Traditionally the sultan's caftans and clothing would be bundled up, labelled and put in store after his death. Stored in the Istanbul Topkapı Palace, the materials in these bundles give extremely helpful information regarding the chronological development of Ottoman textile workmanship. According to the information we have obtained from these materials the oldest cotton and silk cloths originating from Bursa belong to the time of Osman Gazi (r. 1281-1324), founder of the Ottoman State, and his nine caftans of white-cotton cloth were embellished with large yellow pomegranate motifs. In addition to Bursa, which was famous for its silk textiles with their stripes of cotton thread, Ödemiş, Bergama, Soma, and Edirne, too, were important cloth-weaving centres of this period. According to written sources, silk, velvet, taffeta, brocade, and cotton fabrics were exported from Bursa to Europe, Persia, and Russia. The valuable fabrics and caftans in various museums in America and Europe give an idea of the outstanding workmanship of these textiles. Because the textile workers from Bursa had difficulty meeting the demands for their products, people were concerned that the quality might decrease; therefore, an imperial edict binding fabric quality to standards was decreed in 1502. Ottoman fabrics contain seven colours red, blue, green, pink, yellow, black, and cream. Silver and gold thread was also used in the caftans of the sultans and the wealthy. Simple and plain fabrics were used for shirts and underwear.

*Türbe of Murad II, woodwork under the eave, 1451, Murad II, Bursa.*

## Architectural Ornamentation

### Stonework

Stone was the main material used in architecture and architectural decoration of the Emirates and Early Ottoman periods. Stonemasons, who had become extremely skilful during the Seljuq period, continued their success in the 14th and 15th centuries. In the architecture of this period, wall facing was often made of alternating courses of stone and brick, numerous examples of which we see on 13th-century Byzantine structures too. Architectural ornamentation, usually quite plain, is seen much more often on front facades as opposed to the other sides of the building. Portals, casements, window tympana, arches, *mihrab*s and *minbar*s made of stone or marble were ornamented with moulding, relief decorations, lattice work, and *muqarnas*. Rows of bi-chrome stone or marble; columns or piers, column capitals and, also sometimes, *mihrab*s are decorated with stone carvings; floral motifs of this period are much more realistic than they were in the Seljuq period.

Marble, widely used in Mediterranean architecture, was obtained from local quarries or old building remains. Columns and column capitals were commonly re-used materials.

### Stucco and Painted Decoration

In the 14th and 15th centuries it was fashionable to have stucco shelves, niches, and fireplaces decorated with floral and geometric motifs moulded in bas-relief in the *tabhane*s of the mosques (as in the Bursa Yıldırım Mosque (1389-1399) for exam-

*İsa Bey Mosque, detail of the transition to the dome, 1375, İsa Bey, Selçuk.*

ple). Another innovation brought about by this transition period are brown, black, blue, and red coloured *kalemişi* consisting of floral motifs and scripture on plaster, like the examples we see in buildings in Edirne and Bursa. The paintings applied on plaster to internal surfaces such as arches, domes and vaults are called *kalemişi*, just as the painted decoration executed on plaster on wooden structures. In many mosques, the internal surfaces of domes of porticoes surrounding

57

*Yeşil Türbe, tilework şemse, 1419-24, Mehmed I, Bursa.*

the courtyard are decorated with *kalemişi* paintings as well.

In some of the Early Ottoman-period structures in Bursa and Edirne, the wooden ceilings, cornices, window and door wings, *minbar*s, bookstands, and drawers are decorated with lacquered floral and geometric designs in red, dark blue, yellow, green, and white. The designs and compositions on these decorations are the same as those seen on contemporary tiles, ceramics, textiles, and rugs. In later centuries, many wooden items with lacquer ornamentation were produced in Edirne; therefore, lacquer decorations are called "Edirne kari" (Edirne style). The most beautiful examples of this type of decoration are in the Bursa Muradiye Mosque (1426) and on the wooden lean-to roof of the Türbe of Murad II (1451).

## Tiles

It is striking that less tile work was used in the Emirates and Early Ottoman period architectural decoration in comparison with the Seljuq period (with the exception of a few examples in Edirne and Bursa). Apart from these few examples, glazed brick was preferred on the facade decorations of religious structures. The glazed-brick decorations of the minarets of the Birgi Great Mosque (1312/13), Manisa Great Mosque (1367), İznik Yeşil Mosque (1392), and Tire Yeşil İmaret Mosque (1441) are rare examples retaining the Seljuq style. In examples of later dates, the colours yellow, green, and white were added to the turquoise, purple, and dark blue of the Seljuq-period glazed bricks. Tile mosaic decoration, which reached its zenith during the Seljuq period, declined in importance in the 14th and 15th centuries when only a few examples continuing the old tradition successfully. In the tile-mosaic technique, those tiles glazed with turquoise, more uncommonly aubergine purple, cobalt blue, and black, are cut so as to form the desired motif and then put together. Tile mosaics of the Emirates and Early Ottoman periods are different from the Seljuq examples in that the designs are plainer and the pieces that form the designs are larger. In some examples white, green, and yellow were added to the turquoise, black, and cobalt blue of the Seljuq period.

The rare tile mosaic ornamentation of the Emirates period can be seen on the Birgi Great Mosque's *mihrab* (1312/13) and on the pendentives that support the dome in Selçuk İsa Bey Mosque (1375). In some

rly Ottoman buildings tile mosaics
re used together with tiles in the *cuer-
seca* (coloured glaze) technique, rare
amples of which are found on the
lls, arches, casements and *mihrabs* in
e İznik Yeşil Mosque (1392), Bursa Yeş-
Mosque, Yeşil Madrasa and Yeşil Türbe
419-1424) as well as Bursa Muradiye
426) and Edirne Muradiye (1426/27)
osques.

e earliest examples in the *cuerda seca*
chnique appear in structures in Bursa
d Edirne; the design is obtained by
essing a mould into a tile clay or carv-
g out the design and then baking the
ates in a kiln. A mixture of beeswax,
getable oil, and manganese is spread
tween the colours so that they do not
x with one another during the firing.
soon as the beeswax melts, the mix-
re becomes transparent and the red
lour of the clay underneath becomes
sible. According to another method
actised in Spain, thread is placed
tween the different coloured glazes; the
read burns during firing and the con-
urs take the appearance of black lines.
us, the term *cuerda seca* means "dry
read" in Spanish. This technique makes
eation of intricate scriptural and floral
signs easier and the colour scale con-
sting of turquoise, dark-blue, black,
ght purple, white, yellow, pistachio
een, and gold gilding enabled the for-
ation of rich complex designs. We do
t have any definitive knowledge regard-
g the manufacturing centre of *cuerda seca*
es but it is highly probable that masters
ho came with Tamerlane's army from
briz and Samarkand, where this tech-
que was widely used, brought it to Ana-
lia. It is also believed that travelling
aster workmen manufactured the *cuer-*

*da seca* tiles in small workshops established
close to buildings in Bursa, Edirne, and
Istanbul.

In Early Ottoman-period structures, in
addition to tile mosaics and *cuerda seca*
tiles, designs were also made using monochrome glazed plates. Tile plates coloured
turquoise, dark -and light- blue, green,
and white were arranged geometrically
leaving no gaps between the hexagonal,
octagonal, rectangular, square, or triangular plates; sometimes gold leaf or
impressed floral motifs also appear on the
plates.

The Early Ottoman period's highest quality tiles, called the "blue-white" group,
were used especially in buildings in İznik,
Bursa, and Edirne. Ongoing excavations
have proven that these tiles were produced
in İznik in the first half of the 15th century. Successful examples of blue-white tiles

*Türbe of Şehzade
Mustafa and Cem
Sultan, Detail from
mihrab tiles, 1479,
Bursa.*

*Great Mosque, minbar,
1377, Manisa.*

peonies, and cloud or dragon motifs
Far Eastern origin in a realistic sty.
These exhibit similarities with Min
period Chinese Porcelain with rega
to design and colour, and Far Easte
influence can be explained to a lar
degree by imported Chinese porcelai
A great number of blue-white cerami
influenced by Ming porcelain was fou
in the İznik excavations from whi
came most of the blue-white cerami
exhibited in the İznik and Bur
museums.

## Woodwork

Wooden items made from a variety
materials like walnut, apple, pear, ros
and cedar are another important mat
rial that enriched 14$^{th}$ and 15$^{th}$ centu
architecture. Valuable bookrests, *mi
bar*s, window shutters and door wing
banisters and lecterns that decorate
Seljuq structures can also be seen
Emirates and Early Ottoman-peric
structures, although fewer in numbe
Noteworthy works manufactured usin
different techniques are on display
Manisa, Bursa, and Edirne Museums.
Some of the most intricate and master
examples in the art of woodcarving a
on the *minbars* located to the right of th
*mihrabs*. The wood working techniqu
called *kündekari* used on the side surfaces
the Manisa Great Mosque's (1367), Bir
Great Mosque's (1312/13) and Bursa Gre
Mosque's (1400) *minbars* is the legacy
the Seljuq period. Appearing in Egypt an
Syria in the 12$^{th}$ century, *kündekari*
type of basting: wooden pieces in octa;
onal, diamond, and star shapes and dec
rated with carved *rumis* were attached

made with the under-glaze technique can
be seen in the Türbe of Şehzade Mustafa
and Cem Sultan in Bursa (1479), and Üç
Şerefeli (1445) and Muradiye (1426/27)
Mosques in Edirne.

The designs on these tiles have been
worked with blue tones and turquoise
beneath a transparent and colourless
glaze. The clay of the hexagonal or rectangular shaped tile plates is hard and
white like porcelain. Among the most
striking motifs, are spring flowers,

e another without using nails or glue
t by means of rods with mortise.
:ause the pieces are held together with
ortise and tenon (or tongue-and-
oove), once the wood dries, they do
t separate or split. A wooden frame-
ork that reinforces the *minbar* also sup-
rts the surface of the interlocking *kün-
ari*. This technique was used especially
the side surfaces of the *minbar*, and
netimes also on door and window
ngs. A technique that resembles *kün-
ari*, but uses glue or nails to hold the
all wooden pieces together, is called
e *kündekari*.
e most widespread decorations of
th- and 15th-century wood craftsman-
p are floral or geometric motifs and
ilpture with flat or rounded surfaces.
gi Great Mosque's wooden window
ings and *minbar* (1322) are some of the
ost beautiful examples of the period's
oodwork. The surfaces of 15th-century
oden works were also inlaid with
other-of-pearl, bone, ivory and even
le. Woodwork examples with inlaid
d engraved ornamentation are exhib-
d at Edirne, Bursa, and İznik muse-
is. The wood inlay technique was
veloped in the 13th century in Damas-
s and applied to a great number of
orks during the 14th-century Mamluk
riod.

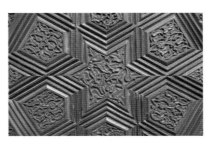

*Great Mosque, detail of wooden door wings, 1400, Bayezid I, Bursa.*

Batuta, the famous traveller who visited Anatolia in the 14th century, says that
Anatolian carpets were praised and
exported to various countries. These
rugs using a special knot, called "Turkish Double Knot" or "Gördes Knot",
which were pure wool carpets. The
main colours are tones of red and blue
together with yellow, cream, purple,
and brown, with green also used to a

*Great Mosque, detail of wooden window shutters, 1312-13, Aydınoğlu Mehmed Bey, Bırgi.*

## ıgs

Islamic countries, carpets and prayer
gs, traditionally donated to mosques,
id mosques a warm atmosphere with
eir lively colours and designs and
est Anatolia was an important carpet-
:aving region in the 14th century. Ibn

61

*Ceramic Plate (Inv. No. 4377), 15ᵗʰ century, İznik Museum.*

lesser degree. The fame of carpets and prayer rugs woven in Milas, İzmir, Uşak, Kula, Gördes, Bergama, Balıkesir, Çanakkale, Ezine, and Bandırma still continues today. Milas Great Mosque still has some authentic rugs of later dates on the floor and the invaluable pieces from Edirne Muradiye Mosque are on display at Turkish-Islamic Arts Museum in İstanbul. It is a great pity that nowadays monochrome, machine-made carpets are found in most of the West Anatolian mosques.

The Seljuqs brought the carpet-weaving tradition with them. It is highly probable that the first rugs woven in Konya and its environs date back to the 13ᵗʰ century. The carpet-weaving tradition increased in variety as it continued in the 14ᵗʰ- and 15ᵗʰ- century Emirates and Early Ottoman period.

In 1935-36, the Swedish researcher C. J. Lamm found up to 100 carpet fragments large and small in old Cairo (Fustat). Today these fragments are in the Stockholm National Museum, Gothenburg Röhs Museum, and Athens Benaki Museum. Of the examples published by C. J. Lamm, seven are Seljuq, while the others

are 14ᵗʰ- and 15ᵗʰ-century Anatolian ru[g]. Most of these are decorated with abstr[act] animal figures, and some of them w[ith] geometric designs; similar fragments a[re] also found in Istanbul and Konya mus[e]ums.

Today our greatest source of informati[on] about carpets with animal figures a[re] paintings by 14ᵗʰ- and 15ᵗʰ-century Itali[an], Flemish, Dutch, and Spanish painter[s]. Turkish rugs imported from Anatolia a[re] often depicted in paintings of this peri[od] beneath the figures' feet or spread out [on] tables. The rugs, which are painted [in] great detail, have large hexagonal a[nd] octagonal rosettes decorated with abstr[act] geometric tree-of-life patterns, bir[ds], double-headed eagles, stags, and scen[es] of animals fighting. The borders of carp[ets] with animal figures have geometric mot[ifs] or a decoration reminiscent of Ku[fic] script. It is striking that the paintin[gs] depict the carpets down to the fin[est] details while remaining true to the ori[gi]nals.

By the 15ᵗʰ century animal figures on ru[gs] were replaced by large rugs with most[ly] geometric designs and plain prayer ru[gs] as seen in some paintings of the 15ᵗʰ ce[n]tury. There are paintings by Hans H[ol]bein, Lorenzo Lotto, Gentile Bellini, a[nd] Giovanni Bellini, which it is believed we[re] produced in the vicinity of Uşak in W[est] Anatolia. Often seen on Hans Holbei[n] paintings, these have been termed t[he] "Holbein Carpets".

Unfortunately, it is impossible to fi[nd] examples of these historic carpets [in] West Anatolian museums today. T[he] same designs, however, are still used [in] the rather high-quality carpets woven [in] various cities in West Anatolia. This tr[a] tion is also kept alive by quality-carpets ianufactured in villages and carpet-eaving centres. Fabrics and carpets ere exported for centuries from İzmir d its environs to Europe and above all Italy.

## andicrafts Exhibited in the useums of West Anatolian

1e examples of handicrafts from the nirates and Early Ottoman periods at have survived up until today are nple and unadorned. Usually archaeological finds pre-dating the Turkish riod, and ethnographic works belonging to the late Ottoman period, are :hibited in the museums that are tailed in our itineraries. The limited imber of ceramic, metal, carpet, and ooden works dating from the 14th and th centuries makes one think that irkish museums need to attach more portance to building collections of the irkish era. A look at the examples displayed in the museums of West Anatolin will suffice to give us an idea about ndicrafts produced in the Emirates and rly Ottoman periods.

## eramic Arts

ittery from the Miletus, Beçin, lçuk-Ephesus, İznik, and Edirne excations, as well as chance finds, show at ceramics of the Emirates and Early ttoman periods are different from ose of the Seljuq period. The most idespread examples are ceramics lled "Miletus ware" because they were st unearthed and published in the

Miletus excavations. Later finds, however, from the excavations and research on İznik in particular, suggested that these ceramics were produced in İznik. Various examples of "Miletus-ware" ceramics are displayed in Bursa and İznik museums. These red-clay ceramics produced for daily use were decorated with cobalt blue, black, turquoise, green floral designs, rosettes, geometric shapes and radial lines beneath a transparent, achromatic, or sometimes turquoise coloured glaze.

In addition to Miletus ware, examples in the "sgraffito" technique in which abstract shapes are worked with incised lines or examples of designs painted beneath glaze on a paste-like material called "slip" have also been recovered at excavations carried out in West Anatolia. Abstract floral and geometric motifs were used on these ceramics too. In the slip technique, the colours used under the transparent colourless glaze are beige, blue, green, brown or yellow and the motifs are slightly raised.

The colours and designs used in the ceramic group classified as "blue-white" because of its colours were also used on ceramic plates, as we stated earlier. İznik and Kütahya were the manufacturing centres of the blue-white ceramics, which were produced in large quantities in the 15th and 16th centuries. The clay of quality blue-white ceramics is white and hard like porcelain. Once again the designs, worked under a transparent and colourless glaze, are reminiscent of 15th-century Ming-period Chinese porcelain. The design is drawn with blue tones on a white background beneath a hard and high-quality transparent glaze. Various examples of blue-white ceramics and of

"Haliç ware" (Golden Horn ware) ceramics such as bowls, plates and mugs are exhibited in the İznik and Bursa Museums.

Blue-white fragments found on excavations in İznik present an idea of the variety available in this type of ceramic ware. Examples of vases, goblets, cups, sugar bowls, lamps, and so on, together with many tile kiln remains prove that İznik was the main manufacturing centre. According to inscriptions, *fermans*, and recovered fragments, blue-white ceramics were also manufactured in Kütahya, where most of today's ceramics are produced. Blue-white ceramics continued to be manufactured in the classic Ottoman style with more realistic motifs in the 16$^{th}$ century as well.

## Metal Art

Our knowledge of metal art during the Emirates and Early Ottomans period is extremely limited but fragments preserved in various collections and museums show that the Seljuq metal arts tradition continued in this period. In the 13$^{th}$ century, Iranian and Seljuq master craftsmen escaping from the Mongol invasion continued the Great Seljuq metal art tradition while settling in Iraq and Syria. We know from inscriptions that Syrian master craftsmen took orders from Anatolian Emirates in the 13$^{th}$ century, right through to the 15th century and it is thought that some Syrian masters migrating to Anatolia also brought the tradition with them to their new homeland. The 14$^{th}$-15$^{th}$-century examples of metalwork that have survived are made of brass, iron, and bronze; works

made of gold and silver are extremely ra[re]. The craftsmanship of metalwork in Anato[lia] exhibits a wide-ranging variety an[d] exemplifies the extreme care craftsme[n] took with their work. For example, was[h] tubs, bowls, trays, long-spouted ewer[s] vases, candelabra, pen cases, oil lamp[s] incense burners, pestle and mortars, mi[r]rors, belt buckles, and door knockers.

Of the limited quantity of metalwork o[n] display in West Anatolian Museums, it [is] thought that the gold and silver inlai[d] bronze candelabra dating from the end [of] the 13$^{th}$ or beginning of the 14$^{th}$ centu[ry] in the Bursa Turkish and Islamic Ar[t] Museum, were manufactured at Siirt [in] Southeast Anatolia. The bronze brazi[er] found in the same museum is a beautif[ul] example of 14$^{th}$-century metal art. Som[e] of the valuable metal objects belongi[ng] to the Early Ottoman period are exhib[ib]ited in museums in Istanbul and abroa[d] According to its inscription a bronze ca[n]delabrum from the year 1329, current[ly] in the Louvre Museum in Paris, w[as] made for Orhan Gazi. Exhibited in t[he] same museum, a bronze decant[er] belonging to Sultan Mehmed II is amo[ng] the period's finest examples of meta[l] work. The workmanship on some of t[he] inscribed candelabra stored in the Istan[n]bul Topkapı Palace and Turkish an[d] Islamic Arts Museums is striking. A pa[ir] of inscribed bronze candelabrum order[ed] for the mosque of the Bayezid I[I] Mosque Complex in Edirne is also di[s]played in the Turkish Islamic Arts Muse[um]. Although few in number, the[se] examples show that 14$^{th}$- and 15$^{th}$-centu[ry] metal workmanship in Anatolia, whi[le] not inventing a new style, neverthele[ss] formed a foundation for metalwork [in] the Ottoman period.

## ook Art

the 14<sup>th</sup> and 15<sup>th</sup> centuries, the rulers
the Western Anatolian Emirates took
patronage for books and the art of
anuscript illumination. Valuable manu-
ripts illuminated with gilding and
lourful ornamentation can be found in
e Tire Necip Pasha Library.
arsa was famous for the artists, known
*müzehhip*, who decorated manuscripts
d did the bookbinding and who were
ken under the patronage of the
ttoman sultans. Valuable calligraphy
d manuscripts dating to the 14<sup>th</sup> and

*Cast bronze jug (Inv. No. 764), 15<sup>th</sup> century, Bursa Turkish and Islamic Arts Museum.*

15<sup>th</sup> centuries is found in the Bursa
Turkish and Islamic Arts Museum as
well as the Istanbul Topkapı Palace
Museum.

# ultan of the Coasts

### Aydoğan Demir, Yekta Demiralp, Rahmi H. Ünal

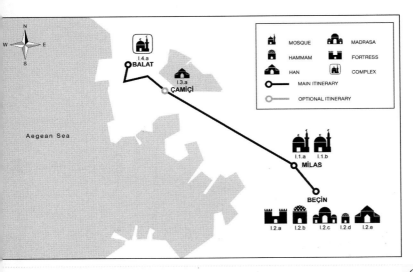

*Ahmet Gazi Madrasa, Lion relief on the left spandrel of the main iwan, 1375, Ahmet Gazi, Beçin.*

The Byzantine Empire, an important power in the Balkans and in West and North Anatolia at the end of the 11th century, found itself unable to overcome the devastating effects of the Fourth Crusade (1204). The Anatolian Seljuq Sultans, who ruled over much of Anatolia, also fell in defeat against Mongolian attacks (1243). Distressed by Mongolian oppression, hundreds of thousands of people under the command of Turcoman *Beys* and some Seljuq administrators broke the resistance of the Byzantines, already greatly weakened in West Anatolia, and settled in the region.

Menteşe Bey and his successors occupied the area that was antique Caria and founded the Menteşe Emirate there (1280 They proceeded to co-operate with th local seamen, that is, the Rums, in orde to develop themselves further by openir up to the seas. They controlled a part Rhodes for a short time until the arriv of the Knights of St. John (1310). Th Ahmet Gazi, who had a beautiful *madra* constructed in Beçin (1375), saw himse deserving of the title "Sultan of th Coasts" must be an expression of his asp ration to establish sovereignty over th seas. Having in hand the important trad ing port of Balat (Miletus), the Menteş Emirate guaranteed peaceful trade b entering into six agreements with th Venetians between the years 1331-1414 According to these agreements, Venetia merchants would be free to trade o Menteşe land, allowed to settle in Bala and able to worship at a church tha would be named Saint Nicholas. Th Venetian Consulate residing in Bala would act as the special trial authority o cases of interest to the Venetians; anoth er Venetian would not be held responsi ble and arrested in place of a Venetia merchant who was in debt because o business. In order to increase the volum of trade, the Menteşe Beys minted silve currency of illustrated Neapolitan typ with Latin script, called "Gigliati". Th Menteşe Emirate's economy, based upo bountiful plains and safe trade, created a important source for the country's devel opment as it aspired to a rich and pros perous condition. Thanks to this health economy, monumental works were con structed in Beçin, Milas, and Balat.

Crossing the Çanakkale Straits (Dard anelles), Ottoman forces conquere Thrace and progressed as far as Kosovo i

*Great Mosque, Entrance facade, 1378, Ahmet Gazi, Milas.*

e 1350s. Then, once they had locked
e Byzantines into Istanbul and its sur-
undings, they proceeded to annex the
nirates in West Anatolia to Ottoman
nd. It has not yet been definitely deter-
ined in which year the Aydın and
enteşe Emirates were conquered. How-
er, it is believed that Balat was captured
the years 1389-90. When Ahmet Gazi
ıssed away in 1391, he was buried in the
adrasa he had built in Beçin. The gover-
or of Menteşe –the region is still named
ter him– under the Ottoman Sultan
eyazid I, Hoca Firuz commissioned the
onstruction of the Firuz Bey Mosque in
lilas, the construction of which was
ompleted on 29 November 1396.

ı 1424 the Ottoman State eradicated the
lenteşe Emirate that had been re-estab-
shed after the Battle of Ankara in 1402.
fter this date, towns like Beçin and Balat
ı Menteşe –an Ottoman *sanjak*
ɔrovince) then– became less important
ıd were eventually abandoned.

A. D.

his itinerary begins in the town centre of
lilas in the ancient region of Caria and con-
nues straight to the north until you reach
ɔur destination in the ancient region of Ionia.
faving looked around Milas town centre and
t the works in Beçin Fortress, continue down
ne main road heading north on D. 525. After
ıssing the rugged territory on the southern
hore of Lake Bafa, you reach Söke Plain,
hich was created by centuries of alluvium
ccumulation from the Büyük Menderes River
ıncient Meandre River). Once you reach Söke,
ɔu need to decide where to spend the night: If
ɔu like, you can spend the night at the start-
ıg point of the next route, Selçuk, or, if you
refer, you can spend the night at the more
vely coastal town of Kuşadaşı. Those visitors

*Silver coin minted in the name of Ahmet Gazi (1359-91), Üstün Erek Collection.*

who decide to continue in the direction of
Selçuk, can stop for a rest at the town of
Ortaklar on the way and drop by one of its
many restaurants for a taste of the region's
famous çöp şiş (a kebab made by grilling very
small cubes of meat that have been strung on a
small skewer over charcoal) and ayran (a drink
made of yoghurt and water) or grilled sucuk (a
very spicy sausage).

If you are using public transport, you may not
be able to complete your visits in a single day.
However, a good transport network exists
between cities in Turkey. You can reach Beçin
from Milas by taking one of the dolmush
minibuses (shared cabs or vans) that leave from
the front of the Great Mosque, opposite the Museum. To get to Balat by bus, you must first go to
Söke and board a Balat or Didim dolmush at
the bus station. Bafa Han is located on the
Milas-Söke main road; however, it is difficult
to visit this building unless you have your own
transport. Be especially careful driving on the
road that stretches along the Söke Plain, there
are tractors on the road loaded with cotton
bales many of which are poorly lit and marked,
especially during harvest season (September-
October).

*Great Mosque, west facade, 1378, Ahmet Gazi, Milas.*

## I.I MİLAS

Known as Mylasa during Antiquity, Milas was the Carian capital in ancient times; however, Halicarnassus (present day Bodrum) assumed this title during the reign of Caria's Persian Satrap Mausolus (4th century BC). Due to the good relations he established with the Persians, Mausolus was able to rule without hindrance. Upon his death, his wife had a monumental grave (mausoleum) constructed for his burial: one of the Seven Wonders of the World, only traces of whose foundations are visible today. Mylasa continued to be important during the Hellenistic period due to the proximity of the religious centre Labranda (13 km. to the east), and later, during the Roman period, it served as an administrative centre. Not very much is known about Milas during the Byzantine period.

We do know, however, that the cit regained its importance with the found ing of the Menteşe Emirate.

### I.1.a Great Mosque (Ulu Cami)

*Hoca Bedrettin District (Mahallesi), İnön Avenue, Milas. Across the street from the Muse um.*

Ruling between the years 1359-1391, th famous Menteşe Emir Ahmet Gaz administered a section of the land that ha been divided up amongst his siblings afte his father's death. Not only did Ahme Bey remain in power longer than an other Menteşe Bey, his period of reig was also the Emirate's most brilliant. / few of the buildings that Ahmet Gazi ha constructed in Beçin, Milas, Balat Fethiye, and Çine, are still standing today Of these, the Milas Great Mosque ha een completely restored in the last few ears and is still open for worship.

he walls of the mosque, which is located in a beautiful garden full of shrubs and rees, were built with bricks, and stones athered from ancient buildings; the ocks with inscriptions and the decorave brickwork here and there are especially noteworthy. Besides the main ntrance in the centre of the north facade, ere is also an entrance on both the east nd west fronts. The stairs located to the ght of the portal on the north facade ere constructed to provide access to the oof for the chanting of the call to prayer. ccording to the Arabic inscription above ae entrance, the mosque's construction as completed in October 1378. Another inscription, written in Ottoman on the op part of the entrance on the west acade, is a *waqf* charter dating from 904. The variety seen in the building's apports and roof shows that it underent important renovations at various mes in history: the rather massive butesses on all of the facades must be later dditions.

oth the plan and roof design of Milas reat Mosque continues the Seljuq tradi-on. Like the Seljuq mosques with basil-al plans, this mosque also has aisles that re perpendicular to the *qibla* wall; while he aisles are covered with various types f vaults, the bay in front of the *mihrab* is istinctly differentiated from the rest with dome. The marble *minbar* decorated vith several rosettes was renovated in 879; however, the inscription of the forner *minbar*, dated January 1380, was opied onto the new one.

R. H. Ü.

### I.1.b **Firuz Bey Mosque**

*Firuz Bey Mosque, view from the northwest, 1396, Hoca Firuz, Milas.*

*Firuz Pasha District (Mahallesi), Kışla Avenue, Milas. Continue north along the main street in front of Great Mosque and turn left at Kışla Caddesi.*

This mosque is located in the middle of a spacious courtyard in the town centre. The *madrasa* cells lined up along the courtyard's western edge lost their special features as a result of renovation and the graves in the mosque courtyard were transferred to another cemetery in the 1930s. The build-

71

*Firuz Bey Mosque, south facade, 1396, Hoca Firuz, Milas.*

*Firuz Bey Mosque, mihrab, 1396, Hoca Firuz, Milas.*

ing, completed in 1396, recently underwen a complete renovation and is still open fo worship. All the external facades are face with blue-veined marble plates. The Turki traveller Evliya Çelebi wrote that, "becaus of the blue-coloured marble, the Turl named the building the 'Gök Camii' (Sk Blue Mosque)". The two rows of window are very attractive: each window has unique decorative composition. The minar usually located on one of the side walls, o the end closest to the entrance side and ri ing from a special base, is here, howeve placed on top of the wall of the prayer hall The portico in front, striking with it elaborate arches, lattice marble ba lustrades with geometric decoration an an elegant portal, is five arched bu three bayed, the central one of which topped with a dome, while the side bay are covered with cradle vaults. The flo ral ornamentation seen around th inscription panel above the entrance an below the portico's central bay are indi cations of a break with the Seljuq tradi tion. A variant of multifunctiona mosques that served as a place of wor ship as well as a guesthouse, the Firu Bey Mosque has *tabhane*s at both its eas and west ends, and the inner cour between the tabhanes and the praye hall are much smaller than normal. Th elegant domes are covered with paint ings of a later date; yet the *mihrab* catch es the eye immediately with its carvings and the plain marble *minbar* has a simpl *Solomon's-knot* (David's-star) motif as dec oration. An architect named Hassan Ibi Abdullah constructed the building while a master craftsman named Mus Ibn Adil executed the ornamentation.

R. H. Ü

*Beçin Fortress, general view from the west, 4ᵗʰ-14ᵗʰ century, Beçin.*

*Milas is a lovely, lively town with a variety of things to offer the visitor: the Museum located in the old town has a small but good collection of works from antiquity; the old town full of Ottoman houses with charming local-style chimneys; the Gümüşkesen Tomb from Roman times; the local market on Tuesdays...*
*The remains of the Mausoleum, one of the Seven Wonders of the World, is located in Bodrum (ancient Halicarnassus), 50 km. from Milas. The St. Peter's Fortress, constructed by the Knights of St. John using stones from the mausoleum, is a worldwide famous Underwater Archaeology Museum today. Bodrum is a charming coastal town that attracts both native and foreign tourists during the summer months.*

*Beçin is situated to the south of Milas, just 4 km. from the city centre. You can reach Beçin by taking one of the Beçin dolmush minibuses that leave from the front of the Great Mosque.*

## I.2 BEÇİN

Built on top of a flat plateau on the edge of the Milas Plain, and 200 m. above, the fortress rises majestically on a weird looking rocky outcrop, like a crown over the head of the modern town. The remains on the top and outskirts of the steep slope to the north have given rise to speculation that this area was used as a necropolis during antiquity. The remains of foundations dating to the Hellenistic period to the east, along with the temple (4ᵗʰ century BC) at the southeast corner of the city walls, are evidence that the fortress existed before the Turkish period.

The town of Beçin was probably a small settlement when it passed into the hands of the Menteşe Beys towards the end of the 13ᵗʰ century. The small dimensions of the Byzantine chapel situated in the ruins of the town supports this thesis. The famous Arab traveller Ibn Battuta, who visited the city in the 1330s, lends further credence

73

*Büyük hammam, general view from the southwest, 14th century, Beçin.*

temple which is thought to be dedicated to Zeus though it still has not been examined in detail. The dilapidated houses inside the fortress, though today deserted, were used up until the 1980s and the oldest of them dates back 100 years at the most. The presence of a deteriorated 14th-century *hammam* makes one think that the settlement inside the fortress should be much older.

R. H. Ü

to this theory when he writes that it was "a newly founded city with new buildings and *masjids*". That the majority of what remains of the ruined city dates back to the Turkish period, is proof that the city developed rapidly during the period. Due to a rapid increase in population and development, the majority of the town's buildings originate in the 14th century.

R. H. Ü.

## I.2.a  Fortress

The road turns right in front of the stairs going up to the fortress. Just in front is a fountain, probably dating to the Menteşe period, and a few steps up on the right is a cistern that provided the water for the fortress. In spite of the large number of water sources and wells in the ruined city of Beçin itself, it was impossible for water to be brought to the fortress because it rises on a steep mass of stone 50 m. higher than the plateau upon which the city lies.

A section of the circular city walls, currently in need of restoration, rest in the south upon the foundations of an ancient

## I.2.b  Büyük Hammam

The famous Turkish traveller Evliya Çelebi, who visited Beçin in the middle of the 17th century, reports that there was no *hammam* in Beçin. However, because the ruins of five *hammams* are visible in the city today, it must be concluded that the baths were either in ruins or no longer operating at the time of Evliya Çelebi's visit.

The Büyük Hammam, literally the Large Hammam, located in the olive grove to the right of the road from the fortress to the Ahmet Gazi Madrasa, is one of the city's most magnificent structures. Although much of its roof has caved in, great portions of the wall are still standing. The vaulted rectangular room to the north is the water depot and on the outside can be seen the stokehole arch through which the fire was fed. The large hall to the east is the *soyunmalık*. Excavations have revealed two fountains, one in the *soyunmalık*, the other in the *ılıklık*. A particularly interesting characteristic of this *hammam* is the existence of two doors that provide access to the outside in the disrobing area, as almost all baths have only one entrance to the disrobing area so as to prevent heat loss.

74

ome Turkish baths were constructed as wo separate, adjoining baths designated or men and women. In these baths, the ntrance to the section set aside for women opens onto a generally not too usy side street so that women could comfortably enter and exit the baths. There are o *hammam*s designated for women only, ther than these double *hammam*s. In case f a single *hammam* only women would be llowed into the baths on one or two days f the week. Of the two entrances seen at he Büyük Hammam, the one on the east ide opens onto the street, while on the west is a secondary entrance of small dimensions not visible from the street. On he days that the *hammam* was set aside for women, the main entrance looking onto he street would probably have been closed o that women customers could enter and xit through this door at the rear of the building.

Passing through the small chamber to the west is the *ılıklık*; to its north it adjoins he *sıcaklık* with three *iwan*s forming a T-hape and in the corners are the *halvet*s. The whole floor is covered with large, re-ised marble blocks and the walls bear races of plaster.

R. H. Ü.

## .2.c **Ahmet Gazi Madrasa**

This *madrasa*, commissioned by the amous Menteşe *Bey* Ahmet Gazi, is the best preserved of all the buildings of the Menteşe Emirate to have survived until he present day. Restoration work, begun n recent years, still continues. According o the Arabic inscription above the entrance, "the Great Ruler, the Sultan of he Coasts Ahmet Gazi" had this *madrasa*

built in the year 1375. Ahmet Gazi's use of the title "Sultan of the Coasts" proves that efforts to establish sovereignty over the Aegean, which were increased during the time of the Menteşe rulers Mesut Bey and Orhan Bey, came to a successful conclusion. The commercial activities and human traffic revived with the Aegean islands, Italy and southern France during this period, resulted in the first appearance of some foreign elements in Turkish architecture. Although it has all the components of the traditional Seljuq portal, there are important differences in detail on the *madrasa*'s entrance. From up close, the numerous mouldings that frame the main niche of the entrance recall portals of the Gothic Order.

The *iwan* of the main entrance is located opposite the main *iwan* of the structure. The *madrasa*'s eight chambers and two *iwan*s open onto a courtyard of lateral rectangular shape. The porticoes that we are used to seeing in most of the *madrasa* courtyards are

*Büyük hammam, soyunmalık after excavation and conservation, 14th Century, Beçin.*

not present here. The two large chambers on either side of the main *iwan* are classrooms. There is a fireplace in each of the cells as well as in the classrooms. On the spandrels of the *iwan*'s main arch are two lion figures which are very simply engraved and each holding a banner in its hands; the lion on the left holds a banner that reads "Ahmed Gazi" in Arabic script. We know that some animal figures like the "eagle" and the "lion" were used as symbols of the sultan during the Seljuq period, too; however, none of these were depicted carrying banners in their hands as they do here. Of the two graves in the main *iwan*, the one closer to the courtyard belongs to Ahmet Gazi. It has been suggested that the grave adjoining might belong to another Menteşe ruler, Şücaeddin Bey. The locals, who believe that these are the graves of great religious people, make offerings and pray when they visit the graves.

R. H. Ü.

### I.2.d **Bey Hammam** (option)

The Bey Hammam is located 25 m. north of a large two-storey mansion located 50 m. to the west of the *madrasa*; the mansion probably belonged to one of the city's prominent people, perhaps even to Menteşe Bey.

Likely to have been constructed at the beginning of the 15th century, Bey Hammam lies approximately 100 m. away from the Büyük Hammam, which is dated to the second half of the 14th century. The close proximity of these two functionally identical structures leads one to believe that Bey Hammam may have been a private bathhouse belonging to the nearby mansion. The ornamental remains, traces of which can still be seen on the plaster inside the structure, shows that the building's workmanship was very fine. Although the superstructure has completely collapsed, a considerable portion of the walls still standing. Excavations have revealed the foundations of the ruined disrobing area.

R. H. Ü.

## 2.e **Kızıl Han**

Directly across from Ahmet Gazi Madrasa in the town centre stands Orhan Mosque (1330-31), the largest one in Beçin. The road continues left round Orhan Mosque, past another fountain on the right, and then arrives at the Kızıl Han.

One of the most important Silk routes stretching from Europe to China traversed Anatolia; since the end of the 12th century, the Turks who ruled over Anatolia realised the material benefits brought about by transit trade and took measures in order to develop it. *Caravanserais*, constructed with this aim of development in mind, ensured traders a safe place to spend the night, while the market places established nearby made trading possible. Trade activities suddenly came alive once the emirates in West Anatolia, which had been in dispute with one another in the 14th century, came under Ottoman rule in the early 15th century and the region was made safe. Thus, the first *han*s constructed in West Anatolian towns like Bergama, Menemen and Tire, date to the 15th century.

The *han*s in West Anatolia are not magnificent and imposing like *caravanserai*s of the Seljuq period. The two *han*s in Beçin, partly in good condition, are also plain, unimposing structures. Kızıl Han is a two-storey structure; its walls are still standing today, although its superstructure has almost entirely collapsed. Its general layout resembles the Döger *Caravanserai* near Afyon. Made up of a single lateral rectangular area, the ground floor is the stable where the pack animals were tethered and where some of the travellers would have spent the night. Traces of a staircase that would have led to two rooms on the upper floor are still visible to the left of the entrance door; travellers spent the night in these upper rooms, too.

R. H. Ü.

*Kızıl Han, south facade, 15th century, Beçin.*

77

*Bafa Han is on the way to Söke from Milas (D.525) and right on the border between Aydın - Muğla provinces, and about 40 km. away from Milas.*

## I.3  ÇAMİÇİ

### I.3.a  **Bafa Han** (option)

The caravan traffic between the Menteşe Emirate's important city port of Balat (Miletus) and the capital Beçin was quite heavy. Though this traffic slowly began to decrease after the Emirate ceased to exist, it nevertheless continued for a very long time. Thus the Turkish traveller Evliya Çelebi, who visited Balat in the 1670's, recounts that active maritime trade was taking place in the town. The Bafa Han is located on the caravan route that stretches from Balat to Milas and Beçin. The *han*

is made of a single rectangular area, an[ ] its entrance looks onto the road that pass es in front of it.

The cistern adjoining the *han*, believed t have been built in the 14th centur attracts more attention than the *han*'s sim ple plan. A great number of cisterns exis in the rather rugged territory of Muğ province's rural area. Although not ric in natural water resources, the regio receives the second highest rainfall i Turkey. These cisterns were constructe to collect rainwater in the autumn, win ter, and spring months, to be used durin the summer months, when almost no rai falls. Furthermore, water was alway needed by travellers and pack anima spending the night at the *han*.

In order to collect water for the cistern small channels were constructed on th long sides of the *han* at the level of th eaves. Rainwater that fell on the roof c the *han* was directed to the cylindrical cis

*Kızıl Han, a pendentive in the northern upper-storey room, 15th century, Beçin.*

*Kızıl Han, covered section, 15<sup>th</sup> century, Beçin.*

...rn by means of these channels. The cistern is in good enough condition to be used even today, with the help of some simple renovation.

R. H. Ü.

*The Milas-Söke main road (D.525) runs along the southern shore of Lake Bafa, a National Nature Park today. The steep stone-covered mountains (Beş Parmak Mountains) that descend sharply on the lake's northern shore offer an attractive view. If before reaching the lake you turn north from the village of Çamiçi and follow the shore of the lake, you will arrive at the remains of the ancient city of Heraclea-under-Latmus (today's Kapıkırı).*

*Balat is the Turkish name of the ancient city of Miletus. To get from Milas to Miletus you must take the main road D.525 in the direction of* *Akköy for approximately 55 km. If you are using public transport, go to Söke first and board a dolmush minibus to Balat. İlyas Bey Mosque Complex stands among the magnificent remains of buildings from the ancient world.*

## I.4 BALAT

The ancient city of Miletus, upon which Balat was founded, was one of the most important cities of the Ionian region. In those days, the city was located on a peninsula in the area where Büyük Menderes River (ancient Meandre) poured into the sea; however, today the city is nine km. from the sea because alluvium carried by the river has filled in the region. Laid out according to the famous city planner Hippodamus' grid plan, the

79

*İlyas Bey Complex, view of mosque and madrasa from the north, 1404, İlyas Bey, Balat.*

city became rich with the colonies it founded on the coasts of the Mediterranean and Black Seas and thereby became a chief site in the Ionian world. Although the city had once been home to the famous philosophers Thales, Anaximenes, and Anaximander (7th-5th century BC), and architects like Hippodamus (5th century BC) and Isidorus (who built Ayasofya in Istanbul in the 6th century AD), it only managed to preserve its importance up to the Roman period. After that it began to lose its popularity, once trade came to a halt as its harbours filled up with alluvium and became swamps. From this point on, it searched in vain for its magnificent days of the past. During the Byzantine period, a fortress was constructed on the hilltop where the theatre was located. In fact, the name Balat comes from the Turkish interpretation of the Greek name "Palatia" meaning palace.

At the beginning of the 1390s, the Menteşe Emirate was annexed to Ottoman territory. However, in the war that ensued between Sultan Beyazid I and Tamerlane around Ankara in 1402, İlyas Bey from the Menteşe dynastic house participated as an ally of Tamerlane. Once Sultan Beyazid I was defeated and taken prisoner, Tamerlane reinstated İlyas Bey to the Menteşe throne, as he did with the other rulers who assisted him. The capital of the re-established Menteşe Emirate was transferred from Beçin to Balat. The new capital became a market site where goods like saffron, sesame, honey, beeswax, and rugs were sold, especially during the time of the Menteşe Emirate. Wheat was also exported from here to Cyprus and Rhodes during this period. By the 19th century, however, the city was in a state of complete abandonment.

*he structure can be reached either by pro-
-eding along the ruins of the ancient city of
iletus (by passing through Faustina Baths),
- by taking the main road leading from the
cket office to Balat village, and then fol-
wing the road that turns left approximate-
- 200 m. later. It is necessary for visitors
avelling by car to park at the car park next
) the ticket office.*

the inner courtyard. A tower-like structure to the west of the outer courtyard is
hidden under the large tree behind the
wall. Approaching the entrance to the
inner courtyard, the section seen on the
left, without a window, topped with a
dome is the *dershane* of the *madrasa*; the
large dome in the distance belongs to the
mosque.

## 4.a İlyas Bey Complex

ıe two separate paths that lead from the
ain road and Faustina Baths join up by
e cemetery to the west of the *hammam*.
oing through an opening in the modern
alls one reaches the outer courtyard.
ıst the graves is the entrance to the inner
ourtyard shared by the mosque and the
adrasa. The main entrance of the com-
ex seems to be the gate structure on the
ıst, which is connected via a path to
ıother gate in the northeast corner of

## İlyas Bey Mosque

Although not of any special importance
architecturally, the fine marble workmanship and rich ornamentation of the
İlyas Bey Mosque is especially attractive.
The walls are faced on the outside with
marble from the ruins of Miletus; the
marble work on the facade is similar to
that seen in Milas Firuz Bey Mosque or
the Selçuk İsa Bey Mosque, as well as in
contemporary structures in neighbouring
towns. Although this use of marble was

*İlyas Bey Hammam,
detail from the plaster
decoration in the
halvet, early 15th
century, İlyas Bey,
Balat.*

*İlyas Bey Hammam, sıcaklık, early 15th century, İlyas Bey, Balat.*

the traditional designs of the Seljuq period that continued partially during the Emirates period. Two arches of the three-arched doorway are closed with lattice marble banisters. The arches have elaborate marble work. According to the Arabic inscription located on the central arch, İlyas Ibn Mehmed of the Menteşeoğulları Emirate commissioned the building, which was completed around the middle of the year 1404.

Walls over two 2 m. thick hold up the large, 14 m. diameter dome that covers square prayer hall. The ornamentation seen here on the ceilings of the lower row of windows, consisting bands of calligraphy along with colourful inlaid stones, is present in very few structures. The marble *mihrab* (with a height of over 7 m. and a width of over 5 m.) also has superb stonework. The minaret, which would have been located above the northeast corner and reached via stairs set inside the wall, no longer exists.

## İlyas Bey Madrasa

The *madrasa* cells surrounding the mosque courtyard on the east, west, and north sides are of various dimensions. The chambers' lack of orderly planning is in contradiction to the extremely careful workmanship of the mosque; therefore the *madrasa* must have been constructed after the mosque. The small domed area across from the mosque is the *dershane*. Excavations conducted over the past several years have revealed the foundations of another *madrasa* adjoining the chambers at the west wing of the courtyard. This second *madrasa* is of an even later date.

almost certainly due to the abundance of available marble from ancient ruins in the vicinity it may also be seen as a response to the architectural fashion of the period, a style we see in Italy, as well. On the eastern, western and southern fronts are four windows arranged in two rows; among the rich decorations on these window frames, the colourful stone inlay work is especially worth noting.

The design of the monumental entrance on the northern facade is different from

**...ammam**

...is generally believed that İlyas Bey also ...mmissioned the two *hammam*s north of ...e mosque. It is not known for certain ...hy two separate *hammam*s with a 2 m. ...ide passageway in between were built ...ght next to each other. In written ...urces, there are entries relating to the ...nstruction of *hammam*s, which indicate ...at they would be built first to allow ...orkers involved in the construction of the ...osque to bathe when necessary. Accord...g to Islamic tradition, Muslims are ...quired to wash their bodies completely ...d perform ablutions after sexual inter...urse because a Muslim who goes onto ...e streets without having washed after ...xual intercourse is believed to have com...itted a sin. Thus, it is thought that the ...naller of the two baths here was con...ructed for the use of the workers. How...ver, once it was realised that this bath of

very small dimensions was going to be insufficient, a second, larger bath must have been constructed right next to it. After the construction of the mosque was complete, the newly built Büyük Hammam was supposedly set aside for men and the small one for women. In the Büyük Hammam, the rectangular vaulted chamber on the west is the water tank. The entrance is to the northeast into the *soyunmalık*, which is now in ruins. Going through a small room in the northeast corner, one reaches a small chamber —*ılıklık*— connected to another small chamber to the south —maybe the *traşlık*— and a very small one to the north adjoining the passageway. The large hall to the west is the *sıcaklık* with a T-shaped main section and two *halvet*s in the corners. There are traces of beautiful plaster decoration on the walls formed by pressing moulds onto the wet plaster.

R. H. Ü.

# EDUCATION IN THE *MADRASA*

**Yekta Demiral**

*Madrasa students,
Codex Vindobonensis,
8626, Österreichisches
Nationalbibliothek,
Vienna.*

*Madrasa*s were educational institutions that first appeared in Islamic countries. Before *madrasa*s, mosques were used as schools only outside the hours of worship and the education consisted solely of making students memorise the Koran and giving them religious information. In later times, it was considered inappropriate for mosques, which were used as places of worship, to be simultaneously used as schools, and so *hodja*s began giving lessons in their homes.

The earliest traces of buildings known as *madrasa*s Date to the 10th century and are found in the Khorasan and Transoxiana. These buildings consisted of rooms lined up around an internal courtyard: an *iwan*

in the middle of each side and studen cells located in between. This layout als influenced the plans of *madrasa*s con structed in Anatolia: a courtyard, *iwan* winter *dershane* and student cells ar found in all of the *madrasa*s constructed i this period that have survived up to th present day. In addition to these architec tural elements, some *madrasa*s also hav elements like *masjid*s, *türbe*s, fountains and minarets. Not all of the *madrasa*s con structed during the Anatolian Emirate and especially the Ottoman periods hav the same plan layout.

*Madrasa*s built by wealthy people and hig state officials were not bound to the state therefore, the state did not meet th penses for feeding students or other penses such as employee salaries and e structure's maintenance and repair ork. For this reason, those who had the adrasas built would devote to their adrasas a part of their properties that gularly brought in income so that the adrasa's expenses could be met after eir death as well. As a result, each adrasa was a *waqf* institution.

he lessons taught, the periods when hool was in session, the hours of daily ssons, and holidays differed from one adrasa to another. A *madrasa* was named cording to the particular type of edu tion given there: for example, *madrasas* which the sayings of the prophet were ught were called *dDarülhadis*; those in hich people were made to memorise e Koran were called *Darülhuffaz*; and ose where medicine was taught were lled *Darüttıb*. Lessons were taught by achers called *müderris* and in every adrasa, there was one or more *muid* that elped the students and made them :peat the lessons given by the *müderris*. very *madrasa* had a doorman, a cleaning erson, a librarian, and a "pointillist" who hecked the attendance of the *madrasa* aff and students and reported absentees

to the *waqf* board of trustees. Education in various fields was given in the *madrasa*s, which were rated according to the wage of the *müderris*.

Between 20 to 40 students were educated in a single *madrasa*. However, *madrasas* constructed by the Ottoman sultans would accept as many students as there were student cells. In addition to meeting all their expenses, students were also given a small allowance.

Y.D.

*Located 20 km. to the south of Balat, the Didyma Apollo Temple (Didim) still preserves its magnificence in spite of being largely in ruins today. The Altınkum beach is just 5 km. from the temple.*

*16 km. north of Balat, on the Balat-Söke main road, the ancient city of Priene charms its visitors with its magnificent location.*

*Another corner of the region worth visiting is the Dilek Peninsula National Park which functions as a plant and animal reserve and is located 30 km. south of Kuşadası. However, the Büyük Menderes River Delta, part of the National Park, can be visited by turning north at the village of Tuzburgazı; also the old village of Doğanbey will give a taste of Aegean and Mediterranean cultures.*

# rotectors of the Arts and Artists

### Lale Bulut, Ertan Daş, Aydoğan Demir, İnci Kuyulu

*Burial Traditions Among the Turks*

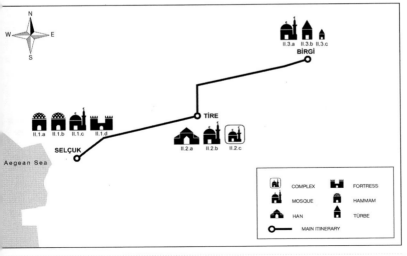

*İsa Bey Mosque, west facade, 1375, İsa Bey, Selçuk.*

on its existence in the Aegean. Becaus
the rulers saw the destruction takin
place on both sides of the war, they di
not hesitate to make peace and sign trad
treaties from time to time: cease-fire
peace, and trade treaties were signe
between Aydın Emirate and Venice for
times between the years 1337-1371.
A large part of the income from boo
brought by these war-filled years, pro
ucts provided by the bountiful land, an
the tariffs, which increased thanks to th
treaties with Venice, were spent on th
construction of monumental works o
religious and social functions. Mehme
Bey's (r. 1308-1334) Great Mosque in Bir
and İsa Bey's (r. 1360-1390) mosque an
hammam in Selçuk are beautiful exampl
that are still with us today. Because Tir
continued to be a lively commercial cen
tre for many long centuries, a great num
ber of *han*s were constructed in additio
to mosques, *madrasa*s, and *hammam*s.
Scholars were held in high esteem in th
Aydın Emirate. When the famous trav
eller Ibn Batuta came to Birgi in 1333, h
was received by Mehmed Bey and treat
ed with great respect. Michael Duca
grandfather of the Byzantine historia
Ducas (1400-1470), and a scholar him
self, took refuge under İsa Bey after h
managed to escape with his life from th
disputes over the throne between th
Cantecuzenus and the Palaeologus dynas
ties in Istanbul. İsa Bey provided Michae
Ducas with everything necessary for h
well-being and treated him like an impor
tant guest. In his book (1381) that he ded
icated to İsa Bey, Hacı Pasha, a famou
physician, introduced him both as a schol
ar and a sultan that supported scholars.
Although he insisted for a long time o
defending his Emirate against th

*Yahşi Bey Mosque,
general view from the
northeast, 1441,
Halil Yahşi Bey, Tire.*

Mehmed Bey, son of Aydın, founded an
Emirate at the beginning of the 14th century (1308) conquering Ayasuluğ (Selçuk-
Ephesus), Tire, and Birgi in West Anatolia and later annexing the city of İzmir in
1317.
The Aydın Beys wasted no time in opening up to the seas; they launched cam-
paigns to Evvoia Island, Peloponnesos
Peninsula, Gelibolu, and Thrace, in particular, with their naval forces stationed
in Ayasuluğ and İzmir. Venice and Genoa
were the states most disturbed by these
developments. Thanks to the Holy Union
that it established against the danger of
Aydın Emirate, Venice was able to carry

Ottomans, in the end, Cüneyd (r. 1405-1426), the last Aydın Emir, had to surrender in 1426. After this date, land belonging to the Emirate was administered by the Ottomans as the Aydın Sanjak.

A. D.

## SELÇUK

We know that throughout history some cities have changed their locations for socio-economic or natural reasons. Ephesus too changed its location at least three times for various reasons. There are different views as to where the exact location of the ancient city of Ephesus, an important trading port beginning in ancient times, was first settled. Not directly connected to the process of relocation, it is also known that the city changed its name frequently too. The ancient settlement of Ephesus, known as Hagios Theologos in the Middle Ages, took the name Ayasuluğ in the Turkish period and the name Selçuk in 1914. The city, which was re-established towards the end of the 4th century BC, in a narrow valley between Panayır Mountain and Bülbül Mountain, lived in prosperity during the Hellenistic and Roman periods. However, as a result of its harbour filling up with alluvium carried by the Küçük Menderes River, its connection to the sea was cut off and therefore, it lost the special feature of being a city port. In addition to being an important religious and commercial centre (the Temple of Artemis, one of the Seven Wonders of the World, was in Ephesus), it is clear that it was an important cultural and artistic centre as well. The large-scale 25,000-person capacity theatre still stands as proof of this. Ephesus is one of the seven churches of Christianity in the Book of Revelation. The spread of Christianity during Saint Paul's lengthy stay here, the presence of the tomb of Saint John, and the claim that the Virgin Mary lived in Ephesus for a while and died there means that the city holds great importance for Christians. Moreover, the Third Ecumenical Council was held in Ephesus in AD 431 debating the divine and human nature of Christ and concluded with the victory of Monophysitism and Nestorianism's conviction as heresy. In 449 a synod also gathered here to enforce Monophysitism. Intense building activity took place in Selçuk, one of Aydın Emirate's important cities that served as the capital of the Emirate between the years 1348-1390. The great majority of the buildings in the city that have survived up to the present day, stem from this period. Mehmed Bey's son İsa Bey commissioned Selçuk's most magnificent edifice, İsa Bey Mosque; some western travellers have thought that the building was converted into a mosque from the church of St. John.

*The second itinerary begins at Selçuk and continues along the Küçük Menderes Plain. Since Ephesus, one of antiquity's most important cities, is also close to Selçuk, you can easily spend a large part of the first half of the day here. If you do not have a private car, you can reach Selçuk, Tire, Ödemiş, and Birgi by means of public transport that you pick up at the towns' bus stations. İzmir, the region's largest city, is a convenient place to spend the night and has accommodation offering various degrees of comfort.*

## II.1.a **Saadet Hatun Hammam**

*The Saadet Hatun Hammam is being used today as the Selçuk-Efes Museum's exhibition hall and is part of the museum's Ethnography Section. The Selçuk-Efes Museum is in the town centre on Ugur Mumcu Sevgi Road, behind the park at the junction. The museum is open between the hours of 08:00-12:00 and 13:00-17:30 in the winter months and 08:30-12:00 and 13:00-18:00 in the sum-*

*Saadet Hatun Hammam, marble basin in the sıcaklık, 14th-15th century, Selçuk.*

*mer months. It is open every day of the week. There is an entrance fee. At the entrance, please inquire whether the hammam section is open.*

Past the courtyard of the museum, first the *külhan* under the water tank is seen on the left. The broken inscription above the south entrance is partially readable and provides no date and a misreading caused this *hammam* to be known with the name Saadet Hatun (Lady Saadet) but this name is not found in archival documents. However, there is mention of a *hammam* that İsa Bey's wife Azize Hatun had built therefore, the "Hatun Hammam" mentioned in the sources might be this one. The entrance opens into the *soyunmalık* enlarged into a rectangle with an additional area by the entrance. The building was restored between the years 1969 1972 and the *soyunmalık* is today used for displaying objects used in the Turkish *hammam* tradition. During the day hammams are generally lit by means of light wells in the superstructure, but during

90

ıe hours when the light is not sufficient ıl lamps and candles were also lit. But ıre, aside from the windows on the ıalls, a polygonal lantern with a cupola ıas placed in the centre of the dome, the ıaklık, however, is lit by light wells in the ome, every single one of which is fitted ıith a glass jar. Past the *ılıklık* and the ıaşlık is the *sıcaklık* consisting of three ıans and two *halvet*s; forming the centre f this fan-like arrangement is a platform, ırmally very hot, on which people used ı lie and sweat and be massaged and ırubbed. The re-used marble basins in ıe *iwan*s and the *halvet*s are attractive ıith their extremely fine decorations ınsisting of oil lamps, water birds, and ıoral motifs. A window opens from the ıntral *iwan* onto the water tank stretch-ıg along the *sıcaklık* for purposes of ıeaning and maintenance.

İ. K.

*After leaving Selçuk-Efes Museum, turn from the parking area in the direction of Kuşadası and then turn right onto Kalinger street 30 m. later. Then 300 m. ahead, past the lonely column of the Artemision on the left, you will see İsa Bey Hammam enclosed by a chain-link fence.*

## .1.b İsa Bey Hammam

*alinger Street, Selçuk.*

is not known for certain whether or not ıis building, to the southwest of İsa Bey's ıosque, belonged to İsa Bey. Today there ı no building inscription, but it is thought ıat an inscribed slab found in the garden f a nearby house and moved to Selçuk-fes Museum might belong to this build-

ing. The inscription describes a *hammam* commissioned by Hoca Ali during the rule of İsa Bey in October-November 1364. Because of this, some researchers suggest that this *hammam* was not commissioned by İsa Bey. We do not have much information about the name Hoca Ali that is mentioned in the inscription; probably an important person of İsa Bey's period, Hoca Ali's gravestone dated 1378 is located in the courtyard of İsa Bey Mosque.

Its environs and interior have been cleaned with the excavation work in the recent years. The building has a plan layout common to the 14th and 15th centuries. Adjoining the *hammam* on the east are the remains of a row of chambers, which are supposedly shops with no organic connection to the *hammam*, although examples of shops adjoining the sides of some Turkish *hammam*s are known. On the south is a low arch opening into the *külhan* under the water depot.

*İsa Bey Hammam, transitional to the ılıklık dome, 14th–15th century, Selçuk.*

91

İsa Bey Mosque, prayer hall, 1375, İsa Bey, Selçuk.

The chambers adjoining the western facade, however, must be later additions. In some Turkish *hammam*s there are special sections called "keçelik" that were constructed for the manufacture of felt. It is thought that of the sections added later, the one on the north might be a "keçelik".

The walls of the *soyunmalık* on the northern side are preserved only at ground level. With two of the four columns still standing, the *soyunmalık* has traces of a star-shaped fountain in the centre of the marble floor. Apart from the *soyunmalık*, the rest of the *hammam* is quite well preserved. The visitor passes from the *soyunmalık* to the corridor, *ılıklık*, and *sıcaklık* respectively. The *sıcaklık* consists of four *iwan*s forming a cross with a dome in the centre and four *halvet*s in the corners, each covered by a dome. Light coming through the wells in the domes, now

without the glass jars, though, creates a exotic play of light and shadow insid The water depot adjoins the souther wall of the *sıcaklık*. As seen in most *ha mam*s, there is a small window on the wa between the *sıcaklık* and the water tan for the purpose of cleaning and mainte nance.

İ. K

## II.1.c **İsa Bey Mosque**

*The building is at the northern end of Kaling Street. It is open all day April-October, b only at prayer times during the winter month*

Kalinger Street ends at a tall wall –th qibla wall of İsa Bey Mosque– with blocked archway in the middle, which said to be the entrance when the struc ture was in use as a *caravanserai* in the 19 ntury. This plain south facade forms a ontrast to the main facade on the west. ocated at the foot of Ayasuluğ Hill, the oad on the right continues up hill to the hurch of St. John and the citadel.

n the west is a superb facade with two ows of windows, a monumental portal, d a row of shops at ground level. The indows have elaborate frames with uqarnas and stone-inlay work. Two ghts of steps crown a fountain beneath d reach the slender portal, which is pecially attractive with its restored oloured marble work and fine crafts-anship. The inscription band reads the me of the founder as İsa Bey, son of ehmed son of Aydın and the date of onstruction as 13 March 1375 by the chitect Ali ibn al Dmashki (Ali, son of e Damascene). İsa Bey, who had this osque built, was the youngest son of ydın Emirate's founder Mehmed Bey, ho divided the administration of the ties he conquered amongst his sons, but cause İsa Bey was very young, he orked alongside his father. İsa Bey came the head of Aydın Emirate after s father and his older brothers Gazi mur Bey and Hızır Bey, and ruled for proximately 30 years. When the ttoman Sultan Bayezid I captured Alaş-ir (ancient Philadelphia, one of the ven churches), İsa Bey showed devotion d obedience to the Sultan. Once Aydın nirate became part of the Ottoman ter-tory, its centre too moved from Ayasu-ğ to Tire. The Ottoman dynasty creased their strength and power by tablishing familial relations with the lers of the Anatolian Emirates. In fact, ace he had captured the lands belonging Aydın Emirate, Sultan Bayezid I mar-ed Hafsa Hatun, İsa Bey's daughter.

The portal still bears the broken minaret; the second of which used to stand on the eastern portal of the courtyard. Selçuk İsa Bey Mosque has two minarets, something rarely seen in mosques of the Emirates period. On entering the courtyard notice the prayer hall to the right, and the east-ern portal straight opposite the western and the northern portal, in the middle of the north wall of the courtyard. The northern and eastern portals are at a high-er level than the courtyard thanks to the sloping terrain; the passageways of the eastern and the western portals have beau-tiful stone ornamentation on their ceil-ings, under the minarets. As understood from the remaining traces, the courtyard was originally enclosed on three sides with porticoes, therefore, it is one of the earli-est examples of this kind of layout encoun-tered before the Ottoman period.

The transept aisle that runs perpendicu-lar to the *qibla* is covered with two domes; the lateral aisles parallel to the *qibla* wall have a pitched wooden roof; this layout is reminiscent of the famous Grand Mosque in Damascus. Both its plan and the colourful stone decorations on its portals and windows exhibit Syrian influ-ence, which is explained by the architect's Damascan origins. There are tile decora-tions on the rim and pendentives of the dome above the transept aisle before the *mihrab*.

The original *mihrab* and *minbar* of this structure were destroyed in the 19th cen-tury. Although it is maintained by some that a section of the *mihrab* is being used again in İzmir Kestanepazarı Mosque, this is not correct, and the fragmented *mihrab* inscription is in the Agora Open Air Museum in İzmir.

İ. K.

*The gravestones described below are displayed in the courtyard of İsa Bey Mosque. The Selçuk-Efes Museum is responsible for them, but they do not have inventory numbers.*

usually not written on the gravestone which makes this one particularly not worthy.

L.

### Gravestone of Hoca Ali Ibn Salih

This is the gravestone of Hoca Ali Ibn Salih, who passed away in the year 1378. The stone is composed of three sections on top of one another, being the cylindrical base, polygonal body, and a polygonal finial. All the surfaces of the stone are ornamented with bands of scripture, which contain information about the "identity of the deceased" as well as terse sayings about death and life. In addition, it is also written that a master stonemason named Halil carved the stone. In Anatolia, the name of the stonemason was

### Gravestone of Hacı Umur Ibn Mente

This magnificent gravestone belongs Hacı Umur Ibn Menteşe, a member of tl Menteşe dynasty, who passed away in tl year 1400. The stone was carved out of ancient column. On each face of the boc arranged with four faces and in two level there are pointed arched inscription pa els. On these inscriptions is written "Tl identity of the deceased" and that "ever living creature on earth is mortal". Insic the curvature of the arches are rosett with flowers filling the spaces betwee them. The sharp corner lines have bee softened with spiral columns. The ba

*Gravestone of Hoca Ali Ibn Salih, 1378, Selçuk.*

*Gravestone of Hacı Umur Ibn Menteşe, 1400, Selçuk.*

on which the body sits is ornamented
ith oyster-shell motifs.

L. B.

### ravestone of Muhlisüddin Hassan

his is the gravestone of a person named
assan, who passed away on 30 August
-39. On the cylindrical marble grave-
one, the inscriptions have been placed in
rtouches. The palmette-like motifs below
d on the edges of the inscriptions are par-
ularly attractive. The owner of the grave-
one, whose name is recorded as Muh-
iddin Hassan on the inscription, asks that
ssers-by will pray for him.

L. B.

### ravestone of Hassan Ibn Kadı
ıba Yulug

is is the gravestone of Hassan Ibn Kadı

Baba Yulug, who passed away in 1439.
The cylindrical gravestone is very plain.
The identity of the deceased and date of
death are stated in the inscriptions written inside cartouches.

L. B.

## II.1.d  Citadel

*The citadel is reached through St. John's
Church on Ayasuluğ hill. However, it is not
open to visitors.*

The history of the Ayasuluğ Citadel stretches back as far as the 4th century AD. During
the time of Byzantine Emperor Justinian
(AD 527-565), a large church was constructed in the name of St. John next to the
fortress and later surrounded by walls. St.
John's Church was enclosed within the
walls when the fortifications were extended

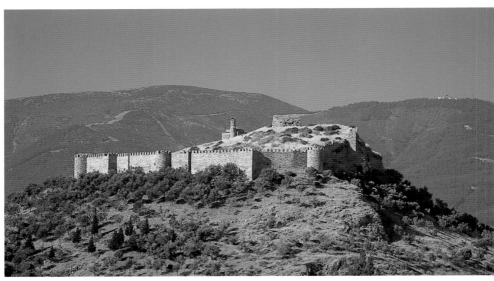

*Selçuk Citadel, general view from the north, 15th century, Selçuk.*

because of the threat of Arab raids. The fortress was reinforced through periodic repairs after the city's fall to the hands of Mehmed Bey, son of Aydın, in 1304. During the Turkish period Ayasuluğ ranked high as one of the East Mediterranean's most lively trading centres and important harbours. Merchants from, for instance, Venice, Genoa and Pisa dealt in international trade here. Evidence of the importance of this town is several-fold: the Venetian Consulate became intensely active in the city beginning in 1337; the Genoese Consulate was founded here in 1351; the number of westerners living in the city increased and trade agreements were made between the Aydın Emirate and westerners.

As its importance continued throughout the Ottoman period, up to 60 military guards charged with protecting the citadel were present in the time of Sultan Mehmed II. At the end of the 16th century, various tax exemptions were granted to those working on the renovation of the citadel. Evli Çelebi, who visited Ayasuluğ in 1671, stat that the citadel, founded on a steep sto outcrop, had a circumference of 300 foc steps (approximately 200 meters) and th about 40 people were on duty.

The walls constructed of re-used mate als are still in good condition today; t main entrance preserves its origin shape; an old Byzantine chapel, sever cisterns, and a small mosque are locat within the walls.

i.

*The village of Şirince, founded by Rums wh left after the Turks took the city, is a long w from the main road and has a calm atmosphe and a beautiful view. Most of the houses, wit their regionally specific architecture, date from the 19th century. There are two churches, or of which was recently restored. Drinking a cu of well-steeped tea at the village café in th public square will make you forget all abou*

*he tiredness of the day. In order to get to Şir-
nce, after leaving Selçuk, heading in the
'irection of İzmir, turn right (east) immedi-
'tely after the city exit.*

## .2 TİRE

Iehmed Bey, who divided his Emirate up
mong his sons, left the administration of
ire, one of the most important towns, to
s fourth son Süleyman Şah. In 1390, Sul-
n Bayezid I, who annexed the Aydın
mirate onto the Ottoman State, forced
a Bey of the Aydın dynasty to reside in
ire. From this point on, the Aydın
ynasty, re-based in Tire, played an impornt role in the town's development. The
attle of Ankara that took place between
ultan Bayezid I and Tamerlane in 1402

resulted in the re-establishment of the Anatolian Emirates, which had supposedly
been wiped off the stage of history. The
battle's victor, Tamerlane, reinstated the
administration of the emirates that Bayezid
had added to Ottoman lands to the former
owners; Musa Bey and his brother of the
Aydın dynasty hosted Tamerlane in Tire
during the winter of 1402-1403.

### II.2.a  Kutu Han

*It is located at Tahtakale Square in Yeni
Mahalle. Every day of the week except Tuesday,
on the second floor of the building, two master
workmen make rope from hemp using extremely simple methods and tools.*

We begin to see city *hans* for the first time
during the Emirates period. The number

*Kutu Han, chambers
on the second storey of
the west wing, 15th
century, Tire.*

*Kutu Han, vault from the stables, 15th century, Tire.*

tures devoted in the *waqf* charter to Yah Bey's İmaret Mosque, like Çöplü Han *Arasta*, Toma Han, and Tahtakale Ham mam are in the neighbourhood of Tah takale (Yenipazar Market), which contin ues to be Tire's commercial centre, just a it was in the 15th century. Halil Yahşi Be must have had Kutu Han built some tim between his appointment as governor c Aydın Province in 1425-26 and 144 when its *waqf* charter was prepared.

Kutu Han is a two-storied city *han* sur rounded on the outside by 9 shops on th south, 11 shops on the west, and 10 shop on the north, which are all shaped lik *iwans* closed off from the street with glas panes. Adjoining the eastern facade is a *arasta* —somewhat altered due to restora tions— consisting a long, narrow covere corridor flanked with a total of 26 shop on both sides.

A broad doorway on the west side open into the square courtyard. Additiona shop areas were formed by closing off th porticoes on the courtyard's eastern western, and southern sides. To the nort of the courtyard are the stables wit attractive cross-vaulted roofs built wit bricks. In the middle of the northern sid of the courtyard is a set of stairs leadin to the terrace over the stables and the to floor. The porticoes located in front c the cells on the top floor and surroundin the courtyard have almost entirely col lapsed. Cells of approximately equal size are lined up behind the porticoes.

İ. K

of *hans* constructed in a city was propor-tionate to that particular town's size and volume of trade activity. City *hans* are generally two-storied buildings consisting a square or rectangular courtyard sur-rounded with porticoes behind which rooms were located. Warehouses and sta-bles were located on the lower floors and the upper floors were most likely to have been used as shops or boarding rooms.

Evliya Çelebi, one of the travellers who visited Tire in the 17th century, writes that 144 mosques and *masjid*s, 30 *madrasa*s, 60 *mekteps*, 13 *hammam*s, 270 fountains, and 27 *hans* were present in Tire. These numbers indicate that Tire was a developed town. Today, the num-ber of *hans* present in Tire is much lower than the figure given by Evliya Çelebi. However, the city's five *hans*, although only partially standing today, are proof of its once lively commercial life.

One of Sultan Murad II's high-ranking offi-cers, Halil Yahşi Bey acted as governor of Aydın Province and made important con-tributions to Tire's development during the Early Ottoman period. All the struc-

## II.2.b  Yahşi Bey (Yeşil İmaret) Mosque

*Cumhuriyet District (Mahallesi) 52, Aydınoğl Street, Tire.*

ışi Bey Mosque, used for a while as the chaeology Museum, is one of the city's ıst important edifices. The mosque was finitely commissioned by Halil Yahşi y, one of Sultan Murad II's high-ranking icers, after Tire was taken under toman rule; however, we do not know ıch about Halil Yahşi Bey. It is under-od from the *waqf* charter dating to 1441 t he turned his vineyards and orchards Ayasuluğ (Selçuk) together with build-s in Tire that provided income like ıs, *hammam*s, shops, etc. over to a *waqf*, order to have this mosque survive ough the centuries. The building must e been complete by the date of the *waqf* ırter or a few years before.

the Tire mosques, the traveller Evliya lebi, who visited Tire in 1671, was ıst interested in the Yahşi Bey Mosque. states that the building was construct-as a centre for the Mevlevi (whirling) vishes and later converted into a ısque; its congregation was large due he large number of *Mevlevi*s residing in vicinity.

proaching from the street on the east, e faces the minaret unusually located on northeast. The building was also given name Yeşil İmaret thanks to the minaret orated with reddish-brown, turquoise green glazed bricks arranged in dia-nd shapes. According to a story, after the ster workman had completed construc-n of the building, he prostrated himself begged Allah, "Forgive me O Lord if I sted any materials I used in the construc-n of this mosque and minaret or if I wingly used too little mortar or plaster". e building was constructed with stone brick; in the north of the mosque is a rtico with five domed bays. Passing ough the plain portal with a canopy of

*muqarnas* one enters the central court sur-mounted with a dome and flanked with a *tabhane* on the east and the west each of which has a single fireplace and niche. The *tabhane*s' wooden door and window wings are ornamented with delicate workmanship as are the door wings of the portal. Accord-ing to the inscription on the entrance wings, the name of the master woodwork-er was İlyas Ibn Mahmud. To the south is the prayer hall, very attractive with its unusual pentagonal shape surmounted with a semi-dome designed as an oyster shell. The wall paintings exposed during the restorations are visible today, along with paintings of a later date; and the *mihrab* is designed as a deep niche projecting out and decorated with paintings as well.

İ. K.

*Yahşi Bey Mosque,
prayer hall, 1441,
Halil Yahşi Bey, Tire.*

### II.2.c  Yavukluoğlu (Yoğurtluoğlu) Complex

*Turan District (Mahallesi) 7, Kaplan Road, Tire. Work has begun in order to convert the mosque complex, which was restored several years ago, into a school for the handicapped. If you request the* Belediye *or* Zabıta, *an official will accompany you and open the complex for you.*

*Following the signpost for Kaplan, Yavukluoğlu Mosque Complex will be on your left, hidden among the olive trees, a little later.*

*Yahşi Bey Mosque, detail of the wooden door of the tabhane on the west, 1441, Halil Yahşi Bey, Tire.*

Another important building in Tire constructed during the Ottoman period is the Yavukluoğlu Mosque Complex.

Although it is not known for certain w had the 15th-century mosque built, it said to be a person by the name of Yavu luoğlu or Yoğurtluoğlu Mehmed Bey. T story goes that Yavukluoğlu Mehmed B ruled over the western section of Ti while the ruler of the eastern section the town was Kazanoğlu Mehmed B who commissioned the Kazanoğ Mosque. In the 15th century these t local potentates became enemies and t attempts of the people of Tire to ma peace between them failed. As time we on, their animosity increased and in t end Yavukluoğlu Mehmed Bey h Kazanoğlu Mehmed Bey killed. Howe er, Yavukluoğlu Mehmed Bey deep regretted his actions and he went to t holy man Buğday Dede's tomb and we Putting his regret into words, he wish for this local Saint to show him the w Buğday Dede appeared before Yoğurt oğlu Mehmed Bey and told him that if held Kazanoğlu Mehmed Bey's funeral, would be cleansed of his ill will. Acco ing to another version of the legend, people of Tire successfully made pea between the two local potentates: th said that Kazanoğlu was going to visit older Yavukluoğlu in person in order make peace. Then as soon as Yavukluoğ accepted the request, they went Kazanoğlu and told him that Yavukluoğ had invited him personally. Wh Kazanoğlu too accepted this offer, th brought the two enemies together a their animosity came to an end.

Consisting a mosque, *madrasa*, *muvakkitha* a soup kitachen or a *mektep* and a *hamma* which has since fallen into ruins, the co plex rises on a slight slope, from north upwards to the south and recently undergone restoration, whi

*Yavukluoğlu Complex, General view from the southeast, 15th century, Yavukluoğlu Mehmed Bey, Tire.*

as completed in 1997 after seven years. f the structures that make up the osque complex, the mosque and adrasa share the same courtyard; the osque placed on the southern side of e courtyard is a simple square structure rmounted by a dome. In the front is a ve-bayed portico, with lovely arches, ading at the minaret on the west; to the st adjoins a room with a *mihrab*, whose nction is not clear but it is suggested at it may be the library. By the eastern ntrance to the courtyard is a room, hich functions as a place to take the ritual ablution. Each *madrasa* cell on the astern and western sides has a fireplace d is covered by a dome; in the front are omed porticoes, a bit shorter in length ough. The courtyard is bounded by a lind wall to the north, pierced with a orway in the middle, which is topped ith a room, presumably the *muvakkithane* the observatory or the clock room. Such ooms are known from ancient times and

were built near mosques and equipped with necessary instruments in order to work out the times of sunrise and sunset for the calls to prayer; the person in charge, a combination of an astronomer and an astrologer, would also give astrological service. In the adjoining area to the north, on the east side, is a two-section building which might have been a soup kitchen or a *mektep*.

İ. K.

*Yavukluoğlu Complex, showing the chambers on the west wing and the portico in front, 15th century, Yavukluoğlu Mehmed Bey, Tire.*

*If you continue along the road up hill instead
of turning back from Yavukluoğlu Mosque
Complex, you will reach the Kaplan area
overlooking the Küçük Menderes Plain. There
are several restaurants here.*

*There is a market twice a week in Tire: at
the Tuesday market all kinds of goods are
sold; at the Friday market, though, the villagers sell fruits and vegetables they have
grown. Tire is famous for its köfte (a kind
of meatball). Strolling in the old parts of
the town with labyrinthine-like streets, you
will find many more mosques, hammams,
old houses —some of which are very dilapidated. The small Archaeological Museum
has an interesting collection of artefacts
from Antiquity and the Middle Ages; the
Ottoman tombstones in the backyard and
the 19th-century Çanakkale pottery are
noteworthy.*

*There are regular dolmush minibuses from
Tire bus station to Ödemiş and from Ödemi
bus station to Birgi.*

## II.3 **BİRGİ**

Mehmed Bey, one of the commanders o
the Germiyan Emirate's army, founded a
Emirate named after his father Aydın, i
the regions of ancient Lydia and Ionia i
West Anatolia and made Birgi his centre
Also known by his nickname "Mübarizüd
din", "the Warrior for the Religion"
Mehmed Bey divided up the regions h
had conquered among his sons. Mehme
Bey carried out various raids on th
Aegean and Rumelian shores with th
naval forces he had established in Ayasu

uğ and İzmir. When Mehmed Bey passed away in 1334, his son Umur Bey took his place.

İbn Batuta, who in the year 1333 visited Birgi, stayed for 14 days at the palace of Mehmed Bey, the founder of the Emirate. According to information the traveller gives about the palace, Mehmed Bey's quarters were located in a high section. At the corners of the pool in the middle of the apartment were bronze statues of lions with water flowing out of their mouths and the inner courtyard was surrounded with rooms side by side. The traveller speaks with praise of 20 young Rum men with long blonde hair wearing satin dresses that welcomed them on arrival at the palace, and of the golden spoons and ceramic bowls he saw there.

## II.3.a  Great Mosque

One of the first works constructed in Birgi during the Aydın Emirate period is the Great Mosque, rising on top of a steep creek bank. Entering the courtyard the visitor is faced with a rather rectangular appearance at first, broken by a triangular pediment above the portal with a lean-to roof. This plain and somewhat unattractive northern facade, built with unhewn stones, is accentuated by the marble frames of the lower windows and the marble portal ornamented with carved rosettes, a tree-of-life motif and an inscription giving the name of the founder as Mehmed Bey, son of Aydın and the date of construction as 1312-13. Going through the portal one enters the central aisle of the prayer hall designed as a basilica with five aisles separated from

*Great Mosque, north facade, 1312-13, Aydınoğlu Mehmed Bey, Birgi.*

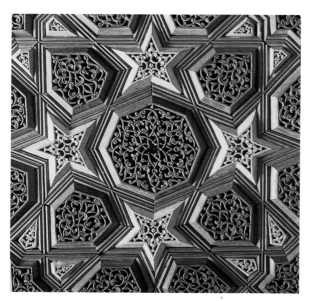

*Great Mosque, detail of wooden minbar, 1322, Aydınoğlu Mehmed Bey, Birgi.*

one another by rows of re-used columns supporting arches. The ceiling and roof, today covered with metal plates, is made of wood; the square area before the *mihrab* is covered with a dome.

The structure has dazzling examples of tile art and woodwork: the *mihrab* in tile-mosaic technique with turquoise and aubergine-purple tiles following the Seljuq tradition; the northern arch of this square area before the *mihrab* is also decorated in tile mosaic.

The building's *minbar* and window wings are exquisite examples of 14th-century wood workmanship. There are different decorations on every single one of the wooden wings attached to the inner side of the lower row of windows; all bear religious inscriptions. The *minbar* made of walnut wood is ornamented in the *kündekari* technique without any nails or glue. There are numerous Arabic inscriptions

on the *minbar*, mainly religious; according to the ones on the right side, the *minbar* was made in 1322 by a master craftsman named Muzaffereddin İbn Abdülvahid. The door wings of the *minbar*, stolen in 1995, were recovered as they were being sold at an auction in London.

On leaving the prayer hall, one should observe the mosque from the outside starting with the east facade. The windows are arranged in two rows; the lower ones on the east have different ornamentation. There is another portal in the middle of the eastern facade, which is quite plain like the northern one. The marble blocks on the eastern and southern facades of the building facing the street are re-used material from earlier structures, as is the statue of a lion placed in the southeast corner. The base of the minaret is built of marble blocks and it adjoins the western end of the southern facade which is entirely faced with marble; its body rising directly from the base is decorated in zigzags and chevrons with glazed bricks and tile mosaics. The western facade is very plain and the building just 1.30 m. to the west is the Türbe of Mehmed Bey.

İ. K.

## II.3.b  Türbe of Aydınoğlu Mehmed Bey

Mehmed Bey, son of Aydın, became ill after falling off his horse during a hunt, and passed away in 1334. The *türbe* in which he is buried is located just to the west of Great Mosque, the mosque he had built. It was most likely to have been constructed while Mehmed Bey was still

althy. The inscription on the *türbe* door
ads 9 January 1334; this must be either
e date of Mehmed Bey's death, or the
te he was buried in the *türbe*.

e modest grave to the right of the
trance door is known among the peo-
e as the King's Daughter's Grave.
cording to one legend, the daughter of
rgi's Byzantine Christian ruler saw
ehmed Bey at war as he besieged the
y and she fell in love with him. She
ote a letter to Mehmed Bey informing
n that she accepted Islam and she was
cretly going to open the city gate. The
ople, who learned that the Christian
ler's daughter had helped Mehmed Bey
pture the city in this way, killed her at
e place where the grave is today. As
on as Mehmed Bey conquered the city,
had the young woman buried at the
ace she had been killed. Similar stories
lating to the conquering of various
zantine fortresses are common.

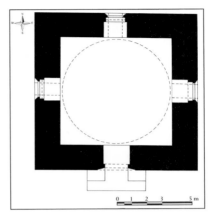

*Plan of Aydınoğlu Mehmed Bey Turbe, Birgi (from R. H. Ünal).*

This plain, square building is faced with
marble blocks and topped with a dome.
There are rectangular windows on the
eastern, western, and northern fronts;
the entrance door, which has a marble
frame like the windows, is in the middle
of the southern facade. The wooden

*Türbe of Aydınoğlu Mehmed Bey, south facade, 1334, Aydınoğlu Mehmed Bey, Birgi.*

*Türbe of Aydınoğlu Mehmed Bey, dome, 1334, Aydınoğlu Mehmed Bey, Birgi.*

lean-to roof above the entrance is a recent addition and the ornamented marble blocks above are re-used Byzantine material. On entering, raise your eyes to the inner side of the dome, which is decorated with concentric rows of glazed bricks, and the band along the edge and medallion in the centre are of tile mosaic.

The graves of four members of the Aydın dynasty are found in the *türbe*. There is no date on the head- or foot-stones; only the names of those buried are given. Once through the entrance, the first grave belongs to one of Mehmed Bey's sons, İsa Bey, who is thought to have died before 1402. The second grave belongs to Bahadır Be sometimes referred to in sources İbrahim Bey, who is thought to ha passed away sometime before 1347. T third grave belongs to Mehmed Bey, s of Aydın; and the fourth is that of Um Bey, Mehmed Bey's second son al known by the name Bahaeddin Bey, w died in battle in 1348.

i. 

*The Türbe of Şah Sultan is opposite th Great Mosque on the south, outside th courtyard. When you exit the mosque courtyard and turn right, you reach th türbe 100 m. ahead. Today it stands in th middle of the road.*

.3.c **Türbe of Şah Sultan** (option)

his hexagonal building, also known as ürbe of Ümmü Sultan, is built with nhewn stones and brick; re-used mate-ials were also used here and there. In ne last renovation, a concrete eve was dded to the structure and the dome's xternal surface was coated with con-rete. A portal slightly protrudes from ne hexagonal body on the south, which flanked with windows on both sides. he building is entered through an arch-ay with a low ceiling, directly above vhich is a two-line Arabic inscription on a marble plaque telling that Mehmed Bey had this *türbe* built for his sister, Sultan Şah Hatun and it was completed in June 1310. The interior is also a regular hexagon in plan, surmounted by a brick dome; there are shallow niches covered by pointed arches made of bricks on each face of the hexagon; some of the arches were damaged during restoration. There is a grave without any special characteristics with broken foot- and headstones inside the *türbe*. There is no sign that might indicate the existence of a crypt.

İ. K.

# BURIAL TRADITIONS AMONG THE TURKS

**Ertan Da**

Shamanism, a religion widespread among the Turks before they accepted Islam, was a kind of belief that fundamentally worshipped nature and supernatural spirits. The religious leader —shaman— would establish a relationship with the supernatural spirits, perform magic, and heal the sick. As in all religions, the shaman religion also believed in the revival of the dead. Thus wealthy followers of shamanism made sheltered graves for themselves so that the bodies present in the grave would not be damaged until the day of resurrection. We also observe that, just as boats were placed in the graves of Egyptian pharaohs so that they would be able to travel on the Nile once they were resurrected, nomadic Turks were buried with their horses.

The Turks continued to be influenced by the beliefs dealing with the burial cult that they acquired in Central Asia even after they converted to Islam. According to Islamic belief, when a person, who is made of earth, dies, he or she is buried in the earth and will return to earth. According to Islamic tradition, the body is buried so that the head is in the direction of the west, his face turned towards the qibla, and the body rests on the right arm. Mummifying the body goes against Islamic belief. Nevertheless, mummified bodies are encountered in some of the türbes in the Anatolian towns of Amasya, Kemah, Harput, etc. In spite of poor conditions of preservation, these mummies have survived until the present day.

Ever since the Karahanid period (842-1212), Turkish architecture has produced extremely interesting burial memorials. Especially during the Seljuq period (12th-13th century) in various examples of kümbets —another name for monumental tombs— the dead were buried in a basement crypt. Closed to visitors, this section is generally covered with earth up half its height; there is a small opening one of the facades providing access to the crypt for maintenance and cleaning; however, beginning in the Emirates period (14th century), the crypt floor slowly disappeared. The body of the kümbet rising over the crypt can have a cubic, polygonal or cylindrical shape; a mihrab and symbolic sarcophagus made of wood plaster, or stone is also found on the floor; the structure is usually covered by a dome. During the Anatolian Seljuq period, the dome was concealed from the outside by a pyramidal or conical spire which slowly began to disappear during the Ottoman period.

During the Seljuq, Emirates, and Ottoman periods in Anatolia, cemeteries were not very far from the town centre. Usually religious men or high-ranking government officials were buried in the small graveyards formed in mosque courtyards.

In Anatolia and most other Islamic countries, a stone is erected at the head and foot ends of graves that are independent or inside türbes. These stones are important documents that give us information detailing the beliefs, aesthetic taste, understanding of art, and even health of the period in which they were made. The ornamentation of gravestones with writing and decorations is a tradition that has been continuous in Anatolia since Seljuq times. In the vicinities of Erzurum and Diyarbakır in the East and Southeast Anatolia respectively there are gravestones of the Akkoyunids and Karakoyunids that are shaped like sheep and rams and embellished with decorative figures

The nomadic tribes of Turcomans carried this tradition into Central Anatolia as far s Afyon and Aydın. In Ahlat, the Seljuq-eriod city famous for its gravestones, nd in some other Anatolian cities, grave-tones bear decorations of figures show-ng traces of shamanist traditions as well s floral and geometric decorations. Bird igures symbolising the spirits' rise to the ky in shaman belief, figure predominant-y on the stones along with other figures, ike lions symbolising strength and power, dragons, and eagles. In the vicinities of Konya and Akşehir there are examples of gravestones with human figures on them howing some of the work the deceased lid in his or her lifetime (a man training a falcon, a woman embroidering with a tambour, etc.). Figurative decorations on gravestones disappeared at the beginning n the Emirates period. During this peri-od, a form of gravestone that closely resembled a *mihrab* became widespread and was in fashion throughout the 14<sup>th</sup> and 15<sup>th</sup> centuries, especially in the West Anatolian Emirates.

Traditional Turkish decorating could not rescue itself from the western influence seen in various branches of art in Anato-lia beginning in the 17<sup>th</sup> century; espe-cially in West Anatolia, although grave-stone forms did not undergo any major changes, the decorating program was heavily influenced by trends like Baroque,

*Yeşil Türbe, tile sarcophagus of Sultan Mehmed I, 1419-24, Mehmed I, Bursa.*

Empire, and Rococo. The few examples we see of gravestones carved in humanoid shapes may have been influenced by Euro-pean sculpture, but they might also be connected to the Central Asian *balbal* tra-dition. While the triangular pediment on women's gravestones (quite common in this period) contains abundant and vari-ous decorations, men's gravestones are much plainer.

Women's gravestones usually get slightly broader from the bottom to the top and end in a triangular pediment. In earlier periods, men's gravestones were shaped like rectangular prisms. During the Ottoman period, a turban-like capital symbolising the occupation of the deceased was added. Men's gravestones in the shape of columns are also encoun-tered.

# Manisa: City of Princes

### Lale Bulut, Şakir Çakmak, Aydoğan Demir, Rahmi H. Ünal

*Trade in Anatolia*

*Great Mosque (Ulu Cami) Complex, madrasa, courtyard, 1378, İshak Çelebi, Manisa.*

111

*Hatuniye Complex, General view of the mosque from the northeast, 1491, Hüsnüşah Hatun, Manisa.*

Saruhan Bey (r. 1305-1345) founded an Emirate in the region of ancient Lydia in the year 1305. In 1313 the city of Manisa, which had been an important trading centre connecting the Aegean Region to Central Anatolia or the Marmara Region since ancient times, became the centre of this Emirate that ruled over the bountiful plains of the Gediz River (ancient Hermus). The presence of large *han*s in the city that have survived until the present day support this view. However, the Saruhan Emirate was unable to establish sovereignty over the seas like the Menteşe and Aydın Emirates did. Since Foça (ancient Phocea), a very busy and sheltered harbour, was under the domination of the Genoese in the 14th century, the Saruhanids had to make do with their harbours of secondary importance. The

Genoese, who controlled Foça, pa[...] taxes though, to the Saruhan Beys [...] order to continue their presence in t[...] area.

The Saruhan Beys used the income fro[...] the fertile Gediz Plain, taxes, and trac[...] to have, among other things, mosque[...] *madrasa*s, *hammam*s, *han*s, *zawiya*s an[...] *türbe*s, built in various cities, beginnin[...] with Manisa. Two of the most famous [...] these structures, Manisa Great Mosqu[...] and Madrasa along with the *Mevlevihan[...]* were commissioned by İshak Bey (r. 136[...] 1388).

In the Ottoman era Manisa was one [...] the most famous cities of the crow[...] princes. In the 14th and 15th centurie[...] quite a few princes became sultans afte[...] first acting as a governor in Manisa. Th[...] Sehzadeler Palace, literally Prince[...] Palace, not a trace of which is left toda[...]

ould have been built after the royal laces in İstanbul and Edirne. The Sul- n Meadow on Spil Mountain was a ace to which the princes migrated in der to rest in the summer heat and joy themselves. The princes would ay together with their mothers, both whom embellished Manisa with mon- nental works: one of the most beauti- l of which is Hatuniye Mosque Com- ex (1491), constructed in the name of üsnüsah Hatun, the wife of Sultan ayezid II (r. 1481-1512) and the moth- of Şehinşah.

fter Sultan Bayezid I (r. 1389-1402) st the Battle of Ankara to Tamurlane . 1369-1405), the ruler of Transoxiana d Persia, the Ottoman State experi- iced a period of internal disorder and cial despair. The disciples of Shaykh edreddin (d.1419), a *Kadıasker* in the ttoman Government, were trying to read a doctrine of religious commu- ism maintaining that food, clothing, wn fields —everything other than omen— must be used communally by e people. In Manisa, Torlak Kemal, a w who converted to Islam and who as a disciple of Shaykh Bedreddin, orked hard to spread these ideas and used an uprising that had a consider- le effect upon the region. The ttoman State only managed to sup- ress the Torlak Kemal Uprising with ifficulty.

he city of Manisa was administered as art of the Saruhan Sanjak during the me of the Ottomans. Manisa, once nportant because of its location on busy ade routes, has preserved its place up to e present day.

A. D.

*You must use your time carefully if you want to visit all the suggested works in this itiner- ary because you cover close to 300 km. in order to reach Bursa, the starting point of the next itinerary. Furthermore, one of the inter- esting buildings you should see is Issiz Han, close to Ulubat on D. 565, which is the highway you will be taking. If you are spend- ing the night in Izmir, you can reach Man- isa easily with the intercity buses. Although the distances between the buildings to be vis- ited are not great, those who want to save time may want to rent a car or take a taxi or the dolmush minibuses. Our recommenda- tion is to pass the first half of the day in Manisa and then head straight for Ulubat stopping on the way for Manisa Kebab for lunch. The highway takes you through West Anatolia's most fertile lands. Those who take a night journey, between Manisa and Akhis- ar in the months of July-August will be amazed at the sight of the burning lights that resemble fireflies in all the fields; these are the lamps of farmers gathering tobacco in the coolness of the evening.*

*Great Mosque (Ulu Cami) Complex, Madrasa, re-used capitals in the courtyard, 1378, İshak Çelebi, Manisa.*

*Pair of armlets, 15th century, Archaeology Museum, Manisa.*

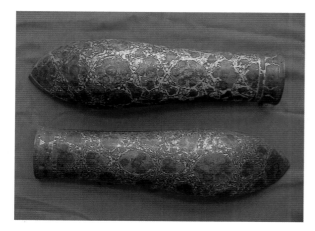

importance until it eventually passed int the hands of the Turks in 1313.

### III.1.a **Archaeological Museum**

*Saruhan District, 107 Murad Avenue. T* *madrasa and imaret sections of the Muradi* *Complex (16th-century Ottoman) are use* *today as the Archaeological and Ethnograph* *cal Museum. The finds from Sardis and nea* *by areas are displayed in the* imaret *and t* *Turkish-Islamic artefacts in the* madrasa. *The museum is open 08:00-12:00 and 13:0(* *16:30 during the winter months and 08:3(* *12:30 and 13:30-17:00 during the summ* *months. There is an entrance fee.*

## III.I **MANISA**

Manisa —Magnesia ad Sipylum of ancient times— was founded by Thessalians towards the end of the 2nd millennium BC on their return from the Trojan War. It exhibits a history parallel to that of West Anatolia. The area passed into the hands of Lydian King Croesus in the 6th century BC but was soon taken over by the Persians in 546 BC. Persian rule came to an end with Alexander the Great's victory at Granicus in 334 BC. In the Hellenistic era the city came under the control of the Pergamene Kingdom. The city and its inhabitants prospered during the time of the Roman Empire and the city preserved its importance during the Byzantine period until the 13th century. Emperor John III Ducas Vatatzes had a fortress built here at the beginning of the 13th century during the Latin occupation of İstanbul and he was buried here, too, when he died. Following the recapture of İstanbul by the Byzantines, the city began to lose its

### Pair of Iron Armlets

During the Ottoman era, soldiers use equipment like armour, armlets, an shields during war to protect their bodie

*Wooden door wings from Great Mosque minbar, 1377, Hacı Mahmud Ibn Abdülaziz, Manisa.*

m sword and arrow blows. The armlet
rn by the warriors was a kind of
nour designed to protect the part of
 arm between the wrist and the elbow.
sically, it is made up of two side wings
d with chain hoops to the main body
t goes over the arm. Because most of
 extant examples are products of fine-
ality workmanship and are richly dec-
ated, it leads one to believe that arm-
s were tools used by high-ranking
diers. The examples displayed in the
nisa Museum consist only of the main
ts, as the wings are missing. The sur-
es of both armlets are decorated with
graving and gold gilding. Although they
k a lot alike, the armlets exhibit dif-
ences regarding decoration. For this
son, it is thought that the two pieces
long to different pairs of armlets. The
nlets are decorated with engraved large
bursts (şemse), cartouches, and tulip
signs, while the area between the
tifs is filled with a gilded plant com-
sition exhibiting even finer workman-
p. These two armlets are dated to the
th century. There are contemporary
amples of armlets similar to these at the
litary Museum in İstanbul.

L. B.

## anisa Great Mosque's Minbar
## oor Wings

e Manisa Great Mosque's *minbar* was
ade by a master named Hacı Mehmed
ı Abdülaziz from Antep in 1377 at the
der of İshak Çelebi, one of the Saruhan
ys; today it is being restored and its
ors are protected in the Manisa Muse-
ı. The *minbar* door wings, made of
ony wood, exhibit quite careful work-

manship. Ornamental panels and panels
with inscriptions are symmetrically
arranged on the door. The large rectangular panels surrounded by ornamental
and inscribed strips are the most interesting components of the composition.
Star and polygonal shapes formed with
long and narrow strips of wood are decorated with mother-of-pearl, ivory, and
wood components of various types and
colours. We learn from the inscriptions
on the door wings that the decorative
composition was prepared by a master
craftsman named Fakih Ibn Yusuf.

L. B.

## III.1.b **Hatuniye Complex**

*On Borsa Avenue in Anafartalar District. Leav-
ing the Museum, follow the Murad Avenue to
the right (east), the complex is a further one
street to the north.*

Manisa, the capital of the Saruhan Emirate, continued to be an important city
after it came under Ottoman rule in
1410. It is one of several Anatolian cities
in which crown princes learned about
state administration. Şehinşah, one of Sultan Beyazid II's sons, was one of the *şehzade*s educated in Manisa. While he was
performing his duties here, his mother
Hüsnüşah Hatun, who was staying with
him, had a large mosque complex consisting of a mosque, a *han*, a *hammam*, an
*imaret*, and a *mektep* built. In order to
meet maintenance and repair expenses,
as well as pay the wages of the people
working at the complex she had built, she
had a *waqf* charter prepared in 1497 and
devoted various real-estate that would
provide the *waqf* with an income. Of the

ing. On the northwest corner of the structure's main body rises the minaret with cylindrical body decorated with zig[...] mouldings, its socle decorated with attractive brickwork. The facade is somew[...] altered with the addition of glass panes [...] closing your eyes to such infelicities, y[...] notice the five-bayed portico support[...] with beautiful re-used Byzantine colum[...] and capitals. Four of the five bays are su[...] mounted with domes, and the central o[...] by a higher flat-topped cross vault. Behi[...] them the high dome of the prayer h[...] rises. Entering the portico, one notic[...] that it is plain without decoration. T[...] inscription over the doorway tells us th[...] the mosque was completed in 1491. T[...] prayer hall was originally designed a[...] square room flanked with two *tabhane*s [...] either side surmounted by domes, b[...] later the separating walls were remov[...] and the *tabhane*s were adjoined. T[...] wooden *minbar*, dated to 1495 accordi[...] to its inscription, is of exclusive craft[...] manship and is decorated with rich ge[...] metric and floral compositions. T[...] mosque was renovated in 1643, 1672 a[...] 1831, and is still open for worship.

*Hatuniye Mosque,
minbar, 1491,
Hüsnüşah Hatun,
Manisa.*

buildings that formed the mosque complex, only the mosque, *han*, and *mektep* have survived up to the present day.

### Hatuniye Mosque

Facing a beautiful park in the market area of the town, the Hatuniye Mosque stands attractively in solitude. At first sight, the walls built with cut-stone (andesite and marble) and brick courses, are breathtak-

### Mektep

Immediately to the west of the mosque[...] a smaller structure with two domes. Th[...] is the *mektep*, believed to have been co[...] missioned by Hüsnüşah Hatun. Howe[...] er, no mention is made of it in the *wa*[...] charter of the mosque complex; there[...] fore, it is generally believed that this pr[...] mary school was built shortly after th[...] establishment of the *waqf* charter in 149[...] It is a small building composed of tw[...] units, each covered by a dome; today, o[...]

it is used as a shop and the other as an ice.

## rşunlu Han

ross the street to the south of the osque stands the Hatuniye Han, the last the complex's buildings that is still nding. It is commonly known as "Kur-nlu Han" or "Lead Han" because its mes are covered with lead sheets. The ain entrance is in the middle of the west le. Built with stone and brick, the build-ʒ –a typical city *han*– is two storied and s a courtyard. Both floors have porticoes ening onto the courtyard but are closed f with glass panes today. There are 36 oms on the ground floor and 38 on the pper floor; all the rooms on the ground oor are covered with vaults, while the oms on the top floor are covered with ults or domes. In all the rooms there is ireplace and niches in which to place longings. The *han*, built to provide come for the mosque complex, is scribed in detail in the 1497 *waqf* char-r, which also states that there were a sta-e and 21 shops. However, the stables, own to have adjoined the eastern cade, have not survived to the present y. Of the shops constructed adjoining e *han*'s north and west fronts, the ones the north were torn down in order to iden a road passing through here. It is own that the building underwent vari-s renovations in 1643 and 1677; it was so thoroughly renovated between the ars 1966-1970. Today it is used as a stu-nt dormitory and can shortly be visited hen accompanied by one of the directors charge.

S. Ç.

### III.1.c **Great Mosque (Ulu Cami) Complex**

*Located on Ulutepe Avenue in İshak Çelebi District. From Hatuniye Complex, continue up hill to the south and reaching Ulutepe Street, turn right. The Complex is located up the hill from the Museum and can also be reached via the staircase-streets behind the Muradiye Mosque.*

Among the many works that were constructed in Manisa during the Saruhan Emirate period, Great Mosque, which forms a complex together with a *madrasa*

*Hatuniye Complex Mektep, general view 1491, Hüsnüşah Hatun, Manisa.*

*Hatuniye Complex Kurşunlu Han, general view, 1491, Hüsnüşah Hatun, Manisa.*

*Hatuniye Mosque, interior, 1491, Hüsnüşah Hatun, Manisa.*

right is hidden behind plane trees. T
complex was constructed by archite
Emet Ibn Osman for Muzaffereddin İsh
Çelebi (1366-1388), the Saruhan Bey.

## Great Mosque

The mosque and the adjoining *madra*
stand on a steep slope; therefore, t
northeast section stands taller than the re
of the complex. Built of re-used mark
blocks, some of which have Byzantine de
oration on them, and roughly cut-stone
the mosque has three portals, one in t
middle of the north side, and one on t
east side, and the other on the west ope
ing into the *madrasa*. The eastern portal
much plainer and has a few re-used Byza
tine pieces as decoration. Today the on
entrance in use is the northern port
which has some very beautiful orname
tation. Most noteworthy are the low ar
of the doorway, the underlying brickwo
of *muqarnas* in the canopy now expose
the rosettes on the side walls and th
inscription itself which records the date
construction for the mosque as 1367. Pa
the portal is the courtyard, one of the ea
liest examples of a courtyard with a po
tico; however, there is no portico in fro
of the prayer hall. The re-used Byzantir
columns and capitals are elaborate, and th
doorway to the west gives access to th
*madrasa*. The prayer hall itself is su
mounted with a large dome supported b
eight pillars and the remaining bays ar
covered with cross- vaults —though the
look different due to thick layers of pla
ter— as are the bays in the courtyard. Th
*minbar*, made in 1377 by an artist name
Hacı Mehmed Ibn Abdülaziz from Antep
and under restoration at the moment,
one of the masterpieces of Turkish art

and a *hammam*, is one of the most important. Approaching from below, past the
*hammam* in ruins now, the mosque comes
into sight first, rising majestically —somewhat obstructed by the ex-fire-watch
tower in front— and the *madrasa* to the

*Great Mosque (Ulu Cami) Complex, Madrasa, türbe door, 1378, İshak Çelebi, Manisa.*

*Great Mosque (Ulu
Cami) Complex,
madrasa, north
façade, 1378,
İshak Çelebi, Manisa.*

*Plan of the Great
Mosque and madrasa,
Manisa
(from Z. Sönmez).*

vood; Bursa Great Mosque's *minbar* is also
he work of the same artist. The minaret,
lecorated here and there with glazed bricks,
s a later addition and can be entered today
rom the roof. Manisa Great Mosque –like
sa Bey Mosque in Selçuk– with its monu-
nental central dome and courtyard with
>orticoes, represents an important step in
he development of Turkish architecture.

## Madrasa

The *madrasa*, adjoining the Great Mosque
>n the west and also known as Fethiye
Madrasa, can be entered either through the

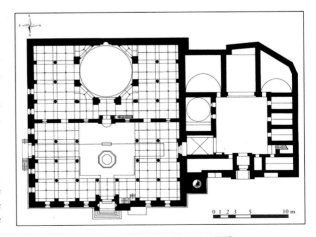

*Great Mosque hammam, west front, second half of the 14ᵗʰ century, İshak Çelebi, Manisa.*

mosque's courtyard, or through the portal on the north side, which resembles the northern portal of the mosque; and the niches on either side of it are fountains. The inscription dates it to 1378 that is later than the mosque. Once inside, the open courtyard without porticoes is surrounded by a two-storey structure; evidently the students' only choice was to concentrate on their studies. In the south is the *dershane* —an *iwan* with a vault; the flaws seen in the plan of the *madrasa* and in its location according to the mosque can be attributed to the sloping terrain of the land.

In the passageway to the mosque is the *türbe* of İshak Çelebi, the founder of the complex; the elegant doorjambs of re-used knotted columns from a Byzantine structure are noteworthy. In the *türbe* there are four symbolic sarcophagi —one belongs to İshak Çelebi, it is not known to whom the other three once belonged.

## Hammam

To the northeast of the mosque is th deteriorated Çukur Hammam, anothe building that belongs to the complex. Th *hammam*, today partially standing, is quit a magnificent building that has a *sıcaklı* with four *iwans*. Sources recount an even that occurred in this *hammam*: Ottoma Sultan Mehmed I, son of Bayezid I, con quered Manisa in 1410 and had Hızırşah the Emirate's last administrator, caugh and executed in this *hammam*: the Saruha Emirate disappeared together with thi event.

Ş. Ç

*This is an excellent place to have a break: sipping a glass of sage tea at the coffee house nearby, enjoy the scenery before you.*

120

## .1.d Karaköy (Sinan Bey) Madrasa (option)

*nca District, 39 Temiz Street. From the Muse-
 continue to the west; at the lights and the
n for "Niobe" turn left; it is in the first street
 the left. From Great Mosque, continue to
utepe Avenue to the west and then to the north;
s in the last street on the right before the lights.*

is known that a great number of *madrasa*s
ere constructed in Manisa during the
ruhan and Ottoman periods. Only four
 these *madrasa*s (Great Mosque [14$^{th}$ c.],
nan Bey [15$^{th}$ c.], Hafsa Sultan [16$^{th}$ c.],
d Muradiye [16$^{th}$ c.] Madrasas) have sur-
ved up to the present day. Of these build-
gs, the only example dating to the early
ttoman period is Sinan Bey Madrasa.
his building, also known as the Karaköy
adrasa, does not have an inscription.
ccording to its *waqf* charter dated 1549,
e *madrasa* together with a *mektep* —which
s not survived— were commissioned by
person named Sinan Bey, who according
 some researchers, was one of the trea-
rers during Sultan Mehmed II's reign
451-1481). According to some other
holars, though, he was one of the same
ltan's *müderris*. Although the *waqf* char-
r dates to 1549, the *madrasa*'s architec-
ral characteristics indicate that it was
nstructed in the middle of the 15$^{th}$ cen-
ry, which is the accepted view.

onstructed out of stone and brick, the
uilding is entered through the monumen-
l entrance in the middle of the north
cade. The courtyard is surrounded with
rticoes on all four sides. On the east and
est wings of the courtyard, there is a total
f 10 student cells, in all of which there is
ne fireplace and various numbers of nich-
s. The cells and porticoes are covered with
ross-vaults, which is striking because this

type of vault, uncommon in Turkish architecture, was quite fashionable and used in
14$^{th}$- and 15$^{th}$-century buildings in West
Anatolian cities like Manisa, Tire and Menemen. To the south of the courtyard is the
*dershane* reached via a set of stairs. In most
of the Anatolian *madrasa*s, the *dershane* area
was also used as a *masjid*. Here, the *dershane*,
together with the portico in front of it, were
raised above the rest of the structure, providing the area with an independent masjid
quality. The *dershane / masjid* is covered with
a dome supported by squinches filled with
*muqarna*s. The Sinan Bey Madrasa was thoroughly renovated in 1985 and is used today
as a Handcrafts Centre in which silver-
working ateliers are found.

Ş. Ç.

---

*Spil Mountain, located just behind the city of
Manisa, offers a rare opportunity for those who
want to rest and be alone with nature. For those
who would like to spend more time in Manisa,
a visit to the Muradiye Mosque Complex and
Sultaniye Mosque Complex (16$^{th}$ century) are
recommended. Manisa also offers the "Mesir Fes-
tival", organized every year during the last week
of April. "Mesir macunu" (a gum-like confec-
tion) was first made in the 16$^{th}$ century by Muslihüddin Merkez Efendi, the manager of Sultaniye Mosque Complex at the time. He devised
the mixture for use in the medical treatment of
Hafsa Sultan, the wife of Yavuz Sultan Selim I.
It has become a tradition to distribute "mesir
macunu" to the people every year from the Sultaniye Mosque, across the street from the Museum. This is done with great festivity. It is also
believed that "mesir macunu", which contains
41 ingredients including clover, ginger, corian-
der, cumin, cinnamon, vanilla, orange rind and
sugar, has, in addition to its characteristics as
an energiser and appetiser that eases digestion
and eliminates tiredness, an aphrodisiac quality.*

It is not difficult to reach Ulubat with the intercity buses but Issız Han is on the edge of the lake some way from the main road.

## III.2 **ULUBAT**

### III.2.a **Issız Han**

*The building is used as a warehouse today. The han's main entrance, which looks onto the lake (to the south), is usually locked. The key is at the farm about 100 m. away.*

The caravan route that connected the Ottoman State's second capital, Bursa, to the west and south reaches Karacabey by following the north shore of Lake Ulubat (Apolyont). In 1394, İne (Eyne) Bey, one of the commanding officers during the eras of the Ottoman Sultans Murad I (1362-1389) and Bayezid I (1389-1402),

commissioned the construction of a h[...] on this road. This *han*, located on th[...] shore of Lake Ulubat close to Seyran Vi[...] lage which is part of the Karacabey town[...] ship, is also known among the people [...] the Susuz Han. İne Bey devoted th[...] income of a village and a mill to this h[...] in order to meet the building's mainte[...] nance and renovation expenses and pa[...] the workers' wages. According to th[...] articles of the *waqf* charter, services wer[...] provided to travellers staying at the h[...] free of charge. It is known that in additic[...] to Issız Han, İne Bey also commissione[...] the construction of various structures i[...] Bergama, Balıkesir, and Bursa. İne Be[...] who played an active role during th[...] Interregnum following the Battle [...] Ankara (1402), was killed in 1405 durin[...] throne disputes amongst the sons of Su[...] tan Bayezid I.

Located in the middle of fields, Issız Ha[...] is an interesting building from an arch[...]

*Issız Han, view from the north, 1394, İne (Eyne) Bey, Ulubat.*

*Issız Han, interior, 1394, İne (Eyne) Bey, Ulubat.*

ectural perspective. Its plan, which lacks
, courtyard but has three aisles, is frequently encountered in the Emirates-peri-
od (14$^{th}$-15$^{th}$ century) buildings. On either
ide of the entrance there are two rooms
or special travellers and the others would
pend the night on the bench inside. In the
niddle of the bench are two fireplaces, the
himneys of which rest upon four short
olumns; this is the only *han* in Anatolia
nown to have this type of fireplace. There
s no fireplace by the classic definition in
ny of the *hans* constructed during the
Seljuq period when *tandır*s, consisting of
a clay-lined pit or earthen jar buried in the
ground, were utilised to cook food and for
heating. Furthermore, The fireplaces in
Issız Han are not on the wall, but are
located on the bench in the centre of the
building. In this respect, it can be said that
Issız Han is a building that symbolizes the
transition from the Anatolian Seljuq *han*
with its *tandır*s in the benches to Ottoman
*han*s with normal fireplaces located on the
wall.

Ş. Ç.

123

# TRADE IN ANATOLIA

**Rahmi H. Üna**

Anatolia, forming a crossroads due to its geographic location, has been the stage of lively trade ever since the oldest periods of history. The most important of the various Silk Roads between the East and the West passed through Anatolia. Turkish tribes, raiding Central Anatolia since the 11th century, made great efforts to establish permanent dominance over the region up until the second half of the 12th century. It is only after this point in history, during the period of Seljuq Sultan Kılıç Arslan II, that Anatolia's new rulers could take measures to develop trade in the country. Because the development of trade is impossible in a country where it is not safe to travel, the sultans made the security of travellers' lives and goods a priority. They applied what may be the first insurance in history to the goods of the tradesmen. The Anatolian Seljuqs signed an agreement with the Cypriots in 1213 and with the Venetians in 1220, according to which both parties were mutually committed to indemnify dam age or loss encountered on their own lands by travelling tradesmen from th other country.

Construction of *caravanserais* —or, by thei other name, *hans*— began in the time o Seljuq Sultan Kılıç Arslan II and contin ued apace in the time of Alâaddi Keykubad I and Gıyaseddin Keyhusrev I The Mongols, who took the Seljuqs unde their hegemony in 1243, also considere trade and the construction of *hans* impor tant. On the caravan routes of Silk an Spice Roads, sultans or important gov ernment officials built *caravanserais*, whic were protective buildings that offere travellers minimal comforts. The archi tecture of *hans* of this period reminds on of small fortresses: the majority of the consisting a covered section and a court yard; the only entrance through a monu mental portal opened directly into th courtyard and from the courtyard onl one portal provided access to the covere

*Sultan Han, courtyard, 1229, Alaaddin Keykubat I, Konya–Aksaray caravan route.*

ection. Caravans that wished to spend the night in a safe place after dark would stay in these buildings, which were constructed at certain intervals along the trade routes. The distance between hans outside settlement centres was never more than 40 km; in fact, this distance is sometimes as little as 5-10 km., on rugged terrain. Hence, such hans are called menzil han, literally a han at a day's journey. Small villages arose in the surroundings of some hans that were constructed in previously uninhabited areas. However, once the Seljuqs' central authority began to vanish towards the end of the 13th century, local potentates headed towards West Anatolia began to found emirates. As a result of the appearance of a great number of small emirates in Anatolian territory, safety could no longer be established on the caravan routes and transit trade began to lose its importance. Caravanserais constructed during this politically unstable period were smaller and without courtyards, and could not match the magnificence of the Seljuq caravanserais. Also in this period the city hans began appearing in ever increasing numbers.

After the Portuguese sailor Bartolemeu Dias' discovery of the Cape of Good Hope in 1488, European tradesmen usually preferred the sea route when doing trade with the East. As the routes that tied the East to the West began to lose their importance, the routes that connected the city centres in the central regions of Anatolia to the port cities

*Susuz Han, interior, first half of 13th century, Burdur–Antalya caravan route.*

began to gain importance and hans of small dimensions were constructed along these routes. In connection to these developments hans, intended to meet the needs of storing tradesmen's goods, selling, and even providing places to spend the night, began to be built in the city centres. The magnificent and large-size hans of the 16th and 17th century that have survived to our day reveal that the caravan routes once again reached their previous level of liveliness once political stability had been re-established during the period of the Ottoman Empire. However, the plan layouts of these hans did not resemble the menzil hans lined up all along the caravan routes because they were constructed for a different purpose. City hans are usually two storied with rooms lined up around a courtyard in the centre. In these hans, the rooms on the lower floor were generally used as depots; the rooms on the upper floor, though, were designated as offices or boarding rooms.

# Bursa: City of Sultans

### Lale Bulut, Aydoğan Demir, Yekta Demiralp

## I BURSA

### First Day

### Second Day

*The* Hammam *Tradition*
*The Battle of Ankara*

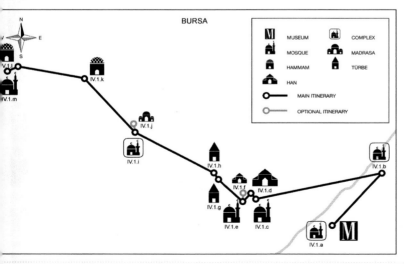

*Great Mosque, Domes, 1400, Bayezid I, Bursa.*

127

*Yeşil Complex, main door, 1419-1424, Mehmed I, Bursa.*

*Orhan Mosque, detail from mihrab, 1339-40, Orhan Gazi, Bursa.*

1113 the Seljuq troops once again to the shores of the Marmara includi Bursa but, as before, they were unable secure their hold on the region.

While various emirates were being esta lished in West Anatolia towards the e of the 13th and the beginning of the 1 century, a Turcoman Bey named Ertuğ (d.1281) and his son Osman (r. 1281-132 were attempting to settle the region ancient Bithynia. Osman's heroes, ren niscent of European knights of the Mi dle Ages, engaged in battles with sm Byzantine landowners; these battles we full of honour and romanticism for bo sides. Nevertheless, after the establis ment of Ottoman dominance over t region, both communities lived in pea for hundreds of years.

Founded by Osman Gazi in 1299, t Emirate captured Prusa, one of the mo important towns of the Byzanti Empire, in the year 1326 during the rei of Orhan Gazi (1324-1362). This ci whose name among the people was tra formed into Bursa, became the centre the newly founded Ottoman State.

In a short time many *hans* were co structed in Bursa, a developed comme cial and industrial centre. The ci became famous as a weaving- and sil production centre in particular.

Bursa, situated on the slopes of Uludağ (Mysian Olympus), with its abundant water supply and fertile plains, has attracted settlers throughout history. An important city of the ancient kingdom of Bithynia, Prusa (today's Bursa) contains evidence of all of the Anatolian civilisations starting from the middle of the first millennium BC. The Anatolian Seljuq State, which was founded in 1075 and had its first centre at İznik (ancient Nicea), established sovereignty over Bursa during its foundation period, even if only for a short time. Once the Seljuqs moved their centre to Konya, having been defeated by the armies of the First Crusade in 1097, they were unable to maintain constant possession of the Marmara region. In

*Yeşil Madrasa, entrance iwan, 1419-24, Mehmed I, Bursa.*

The Ottoman sultans who ruled from the beginning of the 14th century until the middle of the 15th century were Orhan Gazi (1324-1362; also known as Orhan Bey), Murad I (1362-1389; also known as Hüdavendigar), Bayezid I (1389-1402; also known as Yıldırım), Mehmed I 1413-1421; also known as Çelebi), and Murad II (1421-1451), all of whom improved the city by having various religious and public buildings constructed.

At the time of the founding of the state, the Ottoman sultans were broadminded men who lived in a simple manner. After he took Bursa, Orhan Gazi sent a gift of alcoholic drink to Geyikli Baba, a heterodox religious figure who had joined the conquest of Bursa. Sultan Bayezid I was also a sultan who used alcohol; according to legend, when he asked Emir Sultan, a religious leader, whether or not he liked the newly built Great Mosque, Emir Sultan replied: "The mosque has one deficiency: there should be taverns on all four sides so that there's a pretext for you to come".

Bursa is also a city of *türbes*: the first six Ottoman Sultans are buried in *türbes* here. Of these, the *türbe* of Sultan Mehmed I is a dazzling architectural work with its tiles and architecture.

Bursa is famous for its *hammams*, spas, and fountains. The Ottomans tried to make its social services available to all the citizens, regardless of differences in religion and language. For example, after Orhan Gazi captured Bursa, he had pipes installed to bring water to the Jewish quarter of the city.

A. D.

## IV.I  BURSA

### IV.I.a  Yeşil Complex

*Çelebi Sultan District (Mahallesi), on Yeşil Street. An entrance fee is charged for the*

*Yeşil Madrasa, tile vault of western iwan, 1419-24, Mehmed I, Bursa.*

opposition, Mehmed's son, Murad II, con
cealed his father's death until he ascende
the throne. Later, Mehmed's body wa
placed in the *türbe* of his complex, whic
was completed after his death. The *imare*
to the southeast of the mosque was recent
ly restored and is closed to visitors. Th
*hammam,* still in use, to the west of th
*türbe*, is not mentioned in the *waqf* charte

## Yeşil Madrasa (Museum of Turkish and Islamic Arts)

The *madrasa*, about 100 m. to the west o
the mosque, is situated in the middle of
yard and is today used as the Museum o
Turkish and Islamic Arts. Approaching
from the street one reaches the back first
walking past the eastern side observing the
remains of the basic geometric tile deco
rations the window tympana, the entrance
opening to the outside like an *iwan* is in the
middle of the northern side. The columns
and capitals that support the portico were
gathered from various Byzantine buildings
Most of portico's bays, which surround the
courtyard on three sides, are covered with
a single dome each, while the cells are cov
ered with vaults and the vault of the west
ern *iwan* is decorated with lovely turquoise
and dark-blue tiles. Today, a staircase built
to provide access to the upper storey, is
found on the side wings: the *madrasa* was
planned as a two storey structure, but
because of the sudden death of Mehmed I,
the upper storey was never completed.
The domed *dershane* directly opposite the
entrance protrudes outside and it is under
stood from the *mihrab* on the *qibla* wall that
it also served as a prayer room.
The first *müderris* appointed to the *madrasa*
was the son of Molla Şemseddin Fenari,

*madrasa, which is also the Museum of Turkish and Islamic Arts, and the visitor is asked to make a donation at the türbe. The museum is open between 08.00-12.00 and 13.00-16.30 in the winter and 08:30 -12:30 and 13.30- 17.00 in the summer. It is closed on Mondays. The complex is very close to the heart of the town and is a popular place among the locals.*

Today Yeşil Complex is composed of a mosque, a *madrasa*, an *imaret* and a *türbe*. It takes its name, which means "Green", from the turquoise tiles that decorate the mosque, *madrasa*, and especially its *türbe*. After his victory over the power struggle during the Interregnum following the Battle of Ankara (28 July 1402), Mehmed I, also known as Çelebi Mehmed, ascended the Ottoman throne in 1413. He began building the Yeşil Complex a short time later as a potent display of the magnificence of the state, which had just regained its power. However, in 1421, Mehmed fell ill while hunting in Edirne, became paralysed, and passed away shortly thereafter. As a result of the sultan's sudden death, the construction of the complex could not be completed. Because of his fear of the

e renowned Ottoman intellectual. It
ıst have seemed strange for an 18-year-
d to reach a position that required so
ıch responsibility. Thus, at the first lec-
re he gave at the *madrasa*, both students
d learned men from Bursa and environs
rected questions at him in a kind of
amination. After this it became a cus-
m for all *müderris*es of this *madrasa* to be
amined in this way.

ıe museum has a very nice, well dis-
ayed collection with, among other
ings, examples of woodwork, ceramic
ork, metalwork, manuscripts, *fermans*
d embroidery work. The ceramic exam-
es described below are displayed in the
owcases in the western *iwan* and the oth-
s are in the cells on the east.

Y. D.

**eramic Plate** (Inv. Num. 814,
ᵗʰ century)

esearchers agree that İznik white-clay
ramics first appeared in the 15ᵗʰ century.
ese ceramics made of hard, white clay
d thin, smooth transparent glaze were
e result of changes made by tile experts
the preparation of the clay. Some inno-

vations and changes in the decoration of
these ceramics are especially noteworthy.
It is believed that the introduction of Chinese ceramics into the Ottoman court
played an important role in these developments. Deep bowls, large-footed vessels,
wide shallow plates with decorated borders, plates with wavy edges, pitchers, and
jars were the favourite types of ceramics
used in daily life in this period.

This plate of white clay produced in İznik
is of the group of ceramics known as
"blue-white". The centre is indented and
the edges are turned out. The decoration
is done with the under-glaze technique.
The white ornamentation consists of
foliage, large *rumi*s and Chinese clouds in
the centre indentation and the edge, painted on a cobalt-blue background.

L. B.

**Bronze Brazier** (Inv. Num. 107,
15ᵗʰ century)

People have developed various methods
for heating the places they live in. In
the Middle Ages, heating was provided
by fireplaces, clay-lined pit stoves called

*The Koran, 1435, Turkish and Islamic Arts Museum (Inv. Num. 207), Bursa.*

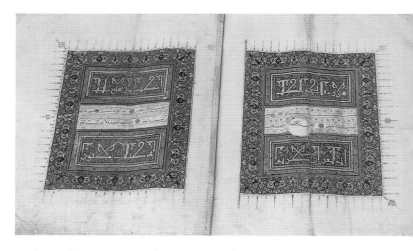

*tandır*s and braziers. Fireplaces were most often used to heat large spaces such as the covered areas in *caravanserais*; because of the loss of heat and the large amount of fuel consumed, this method of heating was used in the residences of the wealthy. The people of lower economic means preferred to heat their living spaces with braziers or *tandır*s.

Braziers are vessels made of baked clay or metal, into which hot coals are placed. The body of the container, in which the fire is set, is placed on a footed stand. To prevent damage that could be caused by red-hot ashes and coals that fall to the ground, large pieces of "brazier board" or a "brazier tray" are placed under the stand. Brazier board was usually made of wood that does not easily catch fire, like hornbeam or oak.

This brazier is cast iron. The hexagonal body rests on six curled feet and has two handles. The six sides are each decorated with symmetrically placed lattice floral motifs.

**The Koran** (Inv. Num. 207, 1435, Sultan Murad II)

Muslims believe that the *Qur'an* (c Koran), the holy book of Islam, is th word of God delivered to Muhammad l the angel Gabriel. The first sura of th *Qur'an* was delivered in 610 and th transaction continued over the next 2 years until the Prophet's death. As th revelations came, they were memorise by Mohammed and other Muslims and, the same time, scribes wrote the vers on various materials like rocks, scapula date leaves, and animal hides. Howeve in the Prophet's lifetime it was neve thought to bring these various text together into one book but after h death, in the time of *Caliph* Abu Bakr, a existing texts were examined and place in one volume.

The *Qur'an* is divided into 114 chapter each of which is called a *sura*; each of th verses that make up the *sura* is called a *ayet* in Turkish. Because of disagreemen about where the verses begin and en ere is no unanimous opinion on the xact number of the more than 6000 rses in the *Qur'an*.

his *Koran* is hand written in the *naskhi* yle of Arabic lettering; the titles and ginnings of the *sura*s are decorated with old; a great amount of gold gilding has en used in the ornamentation. The flo- l motifs on the exterior surface of the own-leather binding with a folded cover ere applied with a mould. On the inner- de surfaces of the covers and the folded ver are decorations in the *katı'* tech- que, the background of which is affixed ith cloth. Floral motifs within rosettes ere applied with paint and gold gilding.

L. B.

*Ceramic vase, 15th century, Turkish and Islamic Arts Museum (Inv. Num. 3374), Bursa.*

## eramic Vase (Inv. Num. 3374, 5th century)

his is an example of İznik "blue-white" eramic ware. Its pear-shaped body nar- ows at the bottom and it has a cylindri- l neck. The designs drawn in the under- aze technique, are repeated on the body d the neck, and consist of stylised cloud otifs and curled leaves applied in blue, n a white background.

L. B.

*Ceramic plate, 15th century, Turkish and Islamic Arts Museum (Inv. No. 813), Bursa.*

## eramic Plate (Inv. Num. 813, 5th century)

his is an example of İznik "blue-white" eramic ware. Though the clay of these eramics is white and hard like porcelain, is not translucent in the same way. The aze is very thin, colourless, transparent nd shiny. Because of these qualities, the aze does not crack during the firing

process. In "blue-white" ceramic ware, the colour contrast between the background and the motifs is what catches the eye. This plate with a depressed centre and a projecting rim is decorated in the under- glaze technique. On the border strip, white *rumi*s and *palmettes* have been paint- ed on a cobalt-blue background. The cir- cular area in the centre of the plate is dec-

*Ferman, 1458, Turkish and Islamic Arts Museum (Inv. Num. 4320), Bursa.*

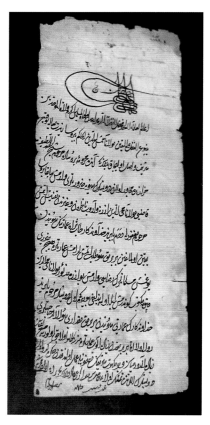

these documents are rare examples of th art of decorative writing. These docu ments bore the *tuğra* or elaborate inscribed signature of the sultan and the contents were ordered according to a ce tain pattern. For example, a *ferman* co sisted of the salutation, *tuğra*, title prayer, narrative, command, the repea ing of the command, and date, in th order. In certain *fermans*, there are als "threat" sentences stating the punishmen to be carried out if the order is n obeyed or the duty is not performe Furthermore, it is interesting that curse in the form of "May earth and heave reject those who disobey this comman are also found on some *fermans*.

The example here is a decree sent fro Edirne by Sultan Mehmed II to the Bur Kadı Şemseddin in 1458. Written in gilde black ink, the *ferman* makes mention dervishes living around the *imaret* built the sultan's great grandfather Murad I, als known as Hüdavendigar. It is understoc from the *ferman* that the *dervishes* requeste some of the water brought to the Hüda endigar İmaret for their own use and that th sultan assented to their request.

L. I

orated with a geometric composition, the empty spaces of which are filled with small-flower and leaf motifs.

L. B.

**Ferman** (Inv. Num. 4320, dated 1458)

*Fermans* are the written orders of the sultans. *Fermans* kept in Ottoman archives, various museums, and private collections supply important information about the administration and the socio-economic condition of the state. At the same time,

**Ceramic Plate** (Inv. Num. 2659, end 14th century, beginning 15th century)

This is an example of the "Miletus type" İznik ceramic ware. This group of ceran ics is distinguishable by the use of cobal blue designs on a white *engobe* back ground. Although free leaf designs, sta motifs in the centre, and radial lines ar frequently seen on these plates, there is n known example where a composition ha been repeated a second time. In th

*Ceramic plate, end of 14th century-beginning of 15th century, Turkish and Islamic Arts Museum (Inv. Num. 2659), Bursa.*

example, a large fish with its body conforming to the circular shape of the bowl is seen among curled branches.

L. B.

## Yeşil Mosque

Approaching from the back, the pale gold of the cut-stone walls gives way to full marble on the northern facade, which is decorated with exquisite stone craftsmanship especially around the windows –though unfinished– and on the portal. On the lower level are four windows and two outdoor *mihrab*s and above them are four loggias. One of the most interesting features of the facade is the absence of a portico: corbels still visible on the front indicate that a portico was planned but, for some reason, never completed. The inscription above the low arch of the portal gives the name of the architect as Hacı İvaz. On entering, there are two corridors on both sides leading to a room in the northern corner and to the steps leading upstairs, which is not open to visitors. There is then is a small and dark *iwan*-like chamber, covered with dark-green tiles which are set with medallions decorated

in the *cuerda seca* technique. Reaching the inner court it is impossible not to be carried away with the decoration –like heaven, as Evliya Çelebi says– so different from other mosques in Bursa of this period. This example of Ottoman tiling to adorn a mosque breaks away from preceding Seljuq examples, setting a style that was to be developed in the following century when the İznik kilns were producing their highest quality, though in a way very different from that seen here.

A soaring dome with a lantern covers the central court. The fountain has a nicely carved marble water jet in the centre. To the east and the west, the two large *iwan*s, whose walls are covered with tiles, are again surmounted with soaring fluted domes. The two recesses flanking the entrance to the north of the central court were for the *müezzin*s; the loggia above the entrance is the royal loge upstairs. All the walls and flat ceilings of these three small recesses are completely covered with tiles; the ones in the royal loge upstairs are particularly richly decorated. Gold floral decorations on the hexagonal tiles on the *iwan*s on the east and west sides are noteworthy, as are those on the

*Decoration on the portal of Yeşil Mosque, Bursa (from Ş. Çakmak).*

*Yeşil Mosque, View from the south, 1419-24, Mehmed I, Bursa.*

*Plan of Yeşil Mosque,
Bursa (from Z.
Sönmez).*

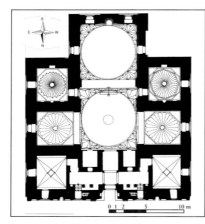

also be seen on the tiles on the *mihrab* as
well as the upper floor chambers. The
mosque was open for worship in 1419
but the decoration was not completed
until 1424. According to the inscription
in the royal loge, Nakkash Ali carried out
the painting of the decorations and super-
vised the ornamentation while the tile
master was Muhammed al-Majnun.

Y. D

## Yeşil Türbe

*To the south of Yeşil Mosque*

Located on a small hillock, Yeşil Türbe
rises at a considerably higher level than
Yeşil Mosque. Almost the entire body of
this octagonal *türbe* is covered with
turquoise tiles; the tympana of the lower
row of the paired windows on each face

walls of two recesses located on the
ground floor.

This mosque was designed to provide
lodging and a meeting area for the wandering *dervish*es who played an important
role in the social and religious life of the
time –though today the whole structure is
used as a mosque. The *tabhane*s located
between the *iwan*s and the prayer hall,
provided with fireplaces and shelving,
were used as lodging for the *dervish*es.
The niches and fireplaces in the *tabhane*s
in the southeast and southwest are
superbly decorated with geometric and
floral motifs in stucco. On the inner surfaces of their domes, traces of wall painting can be seen, as in the domes over the
*iwan*s. The prayer hall to the south, separated from the central court with a "Bursa
arch", is again covered with superb tiles
and the *mihrab* is especially outstanding; as
Evliya Çelebi says, he is incapable of
describing it. According to an inscription
on the upper part of one of the two
columns flanking the *mihrab* niche, the
tiles were manufactured by artisans from
Tabriz (Iran). The Persian influences can

*Yeşil Türbe, Detail
from the mihrab,
1419-24, Mehmed I,
Bursa.*

*Yıldırım Complex, General view from the south, 1389-99, Bayezid I, Bursa.*

f the *türbe* are also decorated with tiles. he tiles, which once covered the facade f the portal, have completely disappeared; yet, the oyster-shell conch resting on Turkish triangles and the niches on he sides are still very attractive. *Kündekari* echnique is used on both wings of the magnificent wooden door. There are six anels in all: two large and four small; xtending around these panels is an inscription that includes the names of Sultan Mehmed I; the architect Hacı İvaz, on of Ahi Bayezid; and the tile master raftsman, Hacı Ali, son of Ahmet, who vas originally from Tabriz.

inside, the lower section of the walls is overed with hexagonal tiles. Between the vindows, there is also one large multicoloured *şemse* sunburst in *cuerda seca* technique. The *mihrab* is also decorated with iles and its rich ornamentation is every bit as glorious as the *mihrab* of Yeşil Mosque. Unique decorative elements are found in he tile-mosaic that adorns the ceilings of

the lower row of casements. The dome rises on a lovely cornice of Turkish triangles. Four of the sarcophagi present in the *türbe* are decorated with tiles; the tile sarcophagus of Sultan Mehmed I located in the centre is especially beautiful, and of the highest standard of workmanship. The other graves belong to his sons Mustafa, Mahmud, and Yusuf, along with the women sultans, including the nanny of the sultan. Currently closed to visitors, the crypt floor has an interesting plan consisting of five areas, three small, and two large; no other example of such a crypt, consisting of several areas, is known.

Y. D.

## IV.1.b  Yıldırım Complex

*Yıldırım District (Mahallesi), Bursa.*

In this complex built by Sultan Bayezid I there is a mosque, a *madrasa*, a *darüşşifa*, an *imaret*, a *hammam*, and a *türbe*; all the

137

*Yıldırım Madrasa, dome with muqarnas on the eastern portico, 1389-1399, Bayezid I, Bursa.*

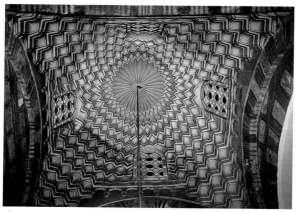

*Türbe of Bayezid I, entrance facade, 1406, Emir Süleyman Çelebi, Bursa.*

structures except the *imaret* have survived to the present day. The whole complex is called "Yıldırım" based on the epithet of Sultan Bayezid I who is also known as Sultan Yıldırım Bayezid. Yıldırım means lightning or thunderbolt in Turkish, suggesting that the sultan was able to move his armies "as quick as lightning" in order to crush his enemies. Hence the name and most of the edifices he had built are called Yıldırım Mosque, Yıldırım Complex, etc. This complex is located on a hill, some way away from the town centre and stands in a lovely park, set on ter-

races due to the slope. The *hammam* hi▮ den among the houses is still in use.

## Yıldırım Mosque

The mosque, the central building of t▮ complex, is built with cut stone. T▮ mosque's present minaret is a later ad▮ tion; the original minarets in the northe▮ and northwest corners collapsed at ▮ unknown time. The five-bayed portico▮ the front is also built with cut stone a▮ surmounted with domes. The two loggi▮ above the outdoor *mihrabs* located ▮ either side of the portal were to provi▮ light for the staircase to the origin▮ minarets. Passing through the plain port▮ *iwan* topped with a tiny dome, o▮ emerges into the inner court covered by▮ soaring dome and flanked with *iwans* ▮ both sides. These *iwans* are also flanked ▮ both sides with rooms covered with fla▮ topped cross-vaults but only the ones t▮ the south, also flanking the prayer hal▮ have furnishings of spectacular stucco fir▮ place and shelving enhanced with embe▮ ded tile pieces. The mosque was designe▮ to respond to the needs of the *Ahi dervishe▮* by providing them with meeting an▮ boarding places; hence the rooms with th▮ fireplace and shelving are the *tabhanes▮* There is a monumental arch separating th▮ inner court from the prayer hall; this is th▮ first example of a "Bursa arch" with its to▮ flat and recessed, another beautiful exam▮ ple of which can be seen in Yeşil Mosque▮ There is no record of construction, but i▮ is believed that building must have take▮ place sometime between Bayezid I's ascen▮ sion to the throne in 1389 and the prepa▮ ration of the *waqf* charter in 1399.

Y. D▮

*Orhan Mosque,
mihrab, 1339-40,
Orhan Gazi, Bursa.*

## Yıldırım Madrasa

The *madrasa*, on a lower terrace to the northwest of the mosque, is today used as a health centre. The attractive walls built with alternating courses of stones and bricks are enhanced with the decoration in the tympana of the windows. The presence of a pair of small niches placed together on the side walls of the entrance to the *iwan*, rising higher than the rest of the structure, is a rarely seen characteristic and its dome is very attractive with its Turkish triangles. The dome covering the portico is very striking with its *muqarnas* decoration. There were latrines in the corner to the right of the entrance, but they were removed during recent repair work. Behind the vaulted porticos are student cells surrounding the courtyard on three sides, and the large *iwan* opposite the entrance fully protrudes and was used as a summer *dershane*. Strangely enough, there is not a winter *dershane* in this *madrasa* as there is in other *madrasas* of this period; in such *madrasas*, during the winter, either the front of the *iwan* was closed with wooden panes or classes were held in the complex's mosque.

Y. D.

## Darüşşifa

The *darüşşifa*, one of the most important buildings in the complex, has been restored in recent years. It is important for it is one of the few Ottoman *darüşşifas* that have survived up to the present day. Built on a steep slope to the east of the mosque, the cells and porticoes on the side wings are graded with steps and the brickwork is noteworthy.

Y. D.

## Türbe

The *türbe* in this complex belongs to Bayezid I, who was defeated and taken prisoner by Tamerlane at the Battle of Ankara (1402). Some historians say he committed suicide; others maintain that he fell ill and died in Akşehir in central Anatolia. After his death, he was buried in Akşehir in the *türbe* of Seyyid Mahmud Hayran, but later his body was handed over to his son Musa Çelebi and sent to

*Koza Han, general view, 1492, Bayezid II, Bursa.*

Bursa at the order of Tamerlane. Because it was his will to be buried near the mosque he had built, his body was buried near the mosque in 1403-1404; in 1406, his son Emir Süleyman Çelebi had the present *türbe* constructed over his grave. During his siege of Bursa in 1413, Karamanid Bey Mehmed II took vengeance on his father's murderer, Bayezid I, by removing his body from the grave and burning it.

The *türbe* of Bayezid I is a simple square building surmounted by a dome and the three-bayed portico in front served as a model for later Ottoman *türbes* with porticoes.

Y. D.

*The following monuments: c, d, e, and f are almost side by side; Orhan Mosque is to the east of the square, a small structure compared to the large Great Mosque at the western end of the square. From Orhan Mosque towards the west is Koza Han; then, past some shops hiding the Bey Hammam of Orhan's Complex, is the Emir Han and Great Mosque. This*

*area, known as Heykel, is the heart of the town and always very lively. Adjoining them on the north are more hans and the bedesten of the Early Ottoman period forming the central market area of Bursa. The hans are closed on Sundays and religious holidays.*

### IV.1.c Orhan Mosque

Orhan, who ascended the throne in 1324, captured Bursa in 1326 and entered the city with a magnificent ceremony. In order to develop the city, which had not yet expanded beyond its city walls, Orhan had the "Lower Fortress" built towards the east as well as the mosque complex that bears his name. Of the buildings that made up the complex, the *madrasa*, *mektep*, and *imaret* have not survived to the present day.

In 1413, while Sultan Mehmed I was away in Rumelia on a military expedition, Karamanid Bey Mehmed II besieged Bursa. Hacı İvaz Pasha withdrew to the tadel and tried to defend the old city. In the last days of the one-month-long siege aramanid Bey Mehmed Bey II set fire to oth Great Mosque and Orhan Mosque. he fire damaged the portico and the ain facade. According to the inscription bove the entrance Orhan had this osque built in 1339-1340, and after the aramanid Bey Mehmed II destroyed it uring his occupation of Bursa, the *Vizier* ayezid Pasha repaired it on the order of ultan Mehmed I in 1417.

he five-bayed portico to the north of Orhan Mosque is very attractive with pandrels decorated in stone and brick. Orhan Mosque was planned to accommodate the needs of the wandering *Ahi ervishes* by providing them with a lodging nd meeting area. The domed *iwans* that lank the domed central court were constructed with this aim in mind. A dome overs the main prayer hall and the *mihrab* s one of the most beautiful, coulourfully ainted examples of an Anatolian stucco mihrab.

## V.1.d  Koza Han

n Bursa, a great number of the *hans* that urvive in good condition today date from he 14th and 15th centuries indicating that Bursa was an important commercial cenre during these centuries. Some *hans* uilt in the commercial centres of Anatoia were given names such as Salt Han, ilk Han, Rice Han, and Copper Han, hus emphasising the particular commodty that each *han* traded. The presence of wo separate *hans* called İpek (Silk) Han and Koza (Cocoon) Han provides evilence that Bursa was an important silk entre in the 14th and 15th centuries, as it

was during the Byzantine era, when it was also known as an active silk centre. The story goes that a Chinese princess who was migrating to Bursa brought some silkworm eggs, then, when she was forbidden to take the eggs out of China, she hid them in her hair.

Silk is a natural fibre obtained from the cocoons of silkworms (*Bombyx mori*). Silk production begins with the incubation of silkworm eggs, two thousand of which weigh only one gram. Under favourable conditions, the silkworms hatch in 11-14 days and feed on mulberry leaves for 24-28 days. Next, they secrete the fibre and imprison themselves in the cocoons within 48-72 hours. The silkworm in the cocoon undergoes metamorphosis and comes out of the cocoon by cutting it as a winged moth. It is necessary to kill the worm before it comes out so that the cocoon fibres are not damaged: this process called "drowning" is done by either treating the cocoons with steam or hot air, or stretching them out to dry in the sun. In the final stage, the cocoons are softened using various methods, the cocoon fibres are caught by a small besom and wound onto spinning wheels and crude silk thread is spun. From each cocoon between 300 and 1400 m. of silk is obtained. As silk is obtained by killing the insect inside the cocoon, silk cloth is religiously unlawful according to Islamic sages.

This two-storey *han* has one entrance to the south opening to the upper floor and an attractive portal to the north opening on to the courtyard, which is surrounded by two-storied porticoes on four sides. The upper portico, made of wood up until recent times, has been renovated in order to resemble the lower one. The

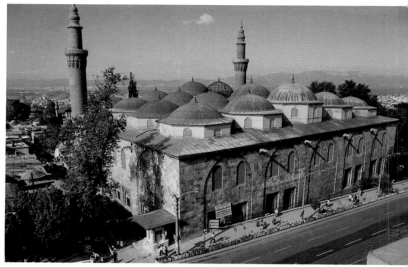

*Great Mosque, general view from the southwest, 1400, Bayezid I, Bursa.*

octagonal two-storey structure in the courtyard has the *masjid* upstairs and the ablution fountain below; an octagonal column in the middle and eight other piers in the corners support the vaulting and the *masjid*. Sultan Bayezid II built Koza Han between 1489-92 in order to provide income for the *imaret* of his mosque complex in İstanbul.

Y. D.

### IV.1.e  Great Mosque (Ulu Cami)

Bayezid I, who ascended the throne after his father Murad I was killed in battle in 1389, constructed the Bursa Great Mosque. Bayezid had his brother, Yakup Çelebi, killed in a struggle for the throne. The story goes that when Sultan Bayezid I defeated the Crusaders at Niğbolu (Nicopolis) on the Danube in 1396, he vowed that he would build 20 mosques with his newly won booty. However, he

was in fact convinced to build one mosque with 20 domes instead and the structure was completed in 1400. It is reported that Tamerlane used the mosque for stabling and storing hay during his occupation of Bursa. And according to another legend, in 1413, during the final days of his 31-day occupation of the city, the Karamanid Bey Mehmed II tried to burn the mosque down by piling wood around it. As a result of the damage done —presumably by this attempt according to some researchers— to the stones in lower part of the walls and the portals, the mosque's exterior surface was plastered with mortar. In the 1950s the ashlars of the facades were completely renewed.

Atatürk Avenue extends along the south *qibla* wall, which is built with cut stones, punctuated by arches and windows, as are the other fronts. The rectangular structure has three entrances: the main portal in the middle of the north facade is more elaborate than the other portals on the east and west fronts. Adjoining the northern corners are two minarets. Once inside, there is a very different atmosphere than the typical Bursa mosques with *tabhanes*: this mosque's large prayer hall is arranged in 20 bays, separated from one other by 12 huge piers aligned in three rows of four, supporting 20 domes of equal size. These piers destroy the integrity of the space and give the mosque a dark and oppressive atmosphere. This example, which continues the Anatolian Seljuq tradition of mosques with equal size multiple bays, lacks the integrity seen in 16th-century Ottoman mosques; another Early Ottoman example with this layout is the Eski Mosque in Edirne. Like the minarets outside, the painted decoration inside is a 19th-century renovation. The real masterpiece here is the *minbar* of walnut wood made in the *kündekari* technique famous for its workmanship and decoration. The sides of the *minbar* are composed of small geometric pieces decorated with floral motifs; these interlocking pieces are held together without the use of glue or any other binding material. According to Evliya Çelebi, it is so beautifully decorated that even if all the artisans of the world come together, they could not have produced anything similar; except the *minbar* of Sinop on the Black Sea coast. Hacı Mehmed bin Abdülaziz of Antep, the artisan of this *minbar*, also made the *minbar* of Manisa Great Mosque.

### 1.f **Emir Han** (option)

Emir Han, also known as Bey Han, is part of the first royal complex of Bursa, commissioned by Orhan Gazi, composing a mosque, *hammam*, *madrasa*, *mektep*, and *imaret*. When the site was chosen, great attention was paid to the development of the town, and the complex was constructed in an empty area to the east. The area was enlivened by the construction of this complex and even today forms Bursa's commercial centre.

Entering the *han* through the simple gate by the northeast minaret of Great Mosque, one arrives on the upper floor; there is another gate on the north opening into the street on the lower level. The *han* consists of rooms, located behind porticoes, and surrounding a courtyard and a small stable downstairs. There are no windows in the 36 lower rooms; in the upper 38 rooms there is a fireplace and a window opening outwards. There is no inscription, but it is believed that it was built in the second half of the 14th century. Emir Han is one of the earliest examples of the Ottoman city *hans*.

### Second day

*The Türbes of Osman Gazi and Orhan Gazi are located in Tophane District (Mahallesi), on Osmangazi Avenue within the old citadel of Bursa. It is also a good area for a stroll, up the hill and past some of the old renovated houses. The view from the terrace, where the türbes are located, is quite magnificent.*

### IV.1.g **Türbe of Osman Gazi**

*Next to the Türbe of Orhan Gazi.*

Osman Gazi, who founded the Ottoman State that bears his name, passed the throne to his son Orhan while he was still alive because of his age and ill health. It is

*Decoration on the portal of Great Mosque, Bursa (from Ş. Çakmak).*

143

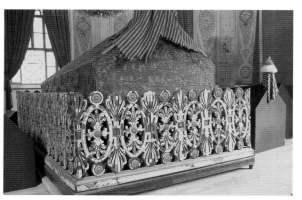

*Osman Gazi Türbe, wooden sarcophagus, 1863, Sultan Abdülaziz, Bursa.*

building there are examples of intrica wall paintings with floral motifs. Of t 17 sarcophagi placed on a marble floc only five have been identified. Osmar sarcophagus, located in the centre, is su rounded with a latticed wooden scree inlaid with mother-of-pearl.

Y. 

### IV.1.h  Türbe of Orhan Gazi

*Next to the* Türbe *of Osman Gazi.*

said that, before the conquest of Bursa, he told his son Orhan Gazi that when he died he wanted to be buried in Bursa beneath the "Silver Dome". It is not certain whether Bursa was conquered before or after Osman's death.

What Osman described as the "Silver Dome" was a Byzantine chapel occupying an elevated area of Bursa; from a distance the structure and its lead-covered dome gave the impression of being made of silver. Osman Gazi was buried here as he had requested but his *türbe* suffered major damage in a fire that destroyed more than half of Bursa in 1801 and it was completely ruined in the earthquake of 1855. It was impossible to repair, so at the order of Sultan Abdülaziz the present *türbe* was constructed on the old foundations in 1863.

The octagonal structure is covered with a dome. Its architectural style and decoration belongs to the "Westernisation Period" of Turkish architecture: from the 17th century onwards, Turkish architecture and decoration fell under the influence of European art; Baroque, Rococo and Empire styles deeply affected traditional Ottoman architecture and design. In this

Orhan Gazi, who ascended the throne 1324 as the second Ottoman Sulta passed away in 1362. In his time, the fir steps were taken to organise the army ar to systemise such matters as the distribu tion of money, clothing, and land. Orh extended Ottoman boundaries with h conquests; he seized Bursa in 1326 ar entered the city with great celebratio and then made it the capital of the your Ottoman Emirate. Immediately after tl conquest, various buildings were co structed which began to improve ar beautify the city and thus the first larg Ottoman mosque complex consisting a mosque, *madrasa*, *mektep*, *hammar imaret*, and *han* was built in Orhan's tim When Orhan died in 1362, he w interred in another Byzantine structu nearby the "Silver Dome" where his fath was buried.

Orhan Gazi's *türbe*, like that of his fathe was damaged in the fire of 1801 ar completely collapsed in the earthquak of 1855; Sultan Abdülaziz had the pre sent *türbe* built on the old foundations 1863. The central section of this squa structure is covered with a dome suppo ted by four huge columns, while the co dors surrounding it are covered with ults. It is understood from the beauti- l *opus sectile* decoration on the floor at a Byzantine building originally occu- ed the place where Orhan Gazi Türbe ow stands. There are 20 other sar- phagi in the *türbe* whereas Orhan's sar- phagus is surrounded with a screen of ttice brass.

Y. D.

*round the Muradiye Complex are other sites f interest like the 17<sup>th</sup>-century Muradiye onak and Hüsnü Züber Evi.*

### .1.i **Muradiye Complex**

*Muradiye District (Mahallesi). Follow the gns for Muradiye.*

mong the buildings constructed by

Ottoman Sultans, mosques occupy an important place. Generally, structures with various functions, such as *madrasas*, *hammams*, *darüşşifas*, *imarets*, etc., were placed in the mosque's surroundings. Thus every sultan commissioned a group of buildings known as a "Complex", which bore the sultan's name and met various social needs. The complex built by Murad II in Bursa consists of a mosque, *madrasa*, *hammam* and *imaret* as well as *türbes* dating from various periods; this is the last impe- rial complex to be built in Bursa.

Y. D.

### **Muradiye Mosque**

In the earthquake of 1855, many histori- cal buildings in Bursa suffered great dam- age and minarets either wholly or par-

*Orhan Gazi Türbe, dome, 1863, Sultan Abdülaziz, Bursa.*

145

*Muradiye Mosque,*
*prayer hall, 1426,*
*Murad II, Bursa.*

*Muradiye Mosque,*
*detail of wooden door*
*wings, 1426, Murad*
*II, Bursa.*

century; the northwest minaret here w
also restored by Parvillé, who remove
the walls dividing the *tabhane*s on the ea
and west from the prayer hall transforn
ing them into *iwan*s. The spandrels of th
five-bay portico are all decorated ver
attractively with geometric motifs impl
mented in stone, brick, and tiles remini
cent of brick ornamentation found on th
facades of late Byzantine buildings. Use (
yellow in the tiles, seen in the portico
window tympana, began in the early 15
century and is characteristic of that per
od. The entrance to the mosque is almo
like a tiny room covered with a flat cei
ing and decorated with tiles and *kalemiş*
According to the inscription above th
entrance, the construction was begun i
May 1425 and completed in 1426. Th
carved ornamentation on the wings of th
wooden door to the prayer hall is a ver
fine example of the period. The Muradiy
Mosque includes all the characteristics c
mosques with *tabhane*s; an interesting fea
ture here is the "U-shaped" corridor, orig
inally the entrance to the *tabhane*s. Th
dome soaring above the central court i
slightly larger than that of the prayer hal
which is supported by very striking con
ical squinches, and the *iwan*s on the side
are also covered with domes. The walls c
the prayer hall are covered with tiles to
certain height, and the painted decoratio
and exotic shape of the windows are fron
19th-century renovations.

Y. D

tially collapsed. At that time, Ahmet
Vefik Pasha, the governor of Bursa,
engaged a French architect by the name
of Léon Parvillé to undertake the repairs.
In many of the buildings, the repairs carried out by this architect were not in
complete accordance with the original
style of the buildings. For example, the
minarets were rebuilt according to the
taste and building traditions of the 19th

## Muradiye Madrasa

*It is used as a TB clinic today; therefore, visi*
*tors are allowed into the courtyard only whe*
*the clinic is open.*

*Muradiye Madrasa, main iwan, 1426, Murad II, Bursa.*

e *madrasa* to the west of the mosque is
e second largest building in the com-
x. Further to the west of the *madrasa*
the third largest building, the *hammam*,
w no longer in use. Immediately to the
uth of the mosque and *madrasa* is a love-
 garden with venerable plane trees and
presses where the *türbe* of Murad II
gether with other *türbes* dating from
rious periods are located.

e *madrasa*, recently extensively
stored, was built with alternating cours-
 of stone and brick. This technique of
ull construction, which has been used in
rkish architecture since the 14th centu-
. made its first appearance in Byzantine
chitecture.

e *iwan*-like portal to the north is
pped with a dome resting upon a cor-
ce of Turkish triangles. Again, the win-
w tympana are decorated with brick
d stonework. There is a domed *dershane*
an on the south side of the square
urtyard surrounded with porticoes on
 e other three sides, behind which lies
 e student cells. Stone and brick deco-
tion similar to that on the portico span-
els of Muradiye Mosque is also found in
 e *madrasa*, especially on the *iwan* facade.
 e *dershane* has a rectangular *mihrab*
che with turquoise and dark-blue tiles
 its south wall showing that this area
as also used as a prayer hall.

nce the classroom would have been used
 the winter as well as the summer, it is
rprising that one side of it is complete-
exposed to the outside. In pre-Ottoman
natolian *madrasas*, there was at least one
inter *dershane* next to the large *iwan*
here lessons were given in the summer.
here are examples in Ottoman *madrasas*
 only one *dershane* for winter or summer,
hile there are also examples of *madrasas*

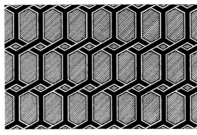

■ Brick  ▨ Stone

*Decoration on the iwan facade, Muradiye Madrasa, Bursa (from Y. Demiralp).*

without a *dershane*; in the latter case,
lessons were given in a nearby mosque or
in the mosque of the same complex. In
those *madrasa*s with only a summer *dershane*, it is supposed that the exposed side
was most likely closed with wooden panes
during the winter months.

Y. D.

## Türbes

*In the courtyard to the south of the mosque and*
madrasa, *there are* türbes *dating from various periods. The most attractive from the point
of view of architectural plan and décor are*

147

*Türbe of Murad II,
entrance facade,
1451, Bursa.*

*Türbe of Murad II,
interior, 1451, Bursa.*

Mehmed II and retired to Manisa to li
in contemplation and mysticisim. Whe
Sultan Mehmed II suffered a crisis becau
of the weight of administration, he invi
ed his father to take the throne agai
According to legend, Sultan Mehmed
said to his unwilling father, "If you are t
Sultan, come and do your duty; if I a
the Sultan, I command you to take t
throne and rule the state". Murad th
returned to the throne, but in 1451, I
fell ill and died in Edirne. According
his will, written in 1446 in Arabic an
Turkish, he asked to be buried in th
ground and near his son, Alaaddin Ali,
Bursa. In the same will it was stipulate
that the *türbe* should have four corners; i
roof should have an opening and i
perimeter closed; no one should b
buried beside him and if he should d
away from Bursa, his body should b
brought back and buried on a Thursda
Sultan Murad II is the last Ottoman Su
tan buried in Bursa; his son Mehmed
and all his successors preferred the ne
capital of Istanbul.

The *türbe* is a square structure built wit
alternating rows of brick and stone an
adjoins another *türbe* to the east. Th
underside of the wooden eaves, above
deep niche-shaped entrance projectin
out from the north wall, is decorated de
icately with *kalemişi* and thin lathes. Th
inside of the *türbe* is very well illuminate
because of numerous windows on th
walls. The simple grave of Sultan Mura
II in the centre is surrounded on all fou
sides by one re-used Byzantine colum
between the pillars in the corners. Th
square area becomes a circle at the to
and has been left open so that, accordin
to the will of Murad II, "the Mercy c
God might come unto him by the shinin

those of Murad II, Hatuniye, Cem Sultan, and
Şehzade Mustafa. *If you find any of them
closed, the guards at the entrance will open up
for you. There is an entrance fee.*

## The Türbe of Murad II

Murad II, who had this mosque complex
built, came to the throne in 1421 but in
1444 he left it to his twelve-year-old son

*Türbe of Şehzade Mustafa and Cem Sultan, interior, 1479, Bursa.*

f the Sun and Moon and falling of the ain and dew of Heaven upon his grave". here is a very plain *mihrab* niche in the outh wall. A door, originally a window, ads to the adjoining *türbe* of his son laaddin Ali, which based on architectural evidence, is believed to have been uilt after that of Murad II.

Y. D.

## he Türbe of Şehzade Mustafa nd Cem Sultan

he *türbe* was built for Sultan Mustafa, on of Sultan Mehmed II. On his return rom the Battle of Otlukbeli in 1473, Sultan Mustafa suffered kidney failure and ubsequently passed away near Niğde in Central Anatolia. His body was taken first o Konya, and then later moved to Bursa, where it was interred in the *türbe* of his uncle Alaaddin Ali. His body was later placed in this *türbe*, constructed in 1479. In 1495 Cem Sultan died in Naples, and in 1499, his body was handed over to Ottoman officials and then buried next to his brother in this *türbe*. After the death of his father, Sultan Mehmed II, in 1481, Cem Sultan fought with his brother Bayezid II for the throne; he was defeated twice and, after the second defeat, sought refuge with the Knights of St. John in Rhodes. He was taken first to Nice and then turned over to the Papacy. When Charles VIII, the King of France, entered Rome in 1495, he gave Cem Sultan his freedom again. Cem Sultan went to Naples with the French king and died there the next day.

This hexagonal structure is built with alternating rows of stone and brick and

149

has an entrance on the north side like a deep, broad niche projecting out. Inside the *türbe*, there is a *mihrab* opposite the entrance. The four plain sarcophagi lined up next to each other beginning at the entrance belong to Cem Sultan; Sultan Mustafa; Sultan Abdullah, a son of Bayezid II; closest to the *mihrab*, is the sarcophagus of Alem Shah, another son of Bayezid II respectively. The light coming through the windows on the central axis of each front, and the lantern in the centre of the dome rising on a cornice of Turkish triangles, causes a play of colour and light on the turquoise and dark-blue hexagonal tiles with gold gilding which cover the walls up to a height of 2.5 m. The upper walls and the dome are decorated with splendid paintings in bright and lively colours that were recently restored to their original condition; among the motifs the stylised cypresses, oil-lamps, rosettes, and religious inscriptions are noteworthy.

Y. D.

enters the outer courtyard and passes fir the *türbe*, a hexagonal building cover with a dome. Its inscription explains th Ahmet Pasha died in 1496-97. Both t türbe and the *madrasa* are built with alte nating rows of stone and brick. T entrance to the *madrasa* is through t middle of the eastern student cells. T courtyard is flanked with student cell both east and west; on the south is t *dershane iwan* protruding out, whereas t north side looks over the plains of Bur and has been left open as a terrace. Vau resting upon columns cover the porti and student cells, each of which has a fir place and a niche. The *madrasa* has r construction inscription; to judge fro the date of Ahmet Pasha's death, it mu have been built towards the end of t 15th century. It is especially interestin that the structure doesn't have a wint *dershane*. As of beginning 2001, th restoration work was about complete an there are plans to use the building as handicrafts centre.

Y. [

### IV.1.j **Ahmet Pasha Madrasa**
(option)

*In Muradiye Mahallesi; just to the north of Muradiye Complex, on Beşikçiler Avenue.*

This building is also known as "Geyikli Madrasa" or "Poet Ahmet Pasha Madrasa", and was built by Ahmet Pasha, who was a *kadı* and a *müderris* in various *madrasa*s. Sultan Mehmed II employed Ahmet Pasha, first as *kadıasker*, and later as *vizier*.
The structure is located directly to the north of the Muradiye Complex and overlooks the plains of Bursa. Approaching from the Muradiye Complex one

### IV.1.k **(Kükürtlü Kaplıca)**
**Sulphur Spas**

*On Kükürtlü Avenue, Bursa. It is current being used as rehabilitation centre by Uluda University and it is not open to visitors but yo may stroll around the peaceful gardens wher it is located.*

According to legend, the spring's nam comes from the sulphur content of th water. It consists of two separate *hammams* one for men and the other for women The men's section was built by Sulta Murad I (1362-1389) while the women' ammam, as well as the men's *soyunmalık,* ere built by Sultan Bayezid II (1481-512). In Ottoman times, *waqf*s were stablished in order to meet repair and maintenance costs, as well as the cost of orkers' wages for the building of structures like mosques and *türbes*. It was the income from structures dedicated to the aqf, like *hammam*s, thermal springs, and ans, that allowed these expenses to be met. Murad I, who commissioned the construction of the men's section of Kükürtlü Kaplıca, did not donate the structure to any *waqf*, and he requested that no payment should be received from those who bathed in the spas. The *soyunmalık* is ample and bright; the central hot platform is in the middle of the *sıcaklık*. Also there are chambers lined with one-person bathtubs for therapy purposes.

Y. D.

## V.1.1 Old Spas (Eski Kaplıca)

*n Çekirge Square, in the courtyard of Ker-ansaray Thermal Hotel. It is open to the pub-ic every day of the week between the hours of 07.30-22.30. Men and women use separate areas of the spa. There is a fee. Non-bathers are welcome to have a look inside.*

Spas are bath complexes built close to therapeutic water flowing from the ground. The plan of these Spas, which were constructed to offer treatment for various discomforts, may be different from that of ordinary *hammam*s. For example, in the *sıcaklık* there is no *halvet*; instead, many of them have a pool filled with therapeutic water. Bursa was a city of spas in Byzantine times too. In the year 525, Empress Theodora,

the wife of Byzantine Emperor Justinian I, came to Bursa with 4000 attendants and stayed for quite a while. According to legend, because the number of existing buildings was insufficient, a quantity of tents had to be pitched in the surrounding area to accommodate so many people. Also known as the "Pear Hammam", Eski Kaplıca was built in the time of Murad I (r. 1362-1389). The *soyunmalık* (apodyterium) built in 1511 by Sultan Bayezid II rises above a basement due to the sloping

*Kükürtlü Kaplıca, general view from the south, 1362-89, Murad I, Bursa.*

*Eski Kaplıca, general view from the northwest, 1362-89, Murad I, Bursa.*

terrain. It is not clear what this area was used for, but some researchers have suggested that it was a stable to house the animals of those who came to the *hammam*.

This structure has very attractive brickwork on the facade, and the larger domes covered with lead sheets are the additions by Sultan Bayezid II. The men's section of Eski Kaplıca is composed of a *soyunmalık* for disrobing, a *ılıklık* (tepidarium), and *sıcaklık* (caldarium). The *sıcaklık* is square on the outside and octagonal on the inside; opposite one another on four of the octagon's walls are semi-circular recesses; the circular pool in the centre is 7 m. in diameter. Many sections of the building, most of all the *sıcaklık*, were built re-using Byzantine architectural pieces; for this reason, some Western scholars have maintained that this was a Byzantine structure.

Y. D.

## IV.1.m  Hüdavendigar Mosque

*In Çekirge Area, in Hüdavendigar Mahallesi. Just up the street to the west of Eski Kaplıca.*

Upon the death of his father, Orhan Gazi in 1362, Sultan Murad I was called to Bursa and ascended the throne. His two brothers challenged him, but Murad had them captured in Eskişehir and then had them killed. In 1368, during his reign, the capital was moved from Bursa to Edirne. In 1386, while fighting at Rumelia, his son Savcı Bey, then governor of Bursa, declared himself sultan; when Sultan Murad I learned of this, he returned to Bursa where he had his son's eyes burned with a red-hot iron and later had him killed. "Hüdavendigar" is the epithet of Sultan Murad I and literally means Sultan. The complex is located on top of a steep slope with a beautiful view of the town below. On the approach is a small domed

*Hüdavendigar Mosque,
view from the
northeast, 1385,
Murad I, Bursa.*

tructure on the left, which once housed
he latrines; the visitor will then be amazed
t the north facade, which has a two-storey
nd five-bayed portico; a two-storied por-
ico on the facade is rarely found in Anato-
an Turkish architecture. A very eye-catch-
ng cornice of arches under the eaves runs
ll around the structure. Columns, elegant
apitals, and decorative elements taken
rom Byzantine buildings can be seen in the
loors, while the brickwork panels are also
ery attractive. Because of the unusual
rrangement of the main facade and the
Byzantine architectural elements, some
Western researchers have suggested that
his building was originally a Byzantine
palace. However, the structure is in the
ight direction for a *qibla* and its architec-
ural layout does not leave this question in
uspension.
Hüdavendigar Mosque is a rare example
n Anatolian Turkish architecture also
rom the point of view that it combines a

*Murad I, Illumination
from Kıyafetü'l-
İnsâniyye fî Şemâili'l'-
Osmâniyye by Seyyid
Lokman Çelebi, 1579,
H.1563, 32b, Library
of Topkapı Palace,
İstanbul.*

153

*Hüdavendigar Mosque, north facade, 1385, Murad I, Bursa.*

mosque and a *madrasa* under a single roof; a *madrasa* was built on the upper level of the structure; the portal on the north facade is used jointly by the mosque and the *madrasa*. According to the inscription above the entrance, the building was renovated in 1904 at the order of Sultan Abdülhamid II. The entrances on the east and west walls were opened later. The *madrasa* upstairs, normally not open to visitors, is reached via the staircase by the entrance foyer of the mosque. The *madrasa* has 16 barrel-vaulted cells aligned around the central court downstairs. As the prayer hall and the central court on the lower floor are two storeys high, the

*madrasa* upstairs has no courtyard. The corridor that runs in front of the cells extends all around the perimeter of the central court and the prayer hall. The fireplaces in the corners of some cells are later additions.

The mosque downstairs was designed to provide accommodation for the itinerant *dervish*es. The entrance foyer opens to a smaller *iwan*-shaped lobby before the central court, which is surmounted with a high dome. To the east and west are a barrel-vaulted *iwan* flanked with barrel-vaulted *tabhane*s on both sides. Opposite the entrance is the prayer hall, another barrel-vaulted *iwan*, with an apse-like *mihrab* iche protruding out. The painted decoations are from later renovations.

This mosque is part of a complex containing a *madrasa*, *imaret*, and a *türbe*. It is
understood from the *waqf* charter that the
founder was Sultan Murad I; there is no
construction inscription; for this reason,
it is generally accepted that the complex
was completed in 1385, the year the *waqf*
charter was prepared.

In the complex, the *imaret*, which is
used as the Tourism Directorate today,
to the west of the mosque, and the *türbe*
to its north both underwent later
restorations.

Y. D.

*Uludag Mountain (2554 m.), which lies
directly behind Bursa, is Turkey's most popular skiing centre. Although there are not
many visitors during the summer months, the
people of Bursa enjoy picnicking there during the holidays. There is a cable car (Teleferik in Turkish) that takes visitors from the
city up to a point close to the summit. You
can take a taxi or the* dolmush *minibuses
from the Heykel square by the Great Mosque
to the cable car station; and* dolmushes *are
also available from the landing station at
Sarıalan to the hotel area, where there is a
ski lift. There are "cook it yourself, eat it
yourself" barbecue restaurants at Sarıalan. If
you prefer the main road, you can take a taxi
or the buses that leave from the city bus station and go up to the summit. The winding
road up to the summit is 36 km. long.
Uludağ is a National Park with a landscape
covered by various types of trees like laurel,
olive, chestnut, elm, oak, Oriental plane,
pine, juniper, and poplar, as well as rich vegetation.
Bursa's peaches, chestnuts (especially chestnut purée), and Iskender Kebab, are as
famous as its towels and silk fabrics. Those
who eat the Iskender Kebab (a local form of
Döner Kebab) should also have a taste of şıra
(very slightly fermented grape juice) made
from dried grapes.*

**Aydoğan Demi**

*Women on the way to the hammam, Ain Turggische Hochzeit, J.2a, 1582, Sächsische Lansdesbibliothek, Dresden.*

During the Middle Ages, the network c water distribution was limited. For th reason, only very rich people could bath in private baths in their mansions, whil the majority of people bathed an enjoyed themselves at *hammams* open t the public. The beauty and spaciousnes of the interior was of first order impor tance for the *hammam*s built during th Emirates and Early Ottoman periods The first building constructed in mosque complex was always the *ham mam*. Thus the hundreds of worker working on the construction of the com plex could benefit from it. Many West ern travellers have praised the spacious ness, beauty, and cleanliness of th Turkish *hammam* interiors.

The Turkish *hammam*s had other function as well as bathing: administrators an poets would come together in them t converse or for a few drinks. For exam ple, during his Anatolian military cam paign (1402), Tamerlane (r. 1370-1405 conversed with the famous poet Ahmet at a *hammam;* Süleyman Çelebi, one o Bayezid I's (r. 1389-1402) sons, enjoye arranging meetings at which alcohol wa served at the Edirne *hammam*s.

*Hammam*s were a place of freedom fo Turkish women, as their appearance ir public was restricted according to Mus lim law. Men had to give their spouse money to go to the *hammam* at least once a week; not giving money to women for the *hammam* counted as grounds for divorce. Wealthy women would take their maidservants with them, and with their embroidered towels, fine shirts, mother- of-pearl inlaid *hammam* clogs, silver bowls, and ivory combs, they would put on a veritable show. One would go to the *hammam* in the morning and return in the

Bath culture, which goes back as far as the second millennium BC in Egypt, Mesopotamia, and Anatolia, experienced its golden age during the time of the Romans. In addition to bathing, sports, and entertainment, literary discussions were also held in Roman baths. The Umayyads (661-750), who conquered the Byzantine Empire's land in the Middle East, also adopted the bath culture. The Islamic religion's stipulation that one must wash his or her entire body after sexual intercourse assisted the spread of *hammam* culture in the Turkish-Islamic world.

vening. Here sweetmeats and savoury ›ods would be eaten, *sherbet* drunk, ιusical instruments played and people ·ould dance. Women with grown-up ›ns would choose potential daughters-ι-law in the *hammam*.

here were regulations governing matters ιch as not re-using a razor after shaving ιe head of someone with scabies and not ιarging more than the official price. ‵leanliness of the *hammams,* which were ᶥso an important source of income for *aqf* foundations, was of the utmost ιportance.

ιrchitecturally, a *hammam* consists of dif-ᵉrent sections: although traditionally ᵉlated to Roman baths, Turkish ham-ιams are quite different from them in lan. Except for the "cold bath" (*frigidar-ım*) section, all the elements of Roman ·aths are also present in Turkish baths. ‵he section of the *hammam* with direct ιccess to the outside is called the *soyun-ιalık* (equivalent of *apoditerium*) where ›eople disrobed or put their clothes back ›n. The *ılıklık* (equivalent of *tepidarium*) ⸱ the warm-bath area and acts as a small ›assage between the *hammam*'s disrobing ιrea and the hot-bath units. In some ham-ιams, there is another small area ·etween the *ılıklık* and *soyunmalık* called ιe *aralık* in Turkish, which simply means ιe "passageway". The *sıcaklık* (the equiv-ᶥent of *calidarium*) section usually con-⸱ists of a central part, where there is gen-ᵉrally a hot platform on which people lie ᶥown to sweat before getting scrubbed ιnd massaged; and private bathing cham-·ers called *halvet*s are usually located in ιe corners. Designed as a separate unit, ιe water depot is where the water is ιeated from underneath as is the build-ng itself.

Some Turkish *hammams* were constructed as two separate, adjoining baths designat-ed for men and women. In these double *hammams*, the entrance to the women's section opens onto a generally not-too-busy side street so that women could comfortably enter and exit the baths. There are no *hammams* designated for women only, other than these double *hammams*. In case of a single *hammam*, one or two days a week there would be a women-only session.

*Woman in the hammam, Abdullah Buhari, 1741-42, Library of Topkapı Palace, YY.1043.*

### Aydoğan Demi

*Ottoman Army on a campaign, Zigetvarname by Nakkaş Osman, 1568-59, H. 1339, fol.103b, Library of Topkapı Palace, İstanbul.*

Anatolia, was faced with an event that was so disastrous for his state that it led to his own enslavement?

Tamerlane's (r. 1370-1405) victory was the cause of a political crisis for the Ottoman State. Tamerlane, known by the title Uluğ Bey or "Magnificent Bey", acquired great political power in West Turkistan which lies today within the boundaries of the Republic of Uzbekistan. Starting out from his own capital, Samarkand, and heading west, Tamerlane began occupying the Middle East. Having already occupied Persia, Azerbaijan, Iraq, and Northern Syria, he wanted to add Anatolia to his empire as well.

Throughout history, all the states that were founded on, or became rulers of the Persian Highlands, wanted to take Anatolia, along with the Black Sea and the Mediterranean: the Medes, Persians, Parthians, Sassanids, Umayyads, Abbassids, and Mongols all followed this policy. It is also worth noting that, beginning with Alexander the Great (356-323 BC), all of the states founded in the West were also in pursuit of domination in the same regions: Rome's famous consuls and emperors occupied the Middle East except Persia; at the end of the 11th century, the Crusaders who were on their way to Jerusalem founded counties and kingdoms in Anatolia and Syria. After World War I (1914-1918), western states also wanted to divide up a large section of Anatolia.

There are many reasons why large states are attracted to Anatolia: Anatolia's important role in the world's trade routes; its strategic location due chiefly to the Istanbul (Bosphorus) and Çanakkale (Dardanelles) Straits; and its temperate climate that makes it suitable

From the founding of the Ottoman State until 1402, the Ottomans continued to pursue an empire by conquering many countries between the Euphrates River in Anatolia and the Danube River in the Balkans. However, with the defeat they faced at the Battle of Ankara in 1402, they reached the very point of disintegration. What happened so that Bayezid I (r. 1389-1402), who was nicknamed Yıldırım –the Lightning– and had gone from victory to victory between Niğbolu (Nicopolis) on the Danube and Erzincan in mid-eastern

r cultivation of all kinds of plants, espe-
ally grains. During an era in which the
ealth of a state was measured by its pos-
ssion of bountiful lands and trade
utes, it cannot be expected that Tamer-
ne would think or act any differently
an the times dictated.

n a hot summer day, 28 July 1402, in
e vicinity of Ankara, Tamerlane's
rces, reinforced with 32 elephants, bat-
ed mercilessly with the forces of
ttoman Sultan Bayezid I that included
ldiers of the Anatolian Emirates con-
ered by the Ottomans. These soldiers
trayed the Ottomans by joining the mil-
ary ranks of their *Beys*, who had taken
fuge behind Tamerlane. As a result of
is betrayal, Bayezid I lost the battle and
as taken prisoner.

fter an extended period of captivity,
ayezid I heard that Tamerlane himself
as going to take him to Samarkand.
ecause of this he became deeply dis-
essed and most likely committed suicide
drinking the poison hidden under the
one in his ring (9 March 1403).

fter Tamerlane departed from Anatolia
1403, Bayezid I's sons Süleyman, İsa,
usa, and Mehmed began disputing the
rone. In 1413, Mehmed I, also known
Çelebi Mehmed, took over the throne
mself and thus put an end to the Inter-
gnum; this event was all but a second
unding of the Ottoman State.

efore leaving Anatolia and in return for
eir support, Tamerlane returned to
ose *Beys*, who had sought protection

Lageyen des Tyrckischen Keyfers

under him, the areas that they had formerly ruled. Thus Germiyan, Saruhan,
Aydın, Menteşe, and Karamanid Emirates
were founded anew; the Candar Dynasty
also took back the land that they had lost.
The Ottomans struggled for a period of
over 50 years to erase these emirates from
the map entirely.

*Ottoman Soldiers,*
*Codex Vindobonensis,*
*Cod. 8626, fol 38,*
*Österreichische*
*Nationalbibliothek,*
*Vienna.*

159

# Orhan Gazi: Sultan of the People

### Lale Bulut, Aydoğan Demir, Rahmi H. Ünal

### V.I İZNİK

V.1.a  Nilüfer Hatun İmaret (İznik Museum)
V.1.b  Yeşil Mosque
V.1.c  Süleyman Pasha Madrasa
V.1.d  İsmail Bey Hammam
V.1.e  Murad II Hammam
V.1.f  Kırkkızlar Türbe

*"Flowers that bloom in fire": 14th–and 15th–century Tile and Ceramic Art
Administration in the Ottoman State*

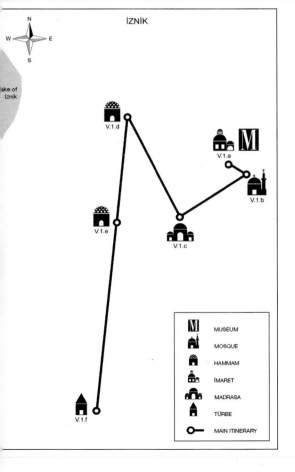

İZNİK

| | |
|---|---|
| M | MUSEUM |
| | MOSQUE |
| | HAMMAM |
| | İMARET |
| | MADRASA |
| | TÜRBE |
| O— | MAIN ITINERARY |

*Yeşil Mosque, minaret,
1378-92, Halil
Hayreddin Pasha,
İznik.*

161

*Nilüfer Hatun imaret, portal, 1388, Murad I, İznik.*

İznik (ancient Nicea), capital of the Anatolian Seljuq State between 1075 and 1097, came under Byzantine rule once again during the First Crusade. However, the second Ottoman ruler, Orhan Gazi, conquered İznik again in the year 1331. According to legend, as Orhan Gazi was entering the city, he asked his own soldiers to marry the widowed Rum women so that the women would not have to experience even more difficulties. One Ottoman writer tells the story as follows: "They carried out the command. The city had homes ready to be lived in, and they gave them to the married war veterans. A ready woman and a house for him too –who wouldn't accept the offer?"

İznik was adorned with various structures during the Ottoman period built by the sultans and many administrators. For example, Murad I had an *imaret* built in İznik in the name of his beloved mother Nilüfer Hatun. Orhan Gazi himself picked up a ladle and distributed food in the *imaret* he had built, and the same sultan also lit the oil lamps with his own hands at the inauguration of the *madrasa* he commissioned in İznik; first Davud of Kayseri, and then Taceddin the Kurd was appointed as the *müderris* in this *madrasa*. The Ottoman sultans considered intelligence and skill important in the administration of the country, and they did no differentiate between races such as Turkish, Kurdish, Albanian, or Circassian.

The Çandarlıs, a distinguished family played an important role in state service ever since the establishment of the Ottoman State. Çandarlı Halil Hayreddin Pasha, an *Ahi* and characteristically a good organiser, was İznik's first *kadı*. The Janissary corps initiated by Çandarlı Halil

yreddin Pasha formed an important
rt of the Ottoman Army. Several of
ndarlı Halil Hayreddin Pasha's sons and
andsons rose to the rank of Grand *Vizier*
d some members of this family that
re able to rise to a good position in the
il service did not forget their city of
th and thus decorated İznik with beau-
ul structures. For example, Yeşil
osque which is a small, extremely fine
d striking structure, was commissioned
Çandarlı Halil Hayreddin Pasha himself.
aykh Bedreddin (d. 1419), whose identi-
and actions have been a topic for debate
centuries, was a government man act-
g as *kadıasker*, and also a learned man of
igion and science who produced works
the field of "Sufism". In 1413 he was
noved from his *kadıasker* duty and forced
live in İznik. Shaykh Bedreddin's disci-
es, Börklüce Mustafa and Torlak Kemal,
rted revolts in Karaburun close to İzmir,
d Manisa respectively. Shaykh Bedreddin
aped from İznik and fled to the Balkans,
ere he started a people's rebellion in
liorman. These revolts were suppressed
the Ottoman State (1419).

ik's importance waned after the 15th
ntury and it continued to exist as a
all Ottoman town. It began to develop
ain in the Republican period, and is
w one of the region's liveliest towns.

A. D.

nik is reached from Bursa via a main road
out 76 km. long. All the works on this itin-
ary are located in the city of İznik. Except for
rkkızlar Türbe, which is a little outside the
y centre, you can reach all the monuments on
ot. For orientation: the town centre surround-
by two superb rings of walls has two main
reets; one in a north-south direction, from
anbul Gate to Yenişehir Gate; and the other

in an east-west direction, from Lefke Gate to Göl
Gate, respectively; at the junction, in the centre, is Ayasofya, the church where the First and
the Seventh Ecumenical Councils were held.

*Murad II Hammam,
basin in the sıcaklık of
the women's section,
15th century, İznik.*

## IV.1  **İZNİK**

The city was founded in 316 BC by
Antigonus I Monophthalmos (380-301 BC),
one of Alexander the Great's generals, and
given the name Antigonia. Another of
Alexander's generals, Lysimachus, captured
the city in 301 BC, and named it after his

*Nilüfer Hatun İmaret,
general view from the
southeast, 1388,
Murad I, İznik.*

deceased wife (Nicea) and made it the capital of the region of Bithynia. After it came under the control of the Romans, the town became one of the most important cities of the Province of Asia. In 325 the First Ecumenical Council gathered in Nicea and laid the foundations of Orthodoxy. In 787, the Seventh Ecumenical Council ended up in moderation between iconodules and iconoclasts. In 1075 the Seljuqs captured Nicea and changed its name to İznik. At the same time, the town became the capital of the Rum Sultanate. However, it changed hands between the Byzantines and the Turks until Ottoman Sultan Orhan Gazi captured it for good in 1331.

### V.1.a  Nilüfer Hatun İmaret (İznik Museum)

*In Eşrefzade District, on Museum Street. It is*

*currently being used as the İznik Museum. T
museum is open 08.00-12.00 and 13.0
16.30 in the winter and 08.30-12.30 a
13.30–17.00 in the summer. It is closed
Mondays. There is an entrance fee. You shou
inquire here about the keys for the İsmail B
Hammam and Süleyman Pasha Madrasa.*

Osman Gazi, the founder of the Ottom
Empire, remained a peripheral *Bey* all h
life, bound to the Seljuqs and Ilkhanid
There is no inscription bearing his nam
as the founder of any structure. Holoph
ra, the local Byzantine princess of Yarh
sar, who married Osman Gazi's s
Orhan Gazi, is said to have taken t
name Nilüfer Hatun after converting
Islam. Although it is said that Bayal
Hatun, one of Osman Gazi's wive
whom the Arab traveller Ibn Bauta m
in İznik, might have been Nilüfer Hatu
this rumour has not been confirme

urces speak of Nilüfer Hatun's taking
interest in philanthropic activities and
ving many *sadaqa* or alms, to poor peo-
e. Likewise, because she had a bridge
uilt across the creek that flows through
e Bursa Plain, this creek is known today
Nilüfer Creek. Nilüfer Hatun, whose
te of death is unknown, was buried in
r husband Orhan Gazi's Türbe in Bursa.
ortly after Nilüfer Hatun's death, her
n Sultan Murad I commissioned the
ilding in İznik known today as Nilüfer
atun İmaret. It is known that the word
aret, which later came to mean "a place
here food is distributed to the poor",
d a general meaning in the beginning,
"any type of building constructed for
od deeds". For this reason, this and
her structures called *imaret*s belonging
the early period should not necessari-
be defined as places where food was
stributed to the poor. Some of these
ecial structures called *imaret*, such as the
e here, were constructed to shelter
ligious missionaries; we encounter
any examples of such structures from
e 14th and 15th centuries. In these struc-
res, which give the impression of a
osque when viewed from the outside,
nly one of the areas was designated for
mmunal worship and this area was
cented with a *mihrab* niche.

ocated 100 m. to the northwest of Yeşil
losque, the building was recently renovat-
d and is currently being used as the İznik
useum. In addition to rich finds of ceram-
s obtained during the ongoing excavations
İznik, Classical, Byzantine and a few
hnographic artefacts are displayed. The
ructure is striking with its exterior wall
ced with brick rows alternating with
urses of stone, and there are a few panels
ith brickwork decoration. Normally in

this kind of structure, the majority of which
are called mosques with *zawiya (tabhane)*, the
five-bay portico extends completely along
the facade, but here empty spaces were left
at two ends; the piers flanking the middle
arch are embellished with distinctive mouldings. The middle bay of the portico is surmounted by a small dome adorned with
beautiful triangles and the rest are covered
with vaults. According to the inscription
above the entrance door, which is accented
with brick-and-stone masonry on the top,
the structure was completed on 8 April
1388. On entering, the visitor stands under
a very large dome. The *tabhane* rooms to the
right and left are used for exhibiting the
ceramic finds of the Ottoman period. The
prayer hall straight ahead, marked with a
small *mihrab* niche on the left, houses the
prehistoric artefacts. In such structures the
prayer hall is usually covered with a dome
but here the roof has been divided into two
parts by a great arch; each part covered by
a single small dome with elaborate transition zones.

R. H. Ü.

*Plan of Nilüfer Hatun
Imaret, İznik (from Y.
Demiriz).*

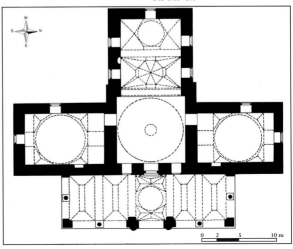

*Ceramic plate,*
*15th century,*
*Nilüfer Hatun İmaret*
*(Inv. No. 1365),*
*İznik.*

### Ceramic Plate (Inv. Num. 1365, 15th century)

This is one of the ceramics produced in İznik called "Miletus ware". First appearing in the 14th century, these red-clay ceramics are also known as "Emirates–Era Ceramics" and have a white background on which are blue designs. The kiln excavations in İznik revealed for certain that the production centre for this type of ceramic was not Miletus, but İznik. It was understood that these red-earth ceramics were produced for a long time as objects for daily use beginning in the 14th century. In this group, most of which are shallow bowls, there are also lamps, bowls, and plates. The inside of the red-clay base is completely lined with *engobe*; the external faces and base are usually not lined. The edges of this example are slightly raised. It was glazed after the designs had been drawn. The ornamentation applied in white upon the dark-blue background consists of concentric circles and stylised *palmette* motifs. Floral motifs were engraved on the blue-painted sections.

L. B.

*Ceramic mug,*
*15th century,*
*Nilüfer Hatun İmaret,*
*(Inv. No. 4609),*
*İznik.*

### Ceramic Mug (Inv. Num. 4609, 15th century)

Produced in İznik, this "blue-whit ceramic mug is decorated in the unde glaze technique, which has been in u since the Seljuq period. The sun-drie ceramic clay was coated with *engobe* firs the decorations were created on top of th coating and the ceramic was baked; th ceramic taken out of the kiln was glaze and then fired again. In this way, the de orations are covered with a layer of shin glaze. Numerous examples of ceramics the under-glaze technique are found many museums all over the world. Th ceramic mug on display here has a cylin drical body that widens towards the to The body is decorated with curlin branches and stylised floral motifs draw in blue, on a white background.

L.

### Ceramic Plate (Inv. Num. 324, 15th century)

First the designs were drawn on this Mile tus-type deep bowl and then it was glaze over. The cobalt-blue designs thoug

three techniques– is also encountered during the Seljuq period. The decorative elements drawn on a red background are made of slip. The designs beneath the coloured transparent glaze layer are slightly raised. This bowl is ornamented with yellow *palmettes* and *rumis* placed on a dark-brown background; on the border there are yellow drop-shape dots.

L. B.

*Ceramic plate,*
*15th century,*
*Nilüfer Hatun İmaret,*
*(Inv. No. 5324) İznik.*

### V.1.b  Yeşil Mosque

*Across the road and to the east of the Nilüfer Hatun İmaret (Museum).*

Halil Hayreddin Pasha, of the Çandarlı family, is among the most famous civil servants to act as *vizier* during the century following the founding of the Ottoman State. In the first days after he was appointed *vizier* in the year 1372, he was awarded the duty of putting down a rebellion initiated by the governor of Selanik (Thessalonica); this is noteworthy because, before him the *viziers* did not interfere with military affairs. Contemporary local and foreign sources relate

were applied on top of the white glaze. The star motif made up of triangles in the centre of the plate is enclosed in a medallion. Parallel lines drawn with brush strokes radiate from the centre to the edges.

L. B.

### Ceramic Plate (Inv. Num. 5304, 14th-15th century)

Produced in İznik, the designs on this bowl are done under the glaze using the slip technique. The slightly raised, beige-coloured large flower motifs placed on a brown background were drawn with slip. The stylised "moving" flowers completely cover the internal surface of the plate. The brown, yellow, and green glazes seen on this group of ceramics appear darker on a red background.

L. B.

### Ceramic Plate (Inv. Num. 5308, 14th-15th century)

Three different techniques were used on red-clay ceramics manufactured in İznik. "Lining décor" (slip) ceramics –one of

*Ceramic plate,*
*14th-15th century,*
*Nilüfer Hatun İmaret,*
*(Inv. No. 5308) İznik.*

167

*Yeşil Mosque, general view from the west, 1378-92, Halil Hayreddin Pasha, İznik.*

that Halil Hayreddin Pasha had quite a lot of influence over Sultan Murad I. After Murad I had ascended to the throne, Halil Hayreddin Pasha was appointed *kadıasker* and he had a positive effect on the new arrangement of the army. Likewise, when not enough soldiers were found for the army, with Halil Hayreddin Pasha's recommendation, young Christian prisoners of war were first educated and then taken into the army. He proposed the establishment of a class of soldiers known as *Yeniçeri Ocağı*, Janissary Corps, that constituted the Ottoman army's main striking forces for centuries thereafter.

*Decoration on the portal of Yeşil Mosque, İznik (from Ş. Çakmak).*

Halil Hayreddin Pasha, who received his education in a *madrasa*, initiated the protection of artists and scholars. He acted as *kadı* in Bilecik, İznik, and Bursa. Yeşil Mosque, which he started building in İznik in 1378, shows elaborate craftsmanship. It is understood that construction of the mosque continued for many years, although the reasons for the delay are not known. The inscription above the entrance of the prayer hall relates that the mosque was constructed by Çandarlı Halil Hayreddin in the year 1378 during the time of Sultan Murad I. However, another inscription above the entrance to the portico reads that the mosque built by the then deceased Hayreddin Pasha, was completed in 1392. This inscription also states that an architect by the name of Haci ibn Musa constructed the building. Standing in a lovely and well-attended park, this beautiful structure with its

mes and coloured minaret is exhilarat-
g. On the outside it is faced entirely
th marble; the roof and domes are cov-
ed with lead sheets. The brick minaret
sting on a prismatic marble base is dec-
ated with zigzags formed by turquoise
d dark-purple glazed and unglazed
icks, and bands of tile mosaic. The
autifully carved frieze along the eaves
d the mouldings on the window frames
minds one of mouldings from ancient
ildings. The portico's marble banisters,
hich suffered significant damage during
e Greek occupation in 1919-1922,
ere replaced in the latest restorations.
he columns bear wonderful capitals,
ith a decoration similar to the band
ong the eaves; and the frame of the
usual false door in the middle is strik-
g. The central bay of the portico is cov-
ed with a fluted dome. On entering the
rayer hall, the visitor is faced with two
her columns and arches, beyond which
the main part surmounted with a dome

rising above a cornice of Turkish triangles.
This is a very interesting feature because
with this additional three-bay area to the
north, the square prayer hall is enlarged
into a rectangle; it is, therefore, one of
the first examples of an enlarged prayer
hall. Yeşil Mosque has an important place
in the history of Turkish architecture. In
the 14th and 15th centuries, the majority
of mosques were covered with either a
single dome or multiple domes, and
attempts were made to widen the prayer
hall with additional areas placed on one,
two, or three sides of the central dome.
The walls of the prayer hall, which is oth-
erwise very plain, but for the lovely marble *mihrab*, are faced with marble to a certain height.

R. H. Ü.

## V.1.c **Süleyman Pasha Madrasa**

*In Yeni District, on Süleymanpasha Street.*

*Süleyman Pasha Madrasa, general view from the south, mid-14th century, Orhan Gazi, İznik.*

the street to the west and is covered with a bigger dome than the rest. On the outside the upper row of round windows catches the eye. The simple entrance of the southeast opens onto the courtyard surrounded on three sides by domed porticoes rising on columns; beyond which are the cells and the *dershane* to the west. This is one of the first *madrasas* constructed during the Ottoman period. Nevertheless, it is quite different from the *madrasas* of the Seljuq period; here the domes replaced the vaults preferred in Seljuq *madrasas*. The use of columns in the porticoes instead of piers is also striking and seldom encountered in Seljuq *madrasas*. Although the definite date of construction is not known, Süleyman Pasha Madrasa probably dates to the mid 14th century. In 2000, the structure was abandoned but a restoration program is planned.

R. H. Ü

Süleyman Pasha was the oldest son of the second Ottoman Sultan Orhan Gazi, born to Nilüfer Hatun. He lived in İznik until 1336, became a *vizier* from that date on, and took part in the conquest of Thrace. Researchers believe that this *madrasa* was built before Süleyman Pasha left İznik; however, Süleyman Pasha was only 20 years old when he left İznik in 1336. Following a fall from his horse, he passed away in 1360, and his father Orhan Gazi was deeply saddened and turned the property of Süleyman Pasha, together with the additional revenue from two villages in İznik, into a *waqf*; this brings to mind that this *madrasa* could have been built by Orhan Gazi in order that his beloved son's memeory live on.

The *dershane* of the *madrasa* extends into

## V.1.d  **İsmail Bey Hammam**

*In Beyler District, on Yeni Street. From the Istanbul Gate to the south, turn east at Ziya Özbek Street. It is easily recognisable with the modern canopy soaring above it.*

Turkish baths, like Roman baths, are structures open for public use. Palace and private residence *hammams*, very few examples of which have survived, are different from the traditional public bath because of their dimensions. The *soyunmalık*, *ılıklık*, and *sıcaklık* of the private *hammams* are of small dimensions. The fundamental bathing area —the *sıcaklık*—that consists of at least three or four connected units in the public *hammams*, usu ly consists of only one unit in these private ones. Large bathing areas in palaces and homes was not necessary since the number of people bathing at once did not generally exceed three to five.

In Islam, both women and men must remove pubic hair, the removal of which every Friday was considered to be *sevap* or grace begetting, as it was considered a non-obligatory yet meritorious good deed. It was deemed necessary to engage in this kind of cleaning at least once every 15 days, while it was seen as a sin if the time in between surpassed 40 days. In almost all *hammam*s, there are private areas called *traşlık* where hair removal is done.

Approaching from the street, the water tank with the collapsed vault to the right, is the first thing the visitor will see. The *külhan* to heat the water is underneath and opens outside. The main entrance is to the back of the path on the left. Being a residential bath dating to the late 14th-early 15th century, the İsmail Bey Hammam has only four small chambers, each one of which is covered by a single dome. The *soyunmalık* is the area the visitor first enters. Observe what remains of the beautiful transition zone. The chamber to the right is probably what was once the *traşlık*; the transition zone to the dome consists of Turkish triangles. After the dis-

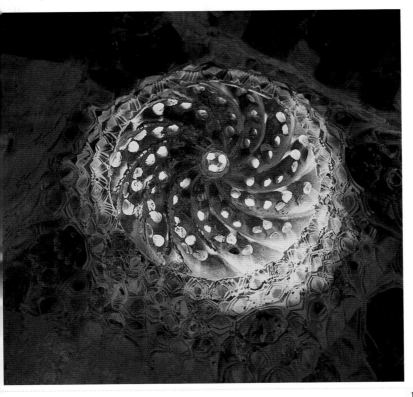

*İsmail Bey Hammam, Dome of the ılıklık, late 14th–early 15th century, İznik.*

171

*Kırkkızlar Türbe, general view from the southeast, 14th century, İznik.*

robing area, the first chamber is the *ılıklık*, the second is the *sıcaklık*, both of which have adorable whorled domes still in very good condition; observe the openings in the domes for glass jars which originally provided light into these chambers; the floors of both chambers are collapsed exposing the heating system under the floor. The *sıcaklık* adjoins the water tank and the furnace, the hot air and gases from the fire, which circulated under the floors and went up through the baked-clay pipes in the walls. All the chambers have remains of superb decorative plasterwork that must have made this *hammam* a delightful place to bathe.

R. H. Ü.

### V.1.e  **Murad II Hammam**

*In Mahmut Çelebi District (Mahallesi). One*

block south of Ayasofya and to the extreme west of the tile-kiln excavation area. At the beginning of 2001, the men's part was fully restored and was still functioning; it can be visited with permission. The key to the ladies' section is at the Iznik Foundation.

While attending to the *Büyük Hammam* in Beçin in Itinerary I, we stated that some public baths were constructed as two separate *hammam*s adjoining each other, and that one of these was designated for men, and the other for women. Murad II Hammam, also known as Hacı Hamza Hammam, is a double *hammam* like this. Of these two *hammam*s, the one in the north is quite a lot smaller in comparison to the other. Like most of the double *hammam*s, the entrances open onto different streets. The *soyunmalık* of the *hammam* in the north for the use of women was built with a recess within so that its female users could comfortably enter and exit without attracting too much attention. The men's bath consists a large disrobing area with beautiful squinches filled with *muqarnas*, an *ılıklık*, a *traşlık*, and a cruciform *sıcaklık* with *halvet*s in the corners. The *soyunmalık* of the women's section, not in use at the time of writing, was employed as a display room by the İznik foundation, which works on the revival of İznik tile and ceramic art. The ladies' bath has not been restored either, but the beautiful old water basins were still there to be seen. The Turkish traveller Evliya Çelebi writes that there were two double *hammam*s in İznik: Tekioğlu Hamamı, and Yeni Hamam. Murad II Hamam (or Tekioğlu Hamamı?) dates to from the 15th century. The other double *hammam*, partially standing and known today as Büyük Hamam (Yeni Hamam?), was, however, constructed in the 15th or 16th century.

R. H. Ü.

## V.1.f  Kırkkızlar Türbe

*In Selçuk District, about 150 m. south of Yenişehir Kapı.*

Putting a dead body in a monumental grave to ensure regular visitors and help keep alive the memory of the person goes against Islamic belief. Considering that in some Orthodox Islamic sects such as the *Wahhabi* it is believed that even the location of the grave must not be obvious, the construction of a special monument for the dead person appears to be rather divergent behaviour. However, in the Islamic world, monumental tombs are closely related to the Turks. The earliest examples of these structures, which have a cubic, polygonal, or cylindrical body covered by a dome, are found in Iran. Some scholars think that this tomb's name, which is *Kırkkızlar* (forty girls), must originally have been *Kırgızlar*, after the tribe of Kyrgyz Turks. In some sources, it is remembered as "Reyhan Türbe" or "Hacı Camasa Türbe". The structure has recently been completely restored. The masonry of brick rows alternating with stone courses is a characteristic that passed from Byzantine architecture to Ottoman architecture. The dodecagon dome drum was raised during later renovations. The structure consists of two rooms, the first of which was covered with a vault in the original construction and the main room is a square surmounted with a dome. The existing sarcophagus-shaped graves are plain and bear no inscriptions, and, therefore, they yield no information about the identity of the deceased. A window was altered and a niche was formed next to it in order to make room for graves built later. The decorative paintings on the inside have lovely floral and candlestick motifs. Although there is no record about the tomb and its owner, it is dated to the 14th-century. This dating is based upon its multi-sided drum, seen in other 14th-century structures such as Hacı Özbek Mosque and Yeşil Mosque in İznik, and also its decorative paintings, which have early Ottoman characteristics.

R.H.Ü.

173

# "FLOWERS THAT BLOOM IN FIRE": 14th–and 15th–CENTURY TILE AND CERAMIC ART

**Lale Bulu**

The tile and ceramic arts experienced a long chain of developments in Anatolia. The tiles that decorated the walls in the Seljuq, Emirates and Ottoman periods are striking for their variety in both technique and design. Only a limited number of Anatolian Seljuq-period tiles have survived to the present day. However, examples that abound beginning in the 15th century, are as much the favoured pieces of domestic and foreign museums as they are of private collections. In Emirates-period structures dating to the 14th and 15th centuries, tile decoration is not frequently encountered. In the limited number of examples there are it is noticeable that the Anatolian Seljuq-period tradition continues without making significant changes. Glazed bricks are used along with tiles in the Birgi Great Mosque's (1312-13), Manisa Great Mosque's (1367), and İznik Yeşil Mosque's (1378-92) minarets.

The tile-mosaic technique –the favourite in the Anatolian Seljuq Period– was not much favoured in the Emirates and Early Ottoman periods; in tile-mosaic ornamentation of this period, which was arranged in larger compositions in comparison with those in the Seljuq period, white was also used in addition to blue, turquoise, purple, and black. The tile mosaics seen on Birgi Grate Mosque' *mihrab* (1312-13) as well as on the transition zone of the dome before the *mihrab* in Selçuk İsa Bey Mosque (1375) are some rare examples of the period, while the ones in İznik Yeşil Mosque (1378-92) Bursa Yeşil Mosque, Yeşil Madrasa, and Yeşil Türbe (1419-24), and Bursa Muradiye Mosque (1426) are some rare examples from the Early Ottoman Period. The decreased use of tiles during the Emirates period did not prevent the appearance of new techniques in the 15th century. The "coloured glaze technique' (also known as *cuerda seca*) that we encounter for the first time during this period is not seen in Anatolian pottery; it was only applied to tiles. A variety of colours like blue, turquoise, deep–blue, black, white, yellow, gold-water, lilac, and pistachiogreen were used on the tiles produced in this technique which is seen particularly in structures at Bursa, Edirne, and Istanbul. The earliest examples of this type are found in Bursa Yeşil Mosque, Yeşil Türbe, and Yeşil Madrasa (1419-24) along with Edirne Muradiye Mosque (1426-27).

Konya, a tile production centre of the Anatolian Seljuq period, began to lose its importance at the beginning of the 15th century, and İznik and Kütahya became the new centres of the tile- and ceramic-art industry. İznik, an important settlement centre since the 4th century BC, was where the Early Ottoman Period's highest quality ceramics were produced. Its location on the route that connects Istanbul to Anatolia ensured its long-lived economic and cultural livelihood. According to various travellers' accounts, around

*Ceramic Vase (Inv. no. 3373), Bursa Museum.*

O tile master-craftsmen were working İznik. Although this may seem exag-rated for such a small town, the num-r of kilns revealed by excavations (for tance, there is an excavation site across street to the east of Murad II Ham-m) and research conducted in the last v years, are proving this rumour to be rrect. Two types of kilns are found in ik: one with a "rectangular firehouse" d the other with a "circular firehouse". the rectangular kilns, the firehouse is vered with a cradle vault and the firing a has holes on its floor. The firing area the circular kiln is covered with a me. Higher temperatures could be ached in circular kilns than could be hieved in rectangular kilns.

e ceramics called "Miletus ware", pro-ced with the under-glaze technique, ve an important place among the 14th- d 15th-century ceramics. Because until cently it was supposed that they were oduced in Miletus, these red-clay ramics were known by this name, but w we know that they were actually anufactured in İznik. In the ceramics of is group, the colours: cobalt blue, dark rple, and turquoise were used, and in addition to decorations in a radial arrangement, decorations with floral and geometric motifs are also seen. For exam-ple, compositions consisting of leaves in a fan shape drawn with thin brush strokes coming out of a rosette in the centre are frequently encountered.

Ceramics that are called "blue-white" appeared after the Miletus type and are a higher quality product, closer to porce-lain. These ceramics are the second inno-vation to appear in the Ottoman period after the coloured glaze technique. This under-glaze technique is rare on tiles, but frequently appears on ceramics for daily use. Produced in İznik until the beginning of the 16th century, in this group of tile and ceramics, the colours blue, turquoise, and deep-blue were applied on a white background; the most prized motifs on these tiles and ceramics, which are remi-niscent of 15th-century Far Eastern Ming porcelain, are peonies, flowers, Chinese clouds, and dragons. On a group of blue-white ceramics mistakenly known as "Haliç ware" (Golden-Horn-ware), though, branches with curled leaves in a helical arrangement on a white back-ground are seen.

*Details from the tile wall-panel, Muradiye Mosque, Edirne.*

# ADMINISTRATION IN THE OTTOMAN STATE

Aydoğan Dem

The Ottoman State administration underwent continuous development from the year it was founded until it finally evolved into a central bureaucratic structure. The tendency to administrate the state according to laws began in the time of Osman Gazi (r. 1281-1324) and continued throughout Ottoman history.

According to our current knowledge, the first Ottoman Sultan to gather the laws in a corpus, or, to put it another way, select and collect them, was Sultan Mehmed II (r. 1451-1481). Mehmed II's law proclamation or constitution of laws begins with these words: "This constitution of laws, is the constitution of my father and my forefathers, and my constitution too". This expression is proof that the Ottoman State had begun to be administered according to laws long before Sultan Mehmed II.

When the Ottoman State conquered a land, one of its first actions was to register every kind of information in deed registers about the region: the population living in the region who would be eligible for the payment of taxes, the fields, orchards, groves, mills, animals, mines, and so on, that would constitute sources of tax. At the very beginning of the register, the laws to which local people had to subscribe would be written. These laws were aimed at protecting the people. After the Ottoman city of Selanik (Thessalonica) had passed into Byzantine hands due to the Interregnum after the Battle of Ankara (1402), the new administrators were unable to lift the Ottoman laws and apply Byzantine laws because they were afraid that the Rum inhabitants would oppose the imposition of Byzantine laws. Although they had been under Ottoman administration for only a short period,

they had got used to a lower, payable t load.

The first thing that comes to mind whe speaking of Ottoman State administratic is the sultanate of the Osman dynasty. the Ottoman State, for a period of mo than 300 years, the sultanate passed fro father to son, and between the yea 1617-1922, it passed to the eldest mem ber of the royal family. For a dynasty manage a state for a period of over 6( years is something rarely seen in histor The Ottoman Sultan, equipped with ve far-reaching authority, administered th state together with an assembly known *Divan-ı Hümayun,* in which the *Grar Vizier, viziers, kadıasker, defterdar* and *ni ancı* worked in their official capacitie When it was considered necessary, th *şeyhülislam* (shaykh al-islam), *yeniçeri ağa* and the *kaptan-ı derya* were called to th meeting and consulted. Until the last da of Sultan Mehmed II's reign, the Sultan presided over the *divan* meetings, and aft this date, the Grand *Viziers* presided.

At the *divan* meetings, all the country issues were discussed; decisions wer taken and submitted for the Sultan approval. After national matters on th agenda had been discussed, a commo Ottoman citizen had the right to enter th *divan*, explain his problems, and reque a solution. For this reason the *divan*, i addition to governmental work, als functioned as a kind of high court.

The Ottoman central administratio made its strength felt in the most remot corners of the empire. Local administra tors (*beylerbeyi* and *sancak beyi*), *kadıs*, an *tımarlı sipahis* would use their administra tive, judicial and military authority as rep resentatives of the Ottoman centra administration everywhere from village

*Divan meeting, Surname-i Vehbi, 3593, fol.176, by Levni, 1720, Library of Topkapı Palace, İstanbul.*

to large provinces. The *kadı*s were not only busy with the judicial problems of the place in which they were located, but also with municipality services. In addi-

tion to the control of the shopping district and notary services, the city's public works services were also part of the *kadı*'s responsibility. During a judiciary decision

178

o one could interfere with the *kadıs*. However, those who were not pleased with their decisions could insist on their rights by applying to the *divan*. According to Ottoman State understanding, "the state cannot exist without a ruler; the ruler cannot exist without soldiers; the soldier cannot exist without money; the people cannot exist without justice". In short, the Ottoman administration appropriated and applied the principle "the state is founded on justice". Christians and Jews, the non-Muslim subjects of the Ottoman State, were able to worship and carry out their religions and traditions in comfort. When the Jews were expelled from Spain in 1492, they took refuge in the Ottoman country. "Escuchis Señor Soldado" (Listen Sir Soldier), a Jewish folk song that explains those days, tells the story of a Jewish woman's search for her husband among the fugitives:

"Listen sir soldier
Are you returning from war?
- Yes ma'am, I am coming from war. From the war with the Spaniards.
I wonder did you run into my husband? Did you see him at all?
- The man you are speaking of may have died a month ago.
Or he may have found his freedom in Istanbul."

Those Ottoman subjects who did not follow Islam, or who had a different faith, and may have spoken a different language too, lived in peace for many centuries thanks to the Pax Ottomana.

*The lake on the edge of the city of İznik known by the same name is Turkey's 5th largest lake. Its average depth is 30 m. A large part of the southern shore is beach and the lake is suitable for swimming.*

# Social Solidarity

**Şakir Çakmak, Aydoğan Demir, Rahmi H. Ünal**

Tabhanes, Zawiyas *and Itinerant Dervishes*

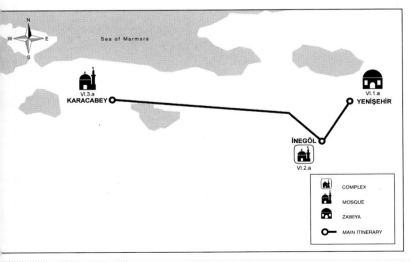

İmaret Mosque, portal,
1457, Karaca Pasha,
Karacabey.

During the period when Osman Gazi was attempting to establish an emirate on the Söğüt Plateau, feudal Byzantine Rulers occupied the surrounding areas. Sometimes Osman Gazi engaged in battle with these rulers; at other times he attended weddings with them and shared their entertainment. At the wedding of the Byzantine Lord of Bilecik, they tried to trap him and take him prisoner. The Byzantine Lord of Harmankaya, Köse Mihail, informed Osman Gazi of the plot against him; Osman Gazi came to the wedding with his armed men disguised as women. With the help of his friend Köse Mihail, Osman Gazi acted first and destroyed the plot. One of the captives, Holophira, was given in marriage to Orhan Gazi, and the Ottoman dynasty was continued by a child of this marriage, Murad I. Holophira, a very charitable woman, who became a Muslim and took the name Nilüfer; in Bursa she had a bridge, a *masjid*, and a *dervish tekke* built; the stream over which Nilüfer had the bridge constructed is called today Nilüfer Çayı.

Osman Gazi's friend Köse Mihail also became a Muslim and entered the service of the state. Köse Mihail, his sons and his grandsons, known as the Mihailoğlu, offered valuable service to the Ottoman State for hundreds of years. İnegöl was among the cities that fell to Osman Gazi as a result of the spoiled wedding plot (1298-1299). İshak Pasha (d. 1485), one of the important statesmen of the 15th century, had a beautiful mosque, *madrasa*, and *türbe* built in İnegöl. Of slave origin, and possessed of intelligence and talent, İshak Pasha performed important duties under Sultans Murad II, Mehmed II, and Bayezid II, acting as governor, an army commander, and a *vizier*. Dedicating the property given to him by the sultans (as well as those bought from his own resources) to the *waqf*s of the institution that he had established, he secured their continued existence for hundreds of years.

After Bilecik and İnegöl, the Ottoman Emirate also took Yenişehir, where Osman Gazi built new houses for his soldiers and thus the city became known as Yenişehir or "New City" (1299). Yenişehir served as the Ottoman capital until the capture of Bursa 27 years later (1326); for this reason 1299 is accepted as the year in which the Ottoman State was founded.

The first Ottoman sultans were very close to some heterodox religious personages who performed important services for the state during the years of its foundation. Sultan Murad I had a *zawiya* built in Yenişehir for Postinpuş Baba, "who wore animal skins", and his *dervish*es. The town of Mihalıç (today Karacabey) came under Ottoman control in 1336. During the reigns of Sultans Murad II and Mehmed II, Karaca Pasha undertook important duties on behalf of the state and rose to the position of Beylerbeyi of Rumelia; he had an *imaret* established and endowed at Mihalıç. In the rooms of the *imaret* that stood apart from the prayer hall, *dervishe*s and learned men were received as guests and were given food without charge. These costs, together with the expenses for the maintenance of the *imaret* and its personnel, were met by the *waqf*. Later Karaca Pasha died in the siege of Belgrade (1456) and the name of Mihalıç was changed to Karacabey in his honour.

A. D

*Postinpuş Baba zawiya, detail from the south facade, 1362-89, Murad I, Yenişehir.*

# VI.I  YENİŞEHİR

### VI.1.a  Postinpuş Baba Zawiya

*In Baba Sultan Park.*

As mentioned above, Turkish chroniclers tell that Sultan Murad I (1362-1389) showed great interest in the *dervish*es and had the Postinpuş Baba Zawiya —also known as "Seyyid Mehmed Dede Zawiya" and "Baba Sultan Zawiya"— built in Yenişehir for Postinpuş Baba and his dervishes. It is said that, when this Muslim holy man who had come to Anatolia from Bukhara passed away in Yenişehir, Sultan Murad I built a *türbe* for him and a *zawiya* for his *dervish*es. In 1555, Hans Dernschwam, a German traveller —providing early written evidence for the structure since it does not have an inscription— briefly mentioned the building; at the beginning of the second half of the 17th century, the Turkish traveller Evliya Çelebi, who travelled around the Near East and Balkans and wrote his memoirs, said of this building that it was the grave of the Shaykh Postinpuş Pasha from Khorasan. In the 1920s the German researcher R. Hartmann wrote that the building was surrounded with a cemetery, of which nothing remains today. The building has recently been restored, but after the earthquake of 1999, it has been abandoned.

Set on a small hill, the structure today stands in solitude, accompanied by trees only. There is no evidence of any other building in the *zawiya*'s close vicinity —only the sad remains of a modern café. Constructed in alternating rows of stone and brick, it has beautiful brickwork panels and decoration on the tympana of the windows and the decoration on the spandrels of the blind arches on the south

183

*Postinpuş Baba
Zawiya, view from the
southeast, 1362-89,
Murad I, Yenişehir.*

front are especially noteworthy. The main facade on the east is totally blind other than the entrance way in the middle, now closed off with glass panes, and the portico that was once here has now disappeared; the traces of an arch on the eastern end of the south wall show that such an area once existed.

An example of "mosques with *zawiyas*," it was designed to offer hospitality to itinerant *dervish*es and other travellers. In these structures, built from the beginning of the 14th century through the middle of the 16th century, the prayer hall was distinctly separate from other areas in the building. For example, in this building the prayer hall is the large hall directly opposite the main entrance and is covered by a large dome; the square rooms on the north and south are reached by a corridor and served as *tabhane*s for guests. Another interesting feature is the building's orientation: in West Anatolia the *qibla* is towards the southeast, while in the East, it is towards the southwest. The main entrance is customarily located on the north, opposite the *mihrab* niche that indi-

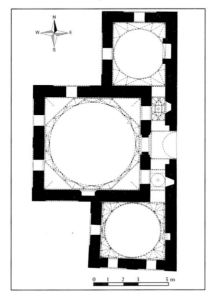

*Plan of Postinpuş Baba
zawiya, Yenişehir
(from S. Emir).*

184

ates the direction of *Kaaba* in Mecca the *qibla*. In the *zawiya* of Postinpuş aba, however, the *mihrab* niche is not on the wall directly opposite the entrance, but on the wall to the left. As mentioned above, the area surrounding the building is now vacant. Although there is nothing to prevent the main entrance from being on the northern side of the building, there is no explanation for the unusual location of the *mihrab* and main entrance in this building.

The north and south *tabhanes* are surmounted by a dome and furnished with a fireplace on their east walls; they both have windows in their two outer walls but their east walls have been left blind; this must have been done in order to provide privacy for the guests staying overnight.

R. H. Ü.

## VI.2 **İNEGÖL**

### VI.2.a **İshak Pasha Complex**

*In Cuma District (Mahallesi), on the Ankara Avenue by the Eski Belediye Square.*

İshak Pasha was an important statesman in the time of Sultans Murad II (1421-1451) and Mehmed II (1451-1481). In the conquest of Istanbul he was an army commander, and later he acted as a governor and Grand *Vizier*. When he died in 1485 at Thessalonica, his body was brought to İnegöl and buried in the conventional cemetery to the south of the mosque he had built in his own name; in 1937 his grave was removed to the *türbe* to the southwest of the mosque. During his years in office he had many buildings

*İshak Pasha Complex, View of mosque and türbe from the northwest, 1476, İshak Pasha, İnegöl.*

185

*İshak Pasha Madrasa, view from the south, 1483, İshak Pasha, İnegöl.*

constructed in several cities, such as Istanbul, Edirne, Kütahya, Bursa and, the income from several *hammam*s, shops, mills, and land rental was dedicated to the *waqf*s for the maintenance of these buildings and to pay the salaries of the staff. The complex built by İshak Pasha in İnegöl consists of a mosque, a *madrasa*, and a *türbe*; although the *waqf* charter mentions a *han* there is no *han* present today.

### İshak Pasha Mosque

This mosque built with alternating rows of stone and brick like the *madrasa* and the *türbe*, has some brickwork decoration and that on the spandrels of the portico is especially noteworthy. The plain portico —closed off with glass panes— has five domed bays separated with brick and

stone piers. The single brick minaret rising on the northwest corner of the building is entered from the western end of the portico. The inscription on the plain portal tells of the repairs carried out in 1877 by Sultan Abdülhamid II. One enters an inner court flanked on the east and west with what were once the *tabhane*s but which are now joined together by removing the walls in between. The rectangular areas that are topped with a vault to the north of these lateral sections, seems to have once been the way leading into the *tabhane*s. The plain prayer hall is to the south. All the domes inside rise above beautiful Turkish triangles. Although there is no inscription, it is believed that the mosque was probably constructed in 1476, based upon the inscription of the *madrasa* and the date of the *waqf* charter established by İshak Pasha.

## Madrasa

The *madrasa* is "U"-shaped opening towards the mosque; this layout reminds us of the Süleyman Pasha Madrasa in İznik. The *dershane* rising higher than the rest of the structure is covered by a dome and also protrudes out on the north. A total of 12 domed student cells flank the *dershane* on both sides; each cell is furnished with a fireplace and a niche for daily use. In front of the student cells is a portico with vaulted bays resting on piers surrounding the open courtyard. According to the construction inscription of the *madrasa*, it was built in 1483, that is, a little later than the mosque. Today (2000) the *madrasa* is used as a Koran school.

## Türbe

The *türbe* to the southwest of the mosque is known to have been built by İshak Pasha for his wife Tacü'n-nisa (Taj al-nisa) Sultan. This hexagonal structure is covered by a dome and has a very plain portal on the north. Inside are three graves, one of which belongs to İshak Pasha; since there are no gravestones, it is not known for certain to whom the other two graves belong. However, taking into account historical documents, it is reasonable to assume that one grave belongs to Tacü'n-nisa. It is said that the third grave belongs to the Pasha's daughter, but this cannot be ascertained.

Ş. Ç.

*İnegöl is famous for its köfte (meatballs). The Thursday market is lively and colourful. The Oylat Kaplıcaları (Spas) 20 km. from İnegöl is well worth a visit for the sulphurous water and the natural scenery. To reach Oylat, take the D200 towards Ankara after 10 km. turn right (south), then 5 km. later, turn right again.*

*İshak Pasha Türbe, view from the north, end of 15th century, İnegöl.*

187

*İmaret Mosque,
northern facade,
1457, Karaca Pasha,
Karacabey.*

## VI.3  **KARACABEY**

The former "Mihaliç" is known as "Kara-cabey" today in honour of the Beylerbeyi of Rumelia, Karaca Pasha, who had a complex built here. Karaca Pasha was a notable statesman at the time of Sultan Mehmed II and took part in the conquest of Istanbul. He died during the siege of Belgrade.

### VI.3.a  **İmaret Mosque**

*Selimiye İmaret Avenue, 12, Karacabey.*

In the 1920s, this building was in ruins and abandoned; only two large domes now remain. When restorations begun in the 1960s, the superstructure was com-pletely missing. Open for worship today the mosque has been reconstructe according to its original plan. Located i a lovely garden, the İmaret Mosque i accompanied by the cubic *türbe* to th west where Karaca Pasha's wife, Bülbü Hatun is buried, along with his brother Approaching from the main street on notices the stone and brick constructio on the mosque and *türbe*, then just goin round, the main facade on the north i beautifully faced in marble with very sof colour contrasts. The portico in the fron is divided into five bays by marble-face piers and whereas the central bay is cov-ered by a flat-topped cross vault, th other bays are covered with domes. The plain portal is also faced in marble bu with stronger colour contrasts. The inscription explains that the mosque wa completed in 1457, after the death o Karaca Pasha.

1 the westernmost bay of the portico is
he grave of Karaca Pasha himself.
According to the inscription on the foot-
tone, which is closer to the portal, he
assed away on 20 July 1456. In Ottoman
urial tradition, the name of the deceased
s not recorded on the footstone, but on
he headstone; and, according to Islamic
aw, the body is buried on its right side
vith the face turned in the direction of
*ibla*; therefore, in this grave, the head is
oward the west and the feet are toward
he east; hence, the footstone is closer to
he entrance of the prayer hall: as such,
nstead of being written on the headstone,
he identity of the deceased was written
on the footstone probably so as to be eas-
ly read by those passing by. Generally,
vealthy individuals who established *waqfs*,
et aside a room for their burial in a build-
ng they had constructed or they had a
eparate *türbe* erected. The purpose of
his was to have visitors remember them
vith good prayers. Therefore, sometimes
here is a window or a door connecting a
*türbe* to an adjoining mosque, *madrasa* or
other building, or the *türbe*'s entrance has
peen incorporated into the *madrasa*.

On entering the inner court one is struck
py the rectangular somewhat elongated
appearance, with a prayer hall to the
south. Like most similar mosques, here
too, the dome of the inner court is larger than that of the prayer hall. An indis-
pensable component of a mosque with
*tabhane*s is an area for visitors to spend the
night; in this mosque, the *tabhane*s lie on
either side of the inner court but separated from it by a wall; however, it is striking that here a corridor runs to the north
providing access to the *tabhane*s, which
are furnished with a fireplace and niches;
the western corridor also leads to the

minaret on the northwest corner, the
other to a staircase for access to the roof.

R. H. Ü.

*For those who wish to rest at the end of the
day and enjoy the beauty of nature, do visit
Manyas Gölü Kuş Cenneti or "Lake Manyas
Bird Sanctuary". To get to the bird sanctuary, head for Çanakkale leaving Karacabey
and 12 km. before reaching Bandırma turn
onto the main road 565 in the direction of
Balıkesir. Two km. later follow the road that
turns to the right until you come to a small
museum. Apart from an observation area and
toilets there are no places to eat or spend the
night in the sanctuary. Picnics are not per-
mitted.*

*In ancient times Lake Manyas was known as
Aphnitis or Daskylitis; it served as a hunting
area for satraps when Anatolia was under Persian rule. The freshwater lake has an area of
166 km² and is at an altitude of 15 m. The
lake is very shallow; towards the end of winter the water level rises and in the spring it
reaches a depth of 10 m. at its deepest point.
In the summer the water level falls to 1.5 m.
White willow is the most common tree found
on the shores of the lake, which is surrounded by villages, and large areas of farmland.
The lake is a safe haven and a rich source of
food for birds. Cormorants, pelicans, geese,
ducks and herons take shelter here. The large
number of fish, frogs, worms and seeds offer
the birds ready access to an abundance of
food. Vegetation is plentiful and healthy. One
of the main reasons that birds gather here is
that one of the migration paths passes over
this lake. Here birds start to brood, pass the
winter or just stop during their migration.
250 species of birds have been identified on
the lake comprising between 2-3 million
individual birds.*

**Şakir Çakmak**

Dervishes, Codex
Vindobonensis,
Cod.8615, fol92r,
Österreichische
Nationalbibliothek,
Vienna.

time was the *Abdalan-ı Rum* (Anatolian Abdals), a society of itinerant *dervishes*.

The Sultans, knowing the importance of the "Turkification" and economic development of conquered cities, and seeing the support these *Ahis* and *dervishes* could lend in this process, patronised them. Some Sultans were even members of a society; and in order to facilitate their religious and vocational efforts, they had special buildings such as *zawiyas*, mosques with *zawiyas* and mosques with *tabhanes* built for the *Ahis* and itinerant *dervishes*.

A 14th-century traveller by the name of Ibn Battuta gives valuable information on *Ahi zawiyas* that he encountered and was entertained in while travelling through some Anatolian cities. These *zawiyas* spread even to most remote villages and, along with giving education in religion, science and morality, they also gave training in various trades.

The mosques with *tabhanes*, which sultans and high-government officials had built for the *Ahis* and itinerant dervish, shed light on the social structures of the Early Ottoman period. The numerous examples of these mosques built from the 14th through to the 16th centuries in areas that fell under Ottoman rule are proof that the government considered such 'socialising' organisations important.

Mosques with *tabhanes* are different from regular mosques whose only function is to provide a place for prayer. In fact, these types of buildings are referred to as *zawiyas* or *imarets* on building inscriptions, *waqf* charters, and other documents. Mosques with *tabhanes* were designed to meet the needs of the *Ahis* and itinerant *dervishes* by providing them with a space for meetings, worship and lodgings.

In Anatolia, beginning in Seljuq times, there were various social organisations influential in military, religious, social and economic affairs and playing an important role during the establishment of the Ottoman State. One of the most important was the *Ahiyan-ı Rum* (Anatolian *Ahis*); it has been suggested that this organisation takes its name from either the Arabic word *akhi* for "brother" or from the Turkish word *akı* for "generous". The *Ahi* society is an extension of the *Futuwwa* supported by the Abbassid Caliph Nasir (1180-1225). Another famous organisation of the

hese buildings, also known as T-shaped osques, are composed of three main ctions: a meeting and transition area lled the "central court" or "inner court" "*sofa*"; a prayer hall; *tabhanes* functiong as guestrooms, whose number varies om two to six.

om the middle of the 15th century, the *ni* organisation began to assume the ature of a guild occupying itself in commercial affairs only. For this reason, the need for mosques with *tabhanes* diminished. The construction of this type of mosque continued until the beginning of the 16th century with a few alterations. From the 16th century on, *tabhanes* became separate buildings in a mosque complex and, as a result of this development, mosques with *tabhanes* were no longer constructed.

# The Lock of the Sea

**Şakir Çakmak, Aydoğan Demir**

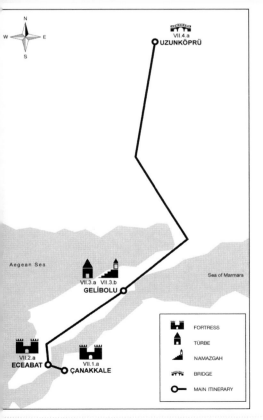

*Azebler Namazgah, minbar, 1407, İskender Ibn Hacı Pasha, Gelibolu.*

*Kilitbahir Fortress, view from the east, 1463, Mehmed II, Eceabat.*

A few kilometres away from the shore on the Anatolian side, at the entrance of the Çanakkale Strait (Dardanelles) that connects the Marmara Sea to the Aegean, on the spot known today as Hisarlık Hill, you can still see the remains of the ancient city of Troy. If you close your eyes for a minute and imagine ancient times, you will see King Priam standing on the city walls of Troy, his wife Hecabe, his famous son Paris, his daughter Cassandra, and his daughter in-law, the beautiful Helen watching with fearful eyes as two men fight. On the other side, there stands Agamemnon, the Achaean King, his brother Menelaus, the king of Sparta, and brave Odysseus, all observing the very same fight with some excitement. Those in battle are well known to both parties: invincible Achilles, son of a goddess and a mortal, and the other is the son of King Priam, namely brave Hector. Homer relates his glorified epic of the Iliad and immortalises the story of the Trojan War into a romantic love story: Paris's abduction of King Menelaus's wife, the beautiful Helen, was the cause of this long war. However, the real reason behind the war was the struggle to take over the Çanakkale Strait, a crucial trade and transportation route connecting the Black Sea with the Aegean Sea.

For many centuries, the Çanakkale and Istanbul (Bosphorus) Straits have been major source of conflict between nations. At the beginning of the 14th century, the Anatolian shores of the Strait were under the sovereignty of the Karasi Emirate. When the Ottomans destroyed the Karasi Emirate around the middle of 14th century, they gained control over the shores of the area. At the same time, the Ottomans gained a base in Gelibolu, on the other side of the Çanakkale Strait in return for helping John VI Cantacuzenus who at the time was struggling to acquire the Byzantine throne (1354). From this date on the Ottomans rapidly acquired all of Thrace. Gelibolu became a much-frequented place for people passing from

natolia to Thrace. Built on the Geli-
olu-Edirne route, Uzunköprü, literally
e Long Bridge, is one of the longest
ridges of Thrace. This bridge indicates
e importance given to the trade and
onquest routes that tied Anatolia and
urope together in the first half of 15$^{th}$
entury.

fter Sultan Mehmed II conquered Istan-
l in 1453, he followed an expansionary
olicy in the Aegean Sea and the Balkans,
hich meant great losses for the mer-
ant communes of Venice and Genoa.
ultan Mehmed II became very popular in
aly, and many legends about him were
assed on. In his *Essays*, Montaigne (1533-
592) says: "Muhammad the Conqueror
elieves himself to be a descendant of the
ojans, just like the Italians, and thus he
astonished that the Italians support the
reeks when they actually ought to work
ith him in order to take revenge for
ector". Since interstate relationships
ould not be resolved by such an
pproach of romanticism and kinship, Sul-
n Mehmed II had ordered the Sultaniye
ortress and Kilidü'l-Bahr Fortress to be
uilt at the narrowest point of the
anakkale Strait against possible Venetian
d Genoese threats.

A. D.

*his Itinerary starts on the Asian continent
nd ends on the European continent. With
he ferryboat that you board at Çanakkale,
ou will reach Eceabat on the Gelibolu
eninsula within 30 minutes. The Gelibolu
eninsula occupies an important place in
oth world and Turkish history. In 1915, the
attle of Çanakkale –the so-called Battle of
allipoli– took place here between the Allied
owers and the Ottoman Empire, and was one
f the bloodiest wars in history. Today this*

*area that witnessed the death of approxi-
mately 500,000 people is a National Park
with monuments erected in various parts so
that the painful experiences of the past will
not be forgotten, and people will reflect on
the great importance of peace. This route
that proceeds through the fruitful land of
Thrace is slightly rugged though the scenery
is peaceful and relaxed. Following the main
road D.550 north from Eceabat, you will
first reach Gelibolu. This road continues
across Uzunköprü via Keşan. To reach
Edirne, you must turn onto the main road
D.100 from Havsa.*

## VII.1  ÇANAKKALE

The city of Çanakkale situated on the
Asian side of the Strait was founded

*Sultaniye Fortress, the
inner court, 1463,
Mehmed II,
Çanakkale.*

*Sultaniye Fortress, the inner court and armoury, 1463, Mehmed II, Çanakkale.*

around the middle of the 15th century, with the building of the Sultaniye Fortress on the Anatolian shore by order of Mehmed II against potential Venetian and Genoese threats. Its citizens named the city Çanakkale because it was a centre of pottery production: in Turkish "Çanak" means earthenware pot and "Kale" means fortress. Pottery produced locally in Çanakkale was popular throughout the country.

> *The famous Troy is just half-an-hour's drive to the south of Çanakkale and some of the finds along with ancient objects from Assos, are on display in the Çanakkale Archaeological Museum.*

### VII.1.a **Sultaniye Fortress**

*The fortress is located in the Kemalpaşa Dis-*

*trict (Mahallesi), on Yalı Avenue; 200 m. t the south of the ferry port. Today it is used a Military (Navy) Museum. Open between th hours of 09.00-12.00 and 13.30-17.00, is closed on Mondays and Thursdays. There an entrance fee (plus an extra fee for the use a camera).*

Following the conquest of Istanbul, Su tan Mehmed II ordered the constructio of two fortresses on the narrowest poir in order to control the Dardanelles; thes fortresses face each other, one on th Anatolian side, and the other on the Thra cian side. Located today in Çanakkale city centre, the fortress on the Anatolia side, Sultaniye Fortress, was built in 146 under the supervision of Yakup Bey, on of Sultan Mehmed II's generals. Th fortress has been restored recently and i surrounding area has been reorganise and turned into a museum.

ast the ticket office on the right is the Nusrat ship used for laying mines during the Battle of Çanakkale in 1915. The main entrance under a tower in the middle of the north side opens into the court. The Sultaniye Fortress, also known as Çimenlik Fortress, is composed of an outer fort, 110 x 160 m., and a three-storey inner castle of 30 x 42 m. and 20 m. high, along with two *masjids* and a circular armoury. The outer wall is fortified with several towers and bastions and supports battlements. On entering the court one faces the inner fort straight ahead, and the round armoury to the left in the distance. The first *masjid* adjoins the tower, under which is the entrance today, and the upper part of its short minaret is in ruins. In the court between the outer fort and the inner castle is an open-air display of cannons and artillery from the first World War. The second *masjid* stands by the southwest corner of the inner castle and according to the inscription, it was built during the reign of Sultan Abdülaziz (1861-1876). The redoubts in the west part of the outer fort were built in the same period. On the landing in front of the main door of the inner castle there is a broken marble seat, on which, according to legend, Sultan Mehmed II sat. This inner castle is a very secure building with walls more than 7 m. thick; according to the writings of researchers, a 38' cannon ball left only a small mark on its wall during the Battle of Çanakkale (1915); today it is used as an exhibition hall housing a display of weapons.

Grelot, a 17th-century traveller, describes Sultaniye Fortress in detail and records that there were 28 large cannons that could shoot cannon balls to the opposite shore, and that Çanakkale was a large village behind the castle, with a population of 3000.

Ş. Ç.

*You can reach Eceabat by taking one of the Turkish Maritime Lines' ferries that leaves every hour from Çanakkale. Just to the south of the port, there are smaller private ferries going directly to Kilitbahir.*

## VII.2  ECEABAT

### VII.2.a  Kilitbahir Fortress

*Kilitbahir Village, Eceabat. There is an entrance fee to the inner fort.*

The fortress of Kilitbahir —or Kilidü'l-Bahr— is the second stronghold that Sultan Mehmed II built to control the Straits of Çanakkale. Built in 1463 along with the Sultaniye Fortress on the Asian side, it is named Kilidü'l-Bahr meaning "the lock of the sea" due to its strategic positioning; the village is also named after the fortress.

This fortress is unique among Turkish fortresses in terms of its architectural plan: the original fortress resembles the letter "D" and has a trefoil-shaped inner fort in the centre from which rises a trefoil-shaped tower. Coming from the ferry port one enters the outer fortress through the north gate; on the left is the shore with the walls now collapsed; and on the right stands the majestic inner fort with its bands of brickwork decoration high up to entice your eye upwards.

*Kilitbahir Fortress, view from the south, 1463, Mehmed II, Eceabat.*

The trefoil-shaped inner fortress, rising higher than the rest, consists of three courtyards separated from each other by gates. Its huge walls are 7 m. thick and 18 m. high. Two of the courtyards have monumental doors opening to the court of the outer fortress. A 30-m. high, seven-storied tower stands in the centre; the court in which this tower stands is not directly linked to the outer fortress. With this innovative architectural plan, the enemy forces that wanted to conquer the fortress would have had to pass through one courtyard to the other. Thus, it was rendered extremely difficult to reach the main tower in the centre. There are bands of brickwork with geometric designs on the upper parts of the tower walls. It is understood that the tower was divided by wooden flooring, and that wooden staircases built into the walls led to each of these floors. Unfortunately, neither the staircases nor the wooden floors have survived to the present day; only the first-floor level is accessible by the staircase in the wall.

The second fortress constructed in 154? in the reign of Süleyman I adjoins the original one –forming an almost irregular figure-eight shape. A monumental tower o? 21 m. in diameter stands in its southernmost corner. The outer circuits of the walls are 4 m. high, although the section along the sea have not survived. It i? known that wide moats existed around the fortress; the fortress was entered throug? two gates, one to the north and one to the south. There were suspended bridges over the moats to reach the gates; because the moats were filled in at some later date they are no longer present today. Past the second fortress extend many emplacements and the remains of more 19th-century walls.

Ş. Ç

*Today the Gelibolu (known as Gallipoli in the West) Peninsula is a National Park full of monuments and cemeteries of Turkish and for-*

eign soldiers who lost their lives in the Battle of Çanakkale. You can take a rather narrow main road to the southern end of the
peninsula where there are Turkish, French
and English monuments. In the direction of
the town of Gelibolu to the north, you can
reach Kabatepe, Anzac Bay and Conk Bayırı
by heading north and then taking a road that
curves to the left. There is a small museum at
Kabatepe, where belongings recovered from the
soldiers of the First World War are displayed.

You can reach Gelibolu by taking the main
road D.550 north from Eceabat.

## VII.3 GELİBOLU

Gelibolu is situated in a strategically
important area, where the Dardanelles

opens into the Sea of Marmara. The city,
first founded by the Thracians, was called
Kallipolis –the beautiful city– after the
Greek colonisation. Alexander the Great
then took the area in 334 BC. The Roman
and Byzantine Empires later ruled the
city, and the Byzantine Emperor Justinian
I repaired the city walls. During the Third
Crusade Friedrich I Barbarossa, the German Emperor, transported his armies
from the port of Gelibolu to the Anatolian side.

Umur Bey of the Aydın Emirate besieged
Gelibolu in 1332 and 1341, but did not
succeed in conquering it. The Ottomans,
who initially landed in Rumelia to help
the Byzantines, later realised the strategic
importance of the area and captured Gelibolu, whose fortress had been destroyed
as a result of an earthquake. The town
changed hands several times until 1367,

*Kilitbahir Fortress,
interior of the
trefoil-shaped tower,
1463, Mehmed II,
Eceabat.*

*Türbe of Ahmet Bican Efendi (Hallacı Mansur), entrance facade, 15ᵗʰ century, Gelibolu.*

when it finally became Ottoman territory. About the middle of the 15ᵗʰ century, Çanakkale took over surveillance of the strait, and Gelibolu thus lost its importance. In the city there are various works constructed in the reign of Murad II (1421-1451) in particular; most of these works have suffered from to neglect and have thus fallen into ruins.

## VII.3.a **Türbe of Ahmet Bican Efendi (Hallacı Mansur)**

*On Keşan Avenue.*

The *türbe* of Ahmet Bican Efendi is one of the best-kept works in Gelibolu. Alhough it is assumed that it was built in the period of Murad II, it is not known for certain to whom it belongs. Some researchers argue that it belongs to Ahmet Bican Efendi, but some say it belongs to a person called Hallacı Mansur. Known to have died in the

middle of the 15ᵗʰ century, Ahmet Bican Efendi was a wise man known for hi works in the theology of Islam and Islami geography. However, Hallacı Mansur is Muslim saint who lived before the con quest of Gelibolu. Although the *türbe* wa allegedly built in his memory, no evidenc has been found to support this belief. hallaç is a person who works cotton o wool with a bow and a mallet so that it i suitable for use in beds, covers, and pil lows. The story goes that once upon time, a bow and mallet used by *hallaçe* were found in the tomb. Thus, the belie that this *türbe* should be attributed to thi person called Hallacı Mansur is based upon this legend.

Stones and bricks are used alternately or the walls of the domed *türbe*, which has square plan. In front of the entrance is single-bay portico covered with a flat topped cross vault. Such porticoes locat ed in front of the entrance of Anatolia *türbe*s are observed to have started in the arly 15th century, as we have already seen n the *türbe* of Sultan Bayezid I (1406) in ursa Yıldırım Complex.

here are two sarcophagi in the tomb. he richly ornamented one that is elieved to belong to Ahmet Bican Efeni has no inscription on it. The other maller sarcophagus is plain.

Ş. Ç.

### /II.3.b  Azebler Namazgah

*t is on the road going east from the* türbe *of Ahmet Bican Efendi, in the Fener District Mahallesi).*

n Ottoman architecture, in addition to overed worship places such as mosques nd *masjid*s, there are also open-air prayer places built for use during the summer nonths. Called *namazgah*s, they are usually situated outside the city in recreation areas, suburbs, or on intercity roads. The term *namazgah* means "a large, open-air place, where prayer is performed". The *namazgah*s were not used only as venues for Friday or daily prayer times: people prayed together for those going into military service or taking part in a military campaign, or for those going on a pilgrimage to Mecca, that they may have a safe journey, and in times of drought people went to these places to pray for rain. Situated along routes between cities or suburbs, *namazgah*s also served as resting areas.

*Namazgah*s have rather simple architecture, the main elements of which are: a *mihrab* indicating the direction to Mecca, or a stone symbolising the *mihrab*; a small well or fountain for ablution; a clean and appropriate place for performing prayer and trees to protect the area from excess heat. There are also examples with a more ornamented and decorated *qibla* wall and a *minbar*.

*Azebler Namazgah, view from the northeast, 1407, İskender Ibn Hacı Pasha, Gelibolu.*

This *namazgah* in Gelibolu was built initially as a common prayer area for the soldiers in the Ottoman Navy, called *Azebs*, and is one of the most elaborate examples of such a structure. The *namazgah* is located on a flat area on top of a ridge, overlooking the Strait at the entrance to Dardanelles, southeast of the city. According to its inscription, it was built by the architect Aşık Ibn Süleyman for İskender Ibn Hacı Pasha in 1407.

The *namazgah* is surrounded by low walls on the east, west and north sides, and is entered through a false marble door on the north. There is a *mihrab* in the centre of the marble *qibla* wall along with two *minbars*, one at each end of the wall. Although it is a simple structure, it has a rich appearance with its fine decoration on the tympanum of the entrance and on the upper section of its *qibla* wall.

Ş. Ç.

## VII.4 **UZUNKÖPRÜ**

### VII.4.a **Uzunköprü Bridge**

Constructed over the Ergene River, the Uzunköprü (literally the long bridge) is positioned at the entrance to Uzunköprü town, formerly known as Ergene. It is one of the longest and most splendid historical Turkish bridges. In the 15th century, the inefficient roads and the strong-flowing rivers were major obstacles for the Ottoman army. Ergene River is one of the most intractable natural obstacles in Turkey. According to historical sources, the area

where the bridge stands today used t be a swamp covered by trees; the wooden bridges over the river were insuffi cient to serve the needs and collapse frequently when the river overflowed Sultan Murad II built a new woode bridge after another flood, but soo realised that it was not strong enoug either and decided that a stone bridg should be built.

A mosque, a *han*, a *hammam* and an *imare* were built near this 1400-m. long, 174 arched magnificent bridge. According t its inscription, which was later moved t a nearby fountain, the construction wa completed in 1444. Historical source state that Sultan Murad II himself attend ed the opening ceremony, which was fol lowed by religious ceremonies, feasts an parades.

There are carvings of elephants, birds an lions on the bridge, as well as decoration with geometric and floral themes. The elephant figure, rarely seen in Turkish architectural decoration, has receive much attention from scholars. There ar various theories regarding the origin o this figure, the most remarkable of which is: Sultan Murad II had his son Mehme married in 1449 in Edirne with a wed ding lasting three months. In a manuscript that is known to have left Istanbul for the library in San Marco, Venice, Sitti Hatun —whose tombstone we will see at the Archaeological Museum in Edirne— the wife of Mehmed, is pictured sitting on a throne positioned on an elephant. Some researchers interpret this as follows: Sitti Hatun might have been brought to Edirne on an elephant passing over Uzunköprü. Thus, the elephant carving on the bridge may have been carried out in memory of this incident.

*Uzunköprü Bridge, general view, 1444, Murad II, Uzunköprü.*

Uzunköprü, attractive for its architecture and decoration, has undergone several renovations, the last one in 1970, and is still in use as part of the main road. Only the part directly above the river becomes humpbacked and has balconies with carvings at the top; the rest of the bridge extends flat over the marshy area. Today due to the alluvium brought by the river a large part of bridge's piers are buried underground.

Ş. Ç.

*Uzunköprü Bridge, lion relief, 1444, Murad II, Uzunköprü.*

**Aydoğan Demi**

*Waqfs* are pious foundations established to meet the construction and operating costs of non-profit structures like mosques, *madrasa*s, hospitals, *imaret*s, fountains, and so on, which an individual has built using his or her movable or real-estate property. In the Middle Ages, funds from the state treasury of Islamic countries were not allocated to the construction of public buildings. Buildings constructed by the rulers, bureaucrats and rich citizens of the town and funded by the *waqf*s embellished the splendid Islamic towns.

In Ottoman administration, a statesman that had such a building constructed determined in detail in the *waqf* charter exactly how the revenues of the foundation ought to be spent. For example:

1. It was determined, in detail, the qualifications and the number of people to be employed in these structures.

2. If there was a *madrasa*, the allowance of the students and the salaries of the staff were determined.

3. If there was an *imaret*, the types of food and the number of people to be served, as well as the specific details of the meals for certain days like religious holidays, were determined.

4. The regular maintenance, cleanin and renovation of the structures wa organised.

5. Cash, farms, stores, houses, an ice depot, blacksmith's shop, soap factory *boza* factory, *han*s, *bedesten*s and all othe property that brings revenue to cover th costs of the service structures were liste one-by-one in the *waqf* charter.

6. The owner of the *waqf* bound th management of the *waqf* to himself as lon; as he was alive, and to one of his sons, o if he had no sons, to one of his daughter or grandsons.

7. All conditions regarding the manage ment of the *waqf* were listed one-by-on in writing, and then signed by witnesses The *waqf* charter then had to be approve by the court. Once the *waqf* charter wa approved, as long as it followed the stat ed conditions, no one could interfer with the content of the *waqf*.

*Waqf*s were established for various purposes: some *waqf*s were to help poor girls prepare the necessary trousseau; some were to get indebted people out of prison; there were some that provided food for prisoners, or food and water for animals, and even some that took care of injured storks.

# THE JANISSARY CORPS

**Aydoğan Demir**

he Ottoman State, founded in 1299, ecame a large empire within 150 years llowing its foundation. The organisation f the state in almost all areas, as well as s continuous legal reforms to protect its itizens, must have played an important ›le in the growth of the state.

eginning with the founding of the state, ilitary problems such as recruiting and ·aining soldiers and protecting their tures were considered within a legal ·amework.

)sman Gazi (1281-1324) gathered vol-nteer and paid soldiers from his coun-rymen. However, soon these soldiers ·ecame insufficient as wars tended to last ›nger and took place farther away from he centre. During the reign of Orhan ;azi (1324-1362), an army was formed f cavalrymen and infantries, who lived ot in the barracks but on the farms pro-ided by the state when they were not way at war.

3esides soldiers that were half-farmer, alf-infantry or half-cavalrymen, there vere also those who owned a *tımar* fief lllocated by the Sultan, through which hey collected certain taxes in their dministrative regions. These soldiers vere called *Tımarlı Sipahis* and constitut-·d the main force of the Ottoman army ıntil the end of the 16th century. The title *Tımarlı Sipahi* was usually passed from ·ather to son.

Around the middle of the 14th century, luring the reign of Murad I (1362-1389), ı new group of infantries called *Yeniçeri* (Janissary) was formed, who were con-sidered the court soldiers of the Sultan ınd were lodged in barracks in the capi-tal. The cavalry formed around the same time as the Janissary corps reported directly to the Sultan himself. The

Jannitcharun

armourers to the military corps, sappers, artillerymen, caisson-drivers, Janissary corps and cavalrymen constituted the mil-itary personnel that were called the *kapıkulus* meaning "the servant slaves of the Porte" since they waited upon the Gate of the Sultan.

Prisoners of war were the original source for the Janissary and cavalry corps. According to the laws in effect at that time, 1/5 of the spoils acquired in war was set aside for the state; since prison-ers of war also qualified as part of the spoils, 1/5 of those captives between the ages of 10-20 who were potential war-

*The Janissaries, Codex Vindobonensis, Cod. 8626, fol 13, Österreichische Nationalbibliothek, Vienna.*

3. The Ottomans were very fond o guessing people's characters by looking a their head, eyebrows, eyes, height, etc This constituted "The Science of Person Appearance". For example, according t the Science of Personal Appearance, it wa believed that short people were clever bu dishonest; people of middle height ha good morals; and people with large head were intelligent. Those who were charge with selecting individuals according to th Science of Personal Appearance would no choose bald or short people, but woul choose beautiful, healthy children of aver age height. Tall children of appropriate build would also be taken for private edu cation in the palace.

4. A child whose mother and father wer deceased would not be taken.

5. The children of Jews dealing in trad would not be taken.

The most select of the recruited childre would be set apart to be educated in th palace, while the rest would be given t Turkish farmer-families with children, with whom they were to spend three t eight years. These children who share their environment with Turkish childre and learned Turkish customs and tradi tions would join the *acemi ocağı* in Geli bolu. These young conscripted Janissarie would work on the construction o important social facilities and on ships, and then later, when their time came, they would become Janissaries.

During times of peace, the Janissarie would live as bachelors in barracks in the capital city; they were first given per mission to marry at the beginning of the 16th century. The Janissaries were paid a salary once every three months. They fought in the middle section of the army alongside the Sultan, and for this they

riors were educated for the state. The Janissary corps was originally formed using this system.

At the time of Sultan Bayezid I (1389-1402), some restrictions were imposed upon the training of war prisoners, and a new regulation was put into effect. According to the new *Devşirme* Law, once every three or seven years, male children were gathered from the Christian villages. It is known that certain procedural laws bound the gathering of these male children from only one out of every 40 households:

1. Only children of noble families or priests, between the ages of 8-20 were recruited.

2. Children were not taken from families with only one son.

so received a special military expedition ratuity. They were also given a special ratuity when a new sultan ascended the rone.

o the janissaries and all the children receiving an education in the Palace chool, all military and state positions ere open; a Serb, Croat, Rum or Albann farmer's child could become Grand izier if he was skilled enough.

Vith the sensibilities of our day, the idea f taking children from their families at a ery young age might be approached with riticism. In his novel *The Drina Bridge*, o Andrić tells the dramatic story of nothers in pursuit of their recruited children. However, it should be remembered that many families also tried in various ways to have their children recruited. There are concrete examples of this in Ottoman archival documents. In his work *L'Empire Ottoman*, the renowned Greek historian Dimitri Kitsikis points out that a process like gathering warriors from villagers was also practised under the Byzantine administration.

Beginning in the 17$^{th}$ century, as the recruitment system broke down and their training was neglected, the Janissaries participated in some revolts. Finally, in 1826, the Janissary corps as an institution was abandoned.

# Music Therapy in the *Darüşşifa*

## Lale Bulut, Aydoğan Demir, İnci Kuyulu

*Palaces*

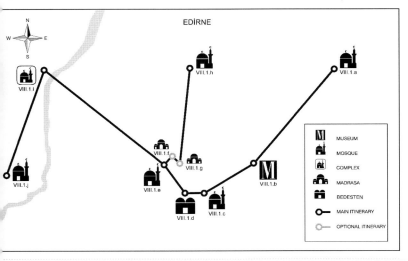

*Bayezid II Complex Madrasa, view from the southeast, 1488, Bayezid II, Edirne.*

*Bayezid II Complex, Mosque, dome in front of the prayer hall portal, 1488, Bayezid II, Edirne.*

Balkans and Europe. When the preparations were complete, the Sultan headed of
to battle from Edirne accompanied b
great ceremony. Sultan Mehmed II accom
plished all his preparations, including th
casting of the cannons in Edirne before h
embarked on the campaign in April 145
to conquer Istanbul and to put an end t
the Byzantine Empire on 29 May 1453.
The Ottoman Sultans and leading officia
embellished Edirne with monuments. I
Edirne, complexes hold an especiall
important place among the *waqf* build
ings. Turkish towns enlarged and deve
oped around such complexes, and th
marvellous structures built by the Sultan
Bayezid I, Mehmed I, Murad II, Mehme
II and Bayezid II are still the source o
great admiration.
The *darüşşifa* of the Bayezid II Complex
a hospital with 50 beds. We learn from i
*waqf* charter that one head doctor, tw
general practitioners, two ophthalmologists
two surgeons, one pharmacist, five nurs
es, one clerk, one purchaser of merchan
dise, one store employee, two cooks, on
cleaner, one launderer, one barber and on
gatekeeper were employed. Two days
week, the outpatients were admitted fo
examination and given medication free o
charge. The famous 17th-century Ottoma
traveller, Evliya Çelebi, praises the atten
tion paid to the patients, as well as th
excellence of the beds and food. He als
relates that music was used in the treat
ment of mental patients, saying that
group of 10 musicians gave concerts thre
times a week as part of music therapy.
Edirne was both an administrative cit
and a strategically located, lively com
mercial centre. For this reason, man
*hans* and *bedestens*, which were a
important source of income for th

The city of Edirne is the crossroads for
various routes that stretch across Anatolia to the Balkans. This city, the object of
many military occupations, fell to the
Ottomans in 1362 and became the capital in 1368. The city retained its importance even after Istanbul was conquered
in 1453 and became the capital soon
after; many Ottoman Sultans made additions to the Edirne Palace and resided
occasionally in this palace on the shores of
the Tunca River. However, after the
Ottoman Sultans abandoned it in 1703,
its days of glory became a part of the past;
as a result of two large fires in the 19th
century, the palace was heavily damaged
and fell totally into ruins.
Edirne was the scene of great preparations
made for military expeditions to the

*Muradiye Mosque, general view from the minaret of Selimiye Mosque, 1426-27, Murad II, Edirne.*

ocial facilities of the *waqf*s, were built the city.

A. D.

## III.I  EDİRNE

*his Itinerary covers the city of Edirne only. Most the monuments are in the centre of town and ithin easy walking distance from one another. 'uradiye Mosque, Yıldırım Mosque and Bayezid Complex, however, are quite a long way from e centre, so transport is recommended.*

dirne was first founded by the Thracians id named Orestia. In the reign of the oman Emperor Hadrian (117-138), it as given City status and took the name adrianople. The city developed as it aped the blessings and advantages of the rosperous Roman Era.
/hen the Roman Empire was divided in 95, Hadrianople was left to the East

Roman (Byzantine) Empire. Raids from the Balkans frequently threatened and destroyed the city.
After the Turks took the city, its name was corrupted to Edirne.

### VIII.1.a  Muradiye Mosque

*On Kıyık Avenue, Furun Street. Follow Mimar Sinan Street from Selimiye Mosque; it can only be visited immediately after prayer times.*

During the period of Sultan Murad II, construction work increased in Edirne; the complex bearing the name of this Sultan stands on a hill in the city's northeast. The story goes that Sultan Murad II dreamt that Mevlana Celaleddin Rumi, the head of the whirling *dervish*es, asked him to build a *tekke* in Edirne. At the time of its construction, the complex was comprised of a mosque, a *mektep*, an *imaret*, and a *tekke*, but only the mosque and graveyard have

211

*Muradiye Mosque, tile
wallpanel, 1426-27,
Murad II, Edirne.*

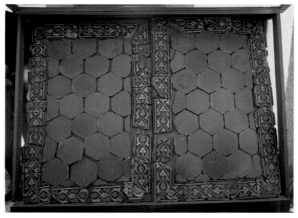

*Tile wallpanel from
Şahmelek Mosque,
1429, Turkish and
Islamic Arts Museum,
Edirne.*

a five-bayed portico, the central bay of
which is covered by a dome, while the
others are covered with flat-topped cross-
vaults. The inscription on the portal gives
the name of Sultan Murad II but does not
provide any date. The portal with a lovely *muqarnas* canopy opens into the central
court covered with a dome and a lantern.
Typical of mosques with *tabhane*s designed
in order to meet the needs of itinerant
*dervish*es, the central court is flanked with
domed *tabhane*s to the east and west while
the domed prayer hall lies to its south.
The Muradiye Mosque's wall paintings,
tiles and wooden decorations are especially noteworthy. The walls of the prayer
hall are covered with tiles up to a certain
height. The hexagonal blue-white tiles are
ornamented with naturalist floral motifs
and among them are placed triangular tiles
glazed in turquoise. The magnificent tile
*mihrab* in *cuerda seca* and tile-mosaic techniques, like those at Bursa Yeşil Complex
is 3.65 m. wide and 6.35 m. high among
the moulded tiles in yellow, white, blue
and turquoise, the yellow is dominant; the
geometric star motifs, *rumi*s, *palmette*s, and
peonies are especially striking. Above are
traces of wall paintings with interlocking
designs, *rumi*s, and various floral motifs
in its day the interior must have looked as
exuberant and glowing as the Green
Mosque in Bursa.

İ. K

survived to the present day. It is known
that the school was standing in the 1920s
and that the *tekke* disappeared after 1935.
The same sultan also built the Üç Şerefeli
Mosque in Edirne and the Bursa Muradiye
Complex, which we have already seen.
The Muradiye Mosque, standing all on its
own on top of a hill, is completely faced
with cut stone on the outside and the
minaret stands on the northwest corner.
On the north side of the mosque, there is

### VIII.1.b **Turkish and Islamic Arts Museum, and Archaeological Museum**

*Today, the* madrasa *situated to the southeast
of Selimiye Mosque is used as the Turkish and
Islamic Arts Museum with a good collection of*

and–crafted artefacts. Just to the east, about [1]00 m. away is the Archaeological and Ethno-graphic Museum. Both museums are open between 08.00-12.00 and 13.00-16.30 dur-ing the winter and 08.30-12.30 and 13.30-[1]7.00 during the summer. There is a separate entrance fee for each museum.

## Wall tiles

The Seljuqs brought with them to Anato-lia the art of tile production and decora-tion, which developed in relationship to architecture. Various techniques were used in the production of Turkish tile art, examples of which span many centuries. The main raw material of tiles, which was an important decorative element in mosques, masjids, madrasas, türbes, and palaces, was clean and good-quality clay.

Clay is cleaned of impurities and made into mud in pools; then it is transferred to a second pool and left to rest for a few days; later it is transported to a third pool. When the liquid-clay dough becomes thicker, it is shaped using moulds in the mould workshops and left to dry. Any rough parts are then cleaned using emery; then the tiles are baked in kilns. The hard-ened tiles are taken from the gradually cooling kiln and designs are drawn on them. They are then covered either with a transparent, coloured or colourless glaze and put back into the kiln.

The tiles on display here in one of the southern cells are from the Edirne Şah-melek Mosque and date back to 1429. They form two rectangular panels, which are filled with turquoise-coloured unor-namented tiles and on the border bands

*Gravestone of Sitti Hatun, 1486, Archaeological Museum, Edirne.*

213

*Eski Mosque, general view from the east, 1414, Mehmed I, Edirne.*

are floral motifs applied in the coloured glaze (*cuerda seca*) technique.

L. B.

**Gravestones**

Displayed in the yard of the Archaeological Museum, is the headstone of Sitti Hatun, daughter of Süleyman, son of Zülfikar; she was married to Sultan Mehmed II and passed away in June 1486. Usually, there is one gravestone at the head and one at the foot of Anatolian graves. In the Seljuq and Emirates periods, both the headstones and the footstones were ornamented with inscriptions. Beginning in the 17th century, figures like cypresses, date palms and grapevines replaced the scriptures on the footstones. In the Ottoman period, the pinnacle of most female graves

ended in a triangular pediment, the inside of which was filled with geometric and floral motifs or depictions of mosques and other buildings. This rectangular gravestone has a top section shaped like, and ornamented with, *palmettes* and *rumis*. A carved niche resembling a *mihrab* is placed on the body of stone, and information about the deceased person is engraved in this niche; a single pinwheel and a rosette are carved in the corners of the niche; the niche is enclosed by a chain pattern.

L. B.

### VIII.1.c  **Eski Mosque**

*In the centre, on Talat Pasha Boulevard, to the west of Selimiye Complex across the park.*

After the tragic death of Sultan Bayezid I,

is sons began fighting over the throne; their struggles calmed for a while when the eldest brother Süleyman Çelebi emerged victorious and ascended the throne. However, in 1411, his brother Musa seized the capital Edirne. Then in 413, Mehmed I, also known as Çelebi Mehmed, took the city from his brother. The construction of Eski Mosque began n 1403 during the time of Süleyman Çelebi, it continued during the period of Musa and was finally finished in 1414 during the reign of Sultan Mehmed I. The inscription on top of the west entrance floor tells us that the architect of this building was Hacı Alaaddin of Konya and his assistant was Omar Ibn Ibrahim. As he inscription above the false door of the portico informs us, the mosque was damaged in a fire of 1745 and then by an earthquake in 1752, and was thoroughly renovated by Sultan Mahmud I in 1753. Frequent renovations were also made in the 20th century, the latest being completed at the beginning of 2001.

Eski Mosque is the first monumental mosque in Edirne constructed in the Ottoman period. The minaret on the east was constructed at the same time as the mosque, while the one on the west is a later addition. The structure is completely faced with cut stone on the outside whereas both cut stone and brick were used in the portico. The central bay of the portico is emphasised with a dome and also has a false doorway. The mosque has nine domes and bears a great resemblance to the 20-domed Bursa Great Mosque, constructed by Sultan Bayezid I in 1400, continuing the Seljuq tradition of mosques with multiple bays of equal size. The domes, each with a diameter of 13.5 m., are supported with four colos-

sal pillars. The three domes on the *mihrab* axis are higher than the others and the northernmost one has a lantern, under which there once used to stand the ablution fountain, as in Bursa Great Mosque. On the walls and pillars are religious inscriptions in very large and bold letters. The wall paintings on the top section of the walls, on the interior of the domes, and on the *mihrab* were probably added during an 18th-century renovation. There is intricate ornamentation on the side surfaces of the marble *minbar*.

İ. K.

### VIII.1.d  Bedesten

*To the west of Eski Mosque, on Talat Paşa Boulevard.*

The *bedesten* is a new building type that

Bedesten, interior, 1413-21, Mehmed I, Edirne.

emerged in the 15th century as a result of the development of commercial life during the Emirates period. Originally constructed to gather fabric sellers called *bezzaz* under one roof, soon other goods began to be sold there as well. Valuable merchandise —like jewellery and money deposited by merchants— was stored and protected in the *bedesten*s, which functioned like the banks of today. Goods were also priced and quality checked in the *bedesten*s, whose officers, chosen among trustworthy persons, also acted as experts in commercial lawsuits.

In general, *bedesten*s are rectangular structures closed to the outside; stores on all four sides completely surround the structure. A door is located in the centre of each front; the interior is divided into equal-size bays, each of which is covered with a dome;

small cells adjoin the interior of the walls; the number of domed sections varies according to the size of the *bedesten*.

One of the most important *bedesten*s, each of which was a *waqf* establishment, is the Edirne Bedesten constructed by Sultan Mehmed I. It is known that this *bedesten* belonged to the Eski Mosque's *waqf*. It has four *iwan*-shaped entrances, one in the middle of each front. Each of the windows on the upper section of the main-body walls has different stonework decoration to offer the observant; 14 lofty domes cover the main rectangular body of the structure; there are 56 stores on its exterior and 36 cells in its interior; the structure, which has been completely restored, is used as a bazaar today. According to a contemporary account by Evliya Çelebi, it was guard-

*Üç Şerefeli Mosque, view from the southeast, 1445, Murad II, Edirne.*

ed by night by 60 Janissaries, with the
our locked gates, for the goods inside
were so valuable.

İ. K.

## VIII.I.e **Üç Şerefeli Mosque**

*In the centre, on Hükümet Avenue, to the north
of Eski Mosque and* bedesten *across the park.*

This very attractive mosque has four
minarets, each of which is different from
the other. At the time of its construction,
the mosque was known as Cami-i Cedid
(New Mosque) and Cami-i Kebir (Great
Mosque) as well. However, the name Üç
Şerefeli Mosque —Mosque with Three
*şerefes*— is also encountered in old documents from the very earliest periods. This
name was most likely derived from the
minaret with three *şerefes* located on the
southwest corner of the courtyard. The
mosque has a total of four minarets,
which makes it the earliest mosque with
four minarets in Ottoman architecture.
The minarets rising from the four corners
of the courtyard have different ornamentation: the northeast minaret has parallel
vertical mouldings whereas the northwest
minaret has spiral mouldings; while the
southeast one has smaller diamond
designs executed in two colours of stone
and the southwest minaret with three
*şerefes* is decorated with large chevrons; a
separate staircase leads to each balcony of
this minaret and with its height of 67.50 m.
It is the second highest of the Ottoman
mosques, after the minarets of the
Selimiye Mosque (approximately 71 m.)
constructed in Edirne by Sinan, the
famous 16th-century Turkish architect.
Approaching it, one notices that the

lower windows are elaborately decorated, and all different from each other.
This courtyard, with a fountain in the centre, surrounded by porticoes on four sides
and three portals opening outside —two on
the sides and one on the *mihrab* axis— is the
earliest example in Ottoman architecture
of a courtyard with this layout, bringing
to mind the courtyards of Manisa Great
Mosque and Selçuk İsa Bey Mosque, both
earlier in date and the work of the Emi-

*Üç Şerefeli Mosque,
portico, 1445, Murad
II, Edirne.*

217

rates Period. This plan shall be employed repeatedly in numerous mosques built later; therefore, the Üç Şerefeli Mosque occupies an important place among the mosques of the Ottoman era. Two windows on the north wall, to the west of the central portal have lovely tile tympana with religious inscriptions; the domes covering the bays vary from each other in size and decoration; some of the painted ornamentation on the transitional elements and the portico domes were renovated during the restoration of 1763-1764.

According to the Arabic inscription on its elegant portal to the prayer hall, the construction of the Üç Şerefeli Mosque was completed in 1445. The beginning and completion dates of the construction given on some other inscriptions present in the mosque, however, indicate various dates with a couple of years difference; the reason for this discrepancy is not known exactly. According to legend, a master workman named "Muslihüddin" was put in charge of the mosque's construction in 1427 and 7000 bags of gold were spent on construction. The mosque, like most of the other structures, was damaged in the Thracian earthquake on 29 July 1752. According to the two inscriptions on both spandrels of the central arch of the portico, the mosque was completely restored in the reign of Sultan Mustafa II in 1763-64. As of beginning of 2001, the latest restoration to the inside that began in 1998 was completed and the courtyard was still under restoration.

The prayer hall opens into the courtyard with three portals, the central one of which is the most monumental; and also there is another doorway by the minaret with three *şerefes* giving direct access to the outside. The central dome with a diameter of approximately 24 m was the largest attempted by the Ottomans to that date and the Üç Şerefeli Mosque is the earliest example of a monumental Ottoman mosque with a central dome. This central dome stands on a hexagonal base supported by two self-standing pillars and four pillars embedded in the south and north walls. This hexagonal area is transformed into a square with the triangular areas in the corners covered by tiny domes and striking vaults. This central section is extended to the east and west, each covered with two domes of equal size separated from each other by an arch; all the domes have various painted decorations. The plain *mihrab* and *minbar* add to the beauty of this spacious mosque. According to legend, 70 camel-loads of dye were brought from Persia for the original 18th-century wall paintings, which is allegedly the work of a Persian artist.

İ. K

### VIII.1.f **Saatli Madrasa** (option)

*Located at 14, Çamaşırcılar Street. Just to the east of the courtyard of Üç Şerefeli Mosque.*

Two *madrasas* located side by side to the east of Üç Şerefeli Mosque are the Saatli Madrasa, which literally means Madrasa with Clock, and Peykler Madrasa, which means Madrasa of Running Footmen. However, there are doubts as to which one is Saatli, and which is Peykler. Neither of the two have construction inscriptions. Sources state that Sultan Murad II built Saatli Madrasa together with the Üç Şerefeli Mosque, while Sultan Mehmed I uilt the Peykler Madrasa. The similar rchitectural features of the two structures nake them difficult to identify. However, ince the *madrasa* on the north is located loser to the Üç Şerefeli Mosque, and the *nadrasa* to the south is situated at a higher levation than the mosque itself, it is believed that the one to the north is the aatli Madrasa that was built at the same ime as Üç Şerefeli Mosque. Therefore, he one located to the south, which is at a arther distance from the mosque, is most ikely to be the Peykler Madrasa.

Today the Saatli Madrasa is largely in ruins. The west wall of the structure is faced vith cut stone, while the rest of the walls re built with alternating rows of cut stone nd brick. The inner surface of the dome hat covers the entrance *iwan* behind the portal on the west is decorated with *nuqarnas*. On one side of the courtyard is he summer *dershane iwan* along with the vinter *dershane* area, and the student cells re found on the remaining sides of the courtyard; each chamber in the *madrasa* vas covered with a dome.

İ. K.

## VIII.1.g **Peykler Madrasa** (option)

*Located on Çamaşırcılar Street, next to the Saatli Madrasa. As at 2000 the structure is closed and not in use. The key is at the Vakıflar (Waqfs) Directorate, which is just to the south of Eski Mosque on Talatpaşa Avenue.*

Historical sources indicate that Sultan Mehmed II built the Peykler Madrasa. The structure is faced with cut stone on both he inside and outside. A dome decorated vith *muqarnas* covers the entrance *iwan* located behind the portal on the west facing the Üç Şerefeli Mosque. However,

today, the small doorway on the northeast on Çamaşırcılar Street is used as the entrance. The courtyard surrounded by porticoes on three sides, the arches of which are very attractive with low but pointed forms. The arch in front of the main portal is of the "Bursa" type. Located to the south is the summer *dershane iwan* protruding out together with a winter *dershane* to its east, while on the remaining three sides are the student cells. Both *dershanes* contain a *mihrab*, which suggests that they were also used as *masjids*. Each *dershane* is covered with a dome while each of the student cells is also covered either by a dome or vault.

İ. K.

## VIII.1.h **Beylerbeyi Mosque**

*On Hükümet Avenue. Continue about 150 m.*

*Beylerbeyi Mosque, prayer hall, 1429, Sinaneddin Yusuf Pasha, Edirne.*

*Beylerbeyi Mosque, view from the northwest, 1429, Sinaneddin Yusuf Pasha, Edirne.*

*further past the Üç Şerefeli Mosque, it is on the right, on a slope, behind a cemetery. It can be visited immediately after prayers.*

Not only the sultans, but high-ranking officials, too, had various structures built for public use. The Beylerbeyi of Rumelia, Sinaneddin Yusuf Pasha, is among these high-ranking officials who commissioned buildings for public benefit. He also had the Beylerbeyi Mosque constructed in 1429, from whose *waqf* charter arranged in 1429 by Sinaneddin Yusuf Pasha, we learn that a *madrasa* and an *imaret* were also built in addition to the mosque, but they have not survived to the present day.

The structure stands on a high terrace behind the cemetery, within which are the ruins of a *türbe*. The mosque, faced entirely with cut-stone, has undergone various restorations and all the cut-stone facing and the minaret rising over the northeast

corner have been renovated. The part o the minaret that lies between the *şerefe* an the spire collapsed in the mid-20th centu ry and has been reconstructed. On th north, facing the cemetery is a five-baye portico, the central bay of which is cov ered by a dome, while the others ar vaulted. Past the plain portal with a frag ment of the inscription remaining, on emerges into the central court covere with a dome of 7 m. in diameter, with lantern at the centre. The prayer hall t the south is divided into two sections b an arch, just like the prayer hall of th Nilüfer Hatun İmaret in İznik. The north ern section, planned in rectangular form is covered with a small dome of 3 m. ir diameter supported by stellar vaults whereas the second section to the soutl containing the *mihrab* is covered with half-dome, shaped like an oyster shell reminiscent of the prayer hall of Yahşi Bey

Mosque in Tire. There are traces of wall paintings, especially on the slanting arch separating the prayer hall from the central court. The central court is flanked on the west and the east with a *tabhane,* each of which is covered by a dome and contains a single fireplace and four niches.

İ. K.

### VIII.1.i  Bayezid II Complex

*It is on the other side of the river. It can be reached by either following the sign on Hükümet Avenue just 50 m. from the junction or by taking a* dolmush *minibus to Y.* İmaret, *which leaves by the Sokollu Hammam 50 m. further on in Hükümet Avenue and passes by the Complex. There is an entrance fee for the Museum of Health and an extra charge for the hexagonal structure.*

Even after the Capital was moved to Istanbul, Edirne maintained its importance for a long time; the Bayezid II Complex, dating from the late 15th century, together with the Selimiye Mosque, a masterly work of Ottoman architecture completed in 1575, are the structures that emphasise the importance given to this city.

Sultan Bayezid II personally attended the ceremonies for the laying of foundations for his complex on 25 May 1484. During the ceremonies animals were sacrificed and their meat was distributed to the poor. The complex was completed in a short time; only four years, and then opened for service with great ceremony in 1488.

There are different opinions regarding the identity of the architect who built the complex. According to some researchers, the name of the architect is Hayreddin, while some others believe that it is Yakub Şah Ibn Sultan Şah.

The Complex of Bayezid II in Edirne, built after another complex of the same Sultan in Amasya, is a large group of buildings spread across an area of 22,000 m$^2$, and consisting

*Bayezid II Complex, Madrasa, general view from the southeast, 1488, Bayezid II, Edirne.*

221

*Bayezid II Complex, Darüşşifa, view from the west, 1488, Bayezid II, Edirne.*

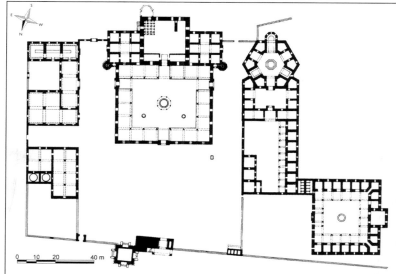

*Plan of Bayezid II Complex, late 15th -century, Edirne.*

*Bayezid II Complex Mosque, view from the courtyard, 1488, Bayezid II, Edirne.*

of a mosque, *madrasa*, *darüşşifa*, *tabhane*, *hammam*, bridge, *imaret* and storerooms. The entrance to the common courtyard, which is surrounded by walls, is through the gates on the north, by the road; to the left of the main gate is the Sinan Ağa Fountain. The mosque is located to the south of the common courtyard; the *darüşşifa* and the *madrasa* are to the west of the common courtyard, whereas to its east is the *imaret*, constructed as two blocks and consisting of a bakery with two ovens, a candle factory, refectory, a larder, and stables; the section containing the ovens and stoves is quite large. In addition to guests and the personnel of the complex, food was also distributed to the poor in the vicinity. Special meals were prepared during Ramadan, religious feasts, and on Fridays; upon the recommendation by a doctor, special food was also prepared for the sick in a separate kitchen.

To the southwest of the complex, outside the courtyard walls, lies the bridge over

Tunca River, This was in order to make the mosque more accessible to those living nearby and thus enlarge the size of the mosque's congregation. The *hammam*, built on the same bank of the Tunca River as the rest of the complex near the bridge, does not exist today; according to historical sources, it was a double *hammam* comprising separate sections for women and men.

*Bayezid II Complex Darüşşifa, view from the west, 1488, Bayezid II, Edirne.*

*Bayezid II Complex, Darüşşifa, interior, 1488, Bayezid II, Edirne.*

*At the beginning of 2001, the imaret complex was closed and in a dilapidated state, while the mosque was closed for restoration, but the darüşşifa and the madrasa are in a very good state and in use by Trakya University as the Museum of Health, and a family health centre respectively.*

## Bayezid II Mosque

Three entrances lead from the common courtyard to the mosque courtyard: one is on the north, and the other two are on the sides. The courtyard is covered with marble plates and surrounded by domed porticoes on all four sides; at the centre of the rectangular courtyard is a marble

fountain. In the seven-bayed portico in the front, the dome covering the central bay in front of the portal, is built higher to emphasise the entrance axis. There are also two outdoor mihrabs in the portico. At the corners of the *tabhanes* adjoining the east and west of the prayer hall are elegant minarets 38 m. in height with a single şerefe and fluted bodies of 3.25 m. in diameter. Both *tabhanes* consist of nine bays, each of which is covered by a dome, with four *iwans* opening onto a central court and rooms in the corners. There is no direct connection between the *tabhanes* and the mosque: the windows in the walls between the *tabhanes* and the mosque are today blocked up.

From the courtyard a portal with an elegant and elaborate canopy filled with *muqarnas* opens into the prayer hall, which covers an area of about 500 m² and is covered with a dome of 20.55 m. in diameter rising upon a polygonal drum. The *mihrab* and the *minbar* are made of marble and the royal loge is noteworthy especially for the forest of reused small columns, on which it rests. The wooden door wings and the cupboard doors and window shutters are elaborately decorated.

## Madrasa

According to most researchers who refer to the complex, the *madrasa* was a medical training institution. Some studies indicate that students who completed their education in the *madrasa* went on to study medicine in the adjoining hospital while continuing to reside in the *madrasa*. However, no clarifying evidence regarding this matter is known from historical sources or the known *waqf* charters of the complex. The Bayezid II Madrasa is a single-storey

ectangular structure with an open court-
ard. The entrance at the centre of the
ast front opens into the courtyard sur-
ounded by domed porticoes on all four
des; there are traces of a fountain that
vas once located in the centre of this
ourtyard. The 18 student cells, each
overed by a dome and each with a fire-
lace, were placed at the north, south,
nd west wings. The *dershane* in the mid-
le of the western side, opposite the
ntrance, is a rectangular chamber pro-
-uding out and covered by a large dome,
nd on its east wall a stone staircase leads
o an interesting balcony, which would
robably have been used as a library.

**)arüşşifa**

o the west of the mosque and southeast
f the *madrasa* lies the *darüşşifa* consisting

of two courtyards and the main structure,
all lined up along the north-south axis.
The western side of the first rectangular
courtyard is lined with domed cells
behind a vaulted portico. On the northern part of the eastern side are domed
chambers that had various functions and
on the southern side two large double-
domed chambers flank the *iwan* giving
access to the second courtyard.

The second courtyard, which is entered
through an *iwan* in the centre of the
southern side of the first courtyard, is
smaller and has two domed *iwans* on the
sides, each flanked with two domed cells.
The cells in the first courtyard and the
eastern cells in the second courtyard are
today used as exhibition halls by the
Museum of Health.

The most attractive structure of the
*darüşşifa* is the hexagonal main building:

*Yıldırım Mosque, view
from the west, 1389-
1402, Bayezid I,
Edirne.*

225

*Yıldırım Mosque, prayer hall looking from east to the west, 1389-1402, Bayezid I, Edirne.*

the central hexagonal hall is surrounded by an *iwan* in the centre of each side and a square room with a fireplace on each corner. The *iwan*s and chambers are each covered by an individual dome and the chambers are entered through the *iwan*s. The hexagonal main hall also has a rather large dome rising on a cornice of *muqarnas*. The central lantern of the dome and the windows on the far walls of the *iwan*s illuminate the main hall. A pool with a fountain is located in the centre of the main hall and the *iwan* opposite the entrance *iwan* is deeper than the rest of the structure and protrudes out. Today the structure is an exhibition hall where scenes of Ottoman daily life are excellently presented with mannequins.

There is some information in historical sources about the function of the various sections of the *darüşşifa*. For example, it is reported that the sections in the first courtyard were used as doctors' rooms, a pantry, a kitchen, isolation rooms for the mentally ill, a laundry and so on, while medicine was prepared and stored in the rooms that opened onto the two *iwan* opposite each other in the second courtyard. Again, based on historical records it is known that on certain occasions musicians performed in the large *iwan* of the hexagonal main structure. According to

gend, the sound of sprinkling water had
soothing effect on the mentally ill, and
as helpful in their treatment.

İ. K.

### III.1.j  **Yıldırım Mosque**

*you are coming from the town centre follow
alatpaşa Avenue in the direction of Kapıkule and
ulgaria; 200 m. after passing over the Tunca
iver, take a right turn and pass over another
mall bridge, you will reach Yıldırım Mosque.
rom Bayezid II Complex, follow the embankment
the west and when you reach the main road
rn right and 200 m. later turn right again, and
ast the small bridge is the mosque.*

dirne, conquered by Sultan Murad I in
362, became the capital of the Ottoman
tate in 1368. Most of the structures built
uring the years following the conquest
ave not survived to the present day. In
dirne, the oldest mosque still standing is
ae one built by and named after Sultan
ayezid I (1389-1402), who is also known
s Yıldırım –the Lightning. According to
aany sources, the Yıldırım Mosque was
onstructed on the foundations of a
aurch. The noticeable errors in the design
f the structure and the placement of the
ihrab seem to verify this. However, some
esearchers argue that the mosque was not
uilt upon the foundations of a church, but
as actually designed and constructed as a
aosque. It is a well-known fact that in the
arly times of Islam, churches in con-
uered cities were converted into mosques
ad used as such. Moreover, it is known
aat before the construction of the Great
aosque in Damascus, Muslims wor-
aipped together with the Christians under
ae same roof for a while. For this reason,

it is quite possible that the Yıldırım
Mosque may have been converted from a
church, and there is no reason why this
should be regarded as odd.

Some sources refer to the Yıldırım Mosque
as the Küpeli Mosque, literally Mosque
with Earrings. According to one legend,
the latter name was attached to the mosque
due to the rings and the chandeliers hang-
ing in the structure, while according to
another story, the second name was given
to it because Sultan Bayezid I's daughter
Küpeli Sultan sold her diamond earrings
and used the money for the mosque.

The structure, built with alternating rows
of brick and stone, has charming brick–
and stone– decoration on the tympana of
the windows. The western part of the
building protrudes out and has a door
opening into the prayer hall. Today the
portico, which originally had a wooden
roof and was located on the eastern side
of the mosque, is in ruins; the door to
the right opens into a *tabhane,* which is
also in ruins but has some lovely stucco
decoration above the fireplace. Passing
through the main doorway on the east,
one enters an *iwan* with a tiny doorway
on the left opening into the second *tabhane,* which is used as a storeroom for
funeral materials today. This entrance
*iwan* opens into a domed area in the centre, which is flanked with three more
*iwans* on the north, south, and west,
thus, giving the prayer hall a cruciform
shape. The *mihrab* has been placed in a
corner of the southern *iwan.* All four
*iwans* have barrel vaults whereas the central area is covered with a dome rising
directly above a cornice of Turkish triangles. The wall paintings derive from a
19th-century renovation.

İ. K.

İnci Kuyul

*Life in the palace,
Surname-i Vehbi,
3593, fol.170a,
Levni, 1720, Library
of Topkapı Palace,
İstanbul.*

alaces (*saray* in Turkish) played an impornt role in reflecting the political, social,
nd cultural character of the periods in
hich they were built. Palace complexes
ere where sultans lived and handled
ffairs of the state. During the Emirates
eriod when Anatolia was politically and
conomically weak, palaces were gener-
lly small and far from monumental. Even
o, palaces, being both residential and
dministrative edifices, had to be built
with more care than other structures.

n Batuta, a North African traveller who
oured Anatolia in the 14<sup>th</sup> century, pro-
ides information about palaces in the
mirate period, although none of these
alaces have survived to the present day.
part from the Aydın Emirate's palace at
irgi, each of the Bey mansions in
lanya, Eğirdir, Antalya, Beçin, Ladik,
nd Bursa were apparently modest
alaces. Sadly, none of these structures
ave survived.

sman Gazi built the first known
ttoman palace in Yenişehir, which was
onquered in 1299 and subsequently
ecame the scene of an extensive con-
truction operation. Of these structures
nly the remains of a *hammam* have sur-
ived to the present day. Another palace
nown from sources was situated in
ursa and dates to the period of Orhan
azi; this structure, enlarged with vari-
us additions since the time of its con-
truction, has not survived either. Locat-
d inside the citadel, the Bursa Palace
vas completely abandoned after Edirne
ecame the capital.

wo palaces were constructed in Edirne,
vhich came under Turkish rule in 1362.
he first was known as Saray-ı Atik, lit-
rally the Old Palace, in which Sultans
ayezid I and Murad II lived. This palace

was constructed by Sultan Murad I, who
conquered Edirne. The 17<sup>th</sup>-century
Turkish traveller Evliya Çelebi recounts
that this palace, located somewhere near
the Selimiye Mosque, was built between
the years 1365-1368 and that several
structures were added subsequently.
Sultan Murad II initiated the construction
of the second palace in Edirne and his son
Sultan Mehmed II had the structure
enlarged and completed. The Yeni Saray
(New Palace), also known variously as
Saray-ı Cedid-i Amire (New Royal
Palace), Tunca Palace (named after the
river) and Hünkar Bahçesi Palace (Royal
Garden Palace), Edirne Saray-ı
Hümayunu (Edirne Royal Palace), was
located in the district presently known as
Sarayiçi. In the 1870s the basement of the
palace was used as a storehouse for
ammunition and in 1876 the palace
exploded when the storehouse was set on
fire. Only some remains of the palace
have survived.
The New Edirne Palace consisted of five
large courtyards with buildings located
around them. Housing about 6000 people, it maintained its importance even
after the capital was moved to Istanbul. It
is known that sultans resided here tem-
porarily from time to time. The palace,
spread across a wide area, continuously
underwent expansion and became a
source of inspiration for palaces built in
Istanbul.
Sultan Mehmed II, also known as
Mehmed the Conqueror for he added
Istanbul to Ottoman territory in 1453,
immediately ordered the construction of
a palace. We know of this palace called
the Saray-ı Atik (Old Palace) where
Mehmed II lived for some years (1454-
1478), through information provided by

*Entertainment in the palace, Külliyat-ı Katibi, 1450-80, R.989, 93a, Library of Topkapı Palace, İstanbul.*

Evliya Çelebi and from manuscript miniatures. Saray-ı Atik was established where Istanbul University stands today, and it is known that the palace was spread across a large area and was surrounded by a circuit of two walls.

Shortly after the first one, Sultan Mehmed II ordered the construction of a second palace. The Saray-ı Cedid (New Palace), known as the Topkapı Palace today, was constructed at Sarayburnu (Seraglio Point), overlooking the Marmara Sea, the entrance of the Bosphorus and the Golden Horn. The Topkapı Palace covers an area of about 700,000 m$^2$ and is a large complex of buildings, resembling the Old Palace of Edirne with regard to its design and the names of some of its pavilions and kiosks. For a while after the construction of the Topkapı Palace, the sultans continued to live in the Old Palace with their families and children, while carrying out the state affairs from the Topkapı Palace. In 1578, Murad III completed the moving of his *harem* to the Topkapı Palace. Thus, when the Old Palace lost its important status, it became a place of exile or a prison for the children, women and the *cariyes* and especially the mother of the deceased or dethroned sultans –the ex-*Valide Sultan*.

Topkapı Palace comprises three sections: the *Birun*, the *Enderun* and the *Mabeyn*. The section that attracts Westerners the most is the *Harem* inside the *Enderun*. Many *cariyes* were housed in this Ottoman palace, having either been bought or taken as slaves and they were kept at hand for private service to the sultan. It is known, however, that when the Ottoman Empire was established the word *harem* had a different meaning than that fancied by most people today: The *harem* consisted of private apartments for the reigning Sultan, apartments for the *Valide Sultan*, other apartments for the use of women, for the Sultan's *ikbal*s, the princes and princesses of the imperial house, the *usta*s, the *kalfa*s and the *cariye*s. The men chosen among those who were either enslaved during conquests or who were bought, were educated in the *Enderun* to serve the state, while the healthy women were given reading, writing, and courtesy lessons in preparation for special services to the Sultan. Although the captives had the status of slaves, they were in a different position from those bought or sold as property.

The palaces are important because of their architectural design; they are also important as buildings that reflect the lifestyles of the Ottoman sultans. The abandonment of the Topkapı Palace and the move to Dolmabahçe Palace in 1853 is the best example of these changes in the lifestyles of Ottoman sultans: the Dolmabahçe Palace and the other palaces are single massive structures built in one stage like European Palaces.

*According to legend, at one time during the 1350s, some Ottoman soldiers stopped to rest on a meadow while crossing from Anatolia to Rumelia. Some 40 of these soldiers paired up to wrestle with each other. Some days after, arriving at the place known as Kırkpınar, they took up wrestling once again. Finally, two of the wrestlers became finalists. When these two wrestled with each other, neither was able to emerge victorious, and eventually both died of exhaustion. They were then buried at the place where they died. Years later, the soldiers who returned to the place to visit the graves of their friends saw that a spring had surfaced where they were buried* and named the place Kırkların Pınarı (Spring of the Forty). Ever since then, wrestling competitions, originally among soldiers but later among wrestlers in general, have been organised at this location, whose name with time has changed to Kırkpınar, literally Forty Springs.

The wrestlers of Kırkpınar rub oil all over their bodies prior to wrestling. They wear trousers called kıspet, the waist and lower parts of the legs of which are tightly bound. Kıspet is usually made of calfskin, and is held around the waist by a thin leather cord or string instead of elastic. The wrestling continues until one of the wrestlers gives up or one of them becomes the winner.

Kırkpınar wrestling matches take place at Sarayiçi every year at the end of June and the beginning of July. The Hükümet Avenue,

Sarayiçi is across the river at the end of the Avenue.

The city of Edirne is embellished with many edifices, the most remarkable of which is the Selimiye Complex in the city centre, to the east of the Eski Mosque, rising on a slope dominating the skyline with its four minarets. Built for Sultan Selim II by the great architect Sinan in the latter half of the $16^{th}$ century, it was considered the masterpiece of his career by Sinan himself.

The area to the west of Eski Mosque is known as Kaleiçi (Citadel). This area was totally rebuilt after a devastating fire in 1905. It is a very pleasant area for a stroll with its old houses and traces of Jewish, Christian and Muslim culture and mosaics.

There are several bridges over the Tunca River, all of them built by the Ottomans. They are all beautiful and worth visiting.

| | |
|---|---|
| Abdalan-ı Rum | The itinerant heterodox dervishes in Anatolia. |
| Acemi ocağı | The barracks where conscripts for Janissary Corps were trained. |
| Ahi | A trade guild organization established by tradesmen and artisans. The members of the organization were called the same. |
| Ahiyan-ı Rum | The *Ahi*s of Anatolia. |
| Akritoi | The Byzantine frontier troops. |
| Aralık | The passageway between the *soyunmalık* and *ılıklık* in a Turkish *hammam*. |
| Arasta | A row of shops aligned along an (un)covered street. |
| Ayet | Verses in the Koran. |
| Balbal | The engraved stone pillars in a human shape that are put on some tombs and tumuli by Turks. |
| Bedesten | A commercial building with two aisles and covered with domes of equal size. The most precious merchandise was kept in the *bedesten*s, which functioned like banks do today. |
| Bey | The ruler of an independent emirate; the governor of a *sanjak;* a title of respect for the men of the upper classes. |
| Beylerbey | The *bey* of the *bey*s: the highest rank in the provincial government of the Ottoman Empire. |
| Beylik | Any district ruled by a *Bey,* so the Emirates are called *Beylik* in Turkish. |
| Bezzaz | Sellers of fabrics. |
| Birun | The public section of the sultan's palace, which includes the administration. |
| Boza | A viscous drink made from fermented barley, maize or wheat. |
| Caliph | From Arabic *Khalifa*, meaning the supreme head of the Muslim community in the line of the Porphet's successors. |
| Cami | Mosque in Turkish. Also transliterated as *jami'*. |
| Caravanserai | Hostel along main travelling routes to accommodate travellers and safeguard their goods. |
| Cariye | "Slave girl", the lowest degree in the hierarchy of the palace harem. |
| Çelebi | A title of respect, given to men of the upper classes; the epithet of Sultan Mehmed I. |
| Cuerda seca | A decorative process used for ceramics. Before firing and imprinting the desired decorative motifs, a dark line of manganese is drawn around them to separate the various colours of the enamel or glaze. |
| Darülhadis | A *madrasa* for studying the *hadith* (*hadis* in Turkish). |
| Darülhuffaz | A *madrasa* for training of memorising the Koran. |
| Darüşşifa | A hospital, sometimes with an asylum for the insane. |

| | |
|---|---|
| Darüttıb | A *madrasa* where the medical sciences were taught. |
| Defterdar | Head of the Treasury. |
| Dershane | A classroom (especially in a *madrasa*). |
| Dervish | A member of a Muslim religious order noted for devotiona exercises. |
| Devşirme | The boys recruited from Christian families to be trained a janissary, or officials for the palace; the system for recruitin these boys. |
| Divan-ı Hümayun | The Imperial Council, chaired by the Grand *vizier* (*vezir* in Turk ish), forming the central organ of the Ottoman government. |
| Emir | Governor, Prince, dignitary. The ruler of an emirate or prin cipality. |
| Enderun | The inner section of the sultan's palace containing the *harem* the Sultan's private apartments, and the Palace School for the education of high-ranking state and palace officials. |
| Engobe | A mixture of non-vitrifiable earth, applied to all or part of a piece of pottery to cover, decorate or outline drawings on it |
| Ferman | An edict of the sultan. |
| Fiqh | Muslim canonical jurisprudence. |
| Funduq | In Northern Africa, a hostel for merchants and their pack ani mals; store for merchandise and a commercial centre, equiva lent of a *caravanserai* or *khan* in Oriental Islam (*Han* in Turkey) |
| Futuwwa | A semi-religious fraternity that originated during the Abbasic Empire and spread across the Muslim lands though the Mid dle Ages. |
| Gazi | A warrior fighting on behalf of Islam. |
| Hacı | In Turkish a Muslim who has been on a pilgrimage to Mecca |
| Hadis | (*Hadith* in Arabic and Lit. "sayings".) Tradition related to acts, say ings and attitudes of the Prophet Muhammad and his companions. |
| Halvet | The private chambers in a public bath. |
| Hammam | Public or private bathhouse. |
| Han | (*Khan* in Arabic) Inn, lodgings for travellers and merchants or the main caravan routes: Store and hostel in large centres. (See also *funduq* and *caravanserai*). |
| Hanikah | A structure built for hosting itinerant *dervishes,* scholars etc. during the Anatolian Seljuq period. |
| Harem | The women's apartments in a Muslim household. |
| Hatun | A title of respect, for women of the upper classes. |
| Hodja | A Muslim teacher. |
| Ibn | Son of (Arabic). |

| | |
|---|---|
| Ikbal | Favourite women of a sultan; the second highest degree in the hierarchy of the palace *harem.* |
| Ilıklık | *Tepidarium*/lukewarm-bath area in a Turkish hammam where bathers would rest after bathing. |
| Imam | One who presides Islamic prayer. A guide, chief, spiritual model or cleric, and sometimes also a politician, in a Muslim society. |
| Imaret | A complex of buildings and institutions supported by a *waqf;* after the 16th century the word was used to mean a soup kitchen for the poor. |
| Iwan | Vaulted hall, walled on three sides with a large opening arch and vaulted recess. |
| Jami' | Main mosque where daily prayer is celebrated and that of Friday. |
| Janissary Corps | (*Yeniçeri Ocağı* in Turkish.) The sultan's standing infantry corps, recruited from the devşirme and paid from the Treasury. |
| Ka'ba | (Litterally. "cube".) Temple in Mecca. Centre of Islamic religion. |
| Kadı | Judge of Islamic canon law and Ottoman law and the governor of a township called *kadılık.* |
| Kadıasker | The highest judicial authority of the empire after the *Shaykh al-Islam.* There were two *Kadıasker,* one for Rumelia and one for Anatolia. Also known as *kazasker.* |
| Kalemişi | The colourful decoration done with a *kalem* (pen) on a plastered surface. |
| Kalfa | The second lowest degree in the hierarchy of the palace harem. |
| Kapıkulu | "Slave of the Porte", a *devşirme* or slave employed in military, administrative or Palace service. |
| Kaplıca | Spas, hot springs used for therapeutic purposes, and facilities on such springs. |
| Kaptan-ı Derya | Grand Admiral of the Ottoman fleet. |
| Katı' technique | A technique which can be described as "paper inlay". The pattern is drawn on either paper or leather then the closed spaces are cut out with a knife. It is then stuck onto paper, leather or glass. |
| Kese | A coarse, cloth bath glove; a small bag or pouch. |
| Khanqa | Monastery or hostel for *sufis* or *derviches.* |
| Koran | (From the Arabic root qr', "to recite, to read".) Sacred text of the Islamic revelation, transmitted by the Archangel Gabriel to the Prophet Muhammad. |
| Külhan | A stoking hole in a *hammam.* |
| Külliye | A complex of several buildings where the mosque is at the centre. The other buildings were the *madrasa, imaret, han, hammam, darüşşifa*, etc. |
| Kümbet | A monumental tomb, usually covered with a dome hidden under a spire. |

| | |
|---|---|
| Kündekari and Fake Kündekari | A woodwork technique. Polygonal pieces decorated with carved floral motifs are held together with rods and mortise without the use of glue or nails. When nails or glue are used it is fake *kündekari.* |
| Mabeyn | A section in an Ottoman palace where the sultan received ambassadors, envoys and the viziers. |
| Madrasa | (*Medrese* in Turkish.) Islamic school of sciences (theology, law, Koran, etc.) and lodgings for students. |
| Masjid | A mosque without a *minbar.* The Friday Service cannot take place in a *masjid* due to the absence of a *minbar.* |
| Mektep | Primary School, also known as *sıbyan mektebi.* |
| Menzil han | A *han* at a day's journey. |
| Mevlevihane | A place for the Mevlevi Order dervishes, also known as whirling *dervishes.* |
| Mihrab | Niche in a *qibla* wall indicating the direction of Mecca towards which worshippers faced when praying. |
| Minbar | Pulpit in a mosque where the *imam* preaches his sermon *(khutba)* to the faithful. |
| Müderris | The chief teacher and administrator of a *madrasa.* |
| Müezzin | Religious Muslim administrator, in charge of announcing the five daily prayers from the top of the mosque's minaret. |
| Mu'id | A tutor in a *madrasa,* who assisted the *müderris.* |
| Muqarnas | Stalactite or honeycomb ornament which adorns cupolas or corbels of a building. |
| Muvakkithane | Clock room equipped with the necessary apparatus to calculate the time for prayer, also where horoscopes were read. |
| Müzehhip | An illuminator of manuscripts. |
| Namaz | Muslim ritual prayers exercised five times a day. |
| Namazgah | An open-air place on inter-city roads or recreation areas for performing the *namaz.* |
| Naskhi | (Lit. "coppied".) One of the most widespread styles of calligraphy used in Arabic script. |
| Nişancı | The secretary of the Imperial Council who checked the *tuğra* to be attached to official orders and letters. |
| Ocak | A fireplace, hearth; a household; any institution for training recruits. |
| -oğlu | "Son of" in Turkish, or "- oğulları" plural. |
| Opus sectile | Stone and / or marble mosaic, in which the pieces are cut in different shapes and sizes and fit side by side forming generally geometric designs. |

| | |
|---|---|
| Qibla | Direction of *Ka'ba*, towards which believers turn to face for prayer. Wall of mosque in which the *mihrab* is situated. |
| Qubba | Dome. By extension, monument erected upon the grave of a saint. |
| Ribat | Fortified enclosure for religious warriors (North Africa); a hospice for pilgrims (Mamluk Egypt, Palestine and Syria). |
| Rumi | Stylised leaf motif; half-cut palmette motif. |
| Sadaqa | Alms. |
| Şadırvan | Fountain with taps and a pool for ritual ablutions. |
| Sancak Bey | The governor of a Sanjak, subdivision of a beylerbeyilik. |
| Şehzade | Prince. |
| Şemse | Sunburst motif. |
| Şerefe | Balcony of a minaret. |
| Sevap | Meritorious in God's sight. |
| Sgraffito | A technique of scratching through one layer so as to reveal another of contrasting colour. |
| Shaykh al-Islam | (*Şeyhülislam* in Turkish.) The head in the hierarchy of the doctors of Muslim canon law, tradition and theology. |
| Sherbet | Sweet fruit drink; a medicinal drink. |
| Sıbyan mektebi | See *mektep*. |
| Sıcaklık | Caldarium/hot-bath area in a Turkish hammam. |
| Şifahane | Hospital; lunatic asylum. |
| Slip | A creamy diluted clay, used for decorating pottery. |
| Solomon's knot | A motif of interlocking broken or curving lines, like a David's star. |
| Soyunmalık | The apoditerium/disrobing hall in a Turkish *hammam*. |
| Spandrel | The triangular area between two arches, or between the outer curve of an arch and the horizontal line from its apex and the vertical line from the pillar supporting it. |
| Squinch | An arch placed diagonally at each corner of a square and filled decoratively with a variety of methods, providing the transition from the cubical walls to the sphere of the dome. |
| Sufi | Mystical or ascetic order in Islam. Mystic, a devotee. |
| Sunna | (Literally "tradition".) For Orthodox Islam, group of traditions of the Prophet in which legal advisers and theologians find support and foundations to establish the content of Islamic Law arising from the Koran. |
| Sunni | Follower of *Sunna*. "Sunnism", a political and religious system opposed to "shi'ism". Sunnites are divided into 4 schools: *maliki, hanbali, hanafi, shafi'i.* |
| Suq | Market place. |
| Sura | Chapter of the Koran. |

| | |
|---|---|
| Tabhane | Guestroom at a mosque for itinerant *dervishes* and other travellers. |
| Tandır | Heating arrangement consisting of a brazier which is put under a table which is covered with a blanket; or in the *hans* of Seljuq period, clay-lined pit or earthenware jar buried in the ground and used for cooking and heating. |
| Tekke | A centre for *dervishes,* where they could gather, worship and live. |
| Tezhip | Art of illuminating the borders of scriptures in a manuscript. |
| Tile Mosaic | Pieces of different colour tile pieces cut in certain shapes and placed in plaster to form a composition. |
| Tımar | Small military fief with an annual value of less than 20,000 akches. |
| Tımarlı Sipahi | Man-at-arms holding a *tımar* fief. |
| Traşlık | A small room in a Turkish *hammam* used the removal of body hair. |
| Tuğra | The sultan's official monogram, attached to state documents to confirm their legality. |
| Türbe | A monumental tomb, sometimes with a crypt downstairs. |
| Turkish triangles | A form of transitional with triangles and chevrons from the cubical walls to the dome. |
| Usta | The third highest degree in the hierarchy of harem women. |
| Valide Sultan | The mother of the reigning Sultan, therefore the most powerful woman in the Empire. |
| Vezir | (Vizier.) Minister. The highest vezir was called the Grand Vezir or Sadrazam. |
| Yeniçeri Ağası | Chief officer of the Janissary Corps. |
| Wahhabi | A sect of Islam, which forbids any mediator like a prophet, saints, veneration of the dead or of their tombs, or votive offerings and supports the belief that the worship to God must be direct. |
| Waqf | (*Vakıf* in Turkish.) Endowment in perpetuity, usually land or property, from which the revenue was reserved for the upkeep of religious foundations. |
| Waqf charter | (Vakfiye in Turkish.) The deed of endowment of a *waqf.* |
| Zawiya | Small *tekke*; a hospice for *dervishes* and travellers. Establishment reserved for religious teaching designed for training *shaykh*s; includes mausoleum of a saint, built on the site where he lived. |
| Zellij | Small enamelled ceramic tiles used to decorate monuments or interiors. |

| Name | Born-Died | Information |
|---|---|---|
| Abdülaziz | 1830-1876 | Ottoman Sultan |
| Abdülhamid II | 1842-1918 | Ottoman Sultan |
| Abu Bakr | c. 570-634 | First caliph after Muhammad |
| Ahmet Gazi | ?-1391 | Emir of Menteşe |
| Ahmet Paşa | ?-1497 | *Müderris, kadı* and poet |
| Ahmet Vefik Pasha | 19$^{th}$ c. | Governor of Bursa |
| Ahmeti | ?-1413 | Poet and author on Ottoman History |
| Ahmet Bican Efendi | 15$^{th}$ c. | Ottoman *sufi* and scholar |
| Alaaddin Ali | ?-? | Son of Sultan Murad II |
| Alâeddin Keykubad I | ?-1237 | Anatolian Seljuq Sultan (1220-37) |
| Alem Şah | 1466-1503 | Son of Bayezid II |
| Andrić, Ivo | 1892-1975 | Yugoslavian author, who won the Nobel Prize |
| Aziza Hatun | 14$^{th}$ -15$^{th}$ c. | Wife of İsa Bey of Aydın Emirate |
| Babinger, Franz | 1891-1967 | German Turkologist and historian |
| Bartolomeu Dias | 1450-1500 | Portugese sailor |
| Bayalun Hatun | 13$^{th}$-14$^{th}$ c. | Wife of Osman Gazi (?) or another name for Nilüfer Hatun |
| Bayezid I | 1360-1403 | Ottoman Sultan, also known as Yıldırım Bayezid, The father of Sultan Mehmed I, and Süleyman Çelebi, İsa Çelebi and Musa Çelebi |
| Bayezid II | 1447-1512 | Ottoman Sultan, the father of Selim I |
| Bayezid Paşa | ?-1421 | Grand *Vizier* |
| Bellini, Gentile | 1429-1507 | Venetian painter |
| Bellini, Giovanni | 1430-1516 | Venetian painter |
| Börklüce Mustafa | ?-1416-19 | Ottoman rebel |
| Bülbül Hatun | 15$^{th}$ c. | Wife of Karaca Pasha |
| Cantacuzenus | ?-1383 | Epithet of Byzantine Emperor John VI, ruled 1341-54 |
| Cem Sultan | 1459-1495 | Son of Sultan Mehmed II |
| Charles VIII | 1470-1498 | King of France |
| Cüneyd | ?-? | Aydın Bey |
| Davud of Kayseri | 14$^{th}$ c. | *Müderris* |
| Dernschwamm, Hans | 1494-1568 | German traveller |
| Devlet Hatun | ?-1414 | Devletşah Hatun, the wife of Sultan Bayezid I |
| Ducas | 1400-1470 | Byzantine chronicler |
| Emir Süleyman Çelebi | ?-1411 | Son of Mehmed I |

| | | |
|---|---|---|
| Emir Sultan | 1368/69-1429/30 | Ottoman *sufi* and son-in-law of Bayezid I |
| Ertuğrul Bey | ?-1281 | Father of Osman Gazi |
| Evliya Çelebi | 1611-1681 | Ottoman traveller |
| Firuz Bey (Hoca) | ?-1402 | Ottoman Commander |
| Friedrich I Barbarossa | c. 1122-1190 | German Emperor, who passed through the Balkans and Anatolia on the Third Crusade and drowned in the Tarsus River. |
| Gazi Umur Bey | ?-1348 | Aydın bey, also known as Bahaeddin |
| Geyikli Baba | 14<sup>th</sup> c. | Heterodox Islamic religious man during the reign of Orhan Gazi |
| Gıyaseddin Keyhusrev II | 1221/22-1246 | Anatolian Seljuq Sultan |
| Grelot | ?17<sup>th</sup> c. | Traveller |
| Gülşah Hatun | ?-1487 | Wife of Sultan Mehmed II; buried at Bursa |
| Hacı İvaz Paşa | ?-1429 | Son of Ahi Bayezid, second *vizier* to Sultan Murad II, supervised the construction of Yeşil Türbe |
| Hacı Umur bin Menteşe | ?-1400 | Member of Menteşe dynasty |
| Hafsa Hatun | 14<sup>th</sup> c. | Daughter of İsa Bey of Aydın Emirate, wife of Bayezid I |
| Hafsa Sultan | ?-1534 | Wife of Sultan Selim I |
| Halil Hayreddin Paşa (Çandarlı) | ? -1389 | Grand *Vizier*, founder of the Janissary Corps |
| Halil Yahşi Bey | 15<sup>th</sup> c. | Governor of Aydın Sanjak |
| Hallacı Mansur | 857-922 | Heterodox Islamic religious man |
| Hartmann, R. | ?-? | German scholar |
| Hızır Bey | 14<sup>th</sup> c. | Son of Mehmed and Aydın Bey (1348-60) |
| Hızırşah | ?-1410 | Last Saruhan Bey (1388-90 and 1403-10) |
| Holbein, Hans | 1460-1524 | Known as "the Elder", German painter |
| Holophira | 14<sup>th</sup> c. | Also Nilüfer Hatun, wife of Orhan Gazi |
| Hüsnüşah Hatun | 15<sup>th</sup>-beginning of 16th c. | Wife of Bayezid II |
| Ibn Battuta | 1304-1369 | Traveller from al-Andalus |
| İlyas Bey | ?-1421 | Menteşe Bey, son of Mehmed |

| | | |
|---|---|---|
| ıe Bey (Eyne Bey) | 14th c. | Ottoman officer |
| a Bey | ?-? | Aydın Bey (1360-90), son of Mehmed Bey |
| hak Çelebi (Muzaffereddin) | ?-1388 | Saruhan Bey (1366-88) |
| ıhak Paşa | ?-1485 | Grand *Vizier* |
| ohn III Ducas Vatatzes | 1193-1254 | Nicean Byzantine Emperor (1222-54) |
| ustinian I | 482-565 | Byzantine Emperor (527-65) |
| ʌaraca Pasha | ?-1456 | Beylerbey of Rumelia, also known as Karaca Bey |
| ʌazanoğlu Mehmed Bey | 15th c. | A local potentate from Tire |
| ʌılıç Arslan II | ?-1192 | Anatolian Seljuq Sultan |
| ʌitsikis, Dimitri | 1935- | Contemporary Greek historian |
| ʌöse Mihail | 14th c. | Ottoman army commander |
| ʌüpeli Sultan | 15th c. | Daughter of Bayezid I |
| ʌotto, Lorenzo | 1480-1556 | Venetian painter |
| ʌahmud I | 1696-1754 | Ottoman Sultan (1730-54) |
| ʌehmed Bey | ?-1334 | Son of Aydın, Aydın Bey (1308-34) |
| ʌehmed I | c. 1389 -1421 | Ottoman Sultan also known as Çelebi Mehmed, father of Murad II |
| ʌehmed II | ?-1423 | Karamanid Bey |
| ʌehmed II | 1432-1481 | Ottoman Sultan also known as Mehmed the Conqueror |
| ʌenteşe Bey | ?-1296 | Originally an admiral of Anatolian Seljuqs who founded the Menteşe Emirate in 1282 |
| ʌesut Bey | ?-1319 | Menteşe Bey |
| ʌevlana Celaleddin Rumi | ?-1273 | Founder of the Mevlevi order of the whirling dervishes |
| ʌichael Ducas | 14th c.-? | Byzantine scientist and doctor |
| ʌichael VIII Palaeologus | 1224-1282 | Byzantine Emperor |
| ʌolla Şemseddin Fenari | 1350-1430 | Ottoman Sheikh-al-Islam and scholar |
| ʌontaigne | 1533-1592 | French author |
| ʌurad I | c. 1326-1389 | Ottoman Sultan also known as Hüdavendigar, the father of Bayezid I |
| ʌurad II | 1403/4-1451 | Ottoman Sultan, the father of Mehmed II |
| ʌusa Bey | ?-? | Aydın Bey |
| ʌusa Çelebi | ?-1413 | Son of Bayezid I |
| ʌustafa II | 1664-1703 | Ottoman Sultan (1695-1703) |
| ʌutasım | 776-842 | Abbasid Caliph |

| | | |
|---|---|---|
| Nilüfer Hatun | 14<sup>th</sup> c. | Originally Holophira, the wife of Orhan Gazi, also known as Bayalun Hatun (?) |
| Nizam al-Mulk | 1018-1092 | Grand *Vizier* of the Great Seljuq Empire |
| | | |
| Orhan Bey | ?- before 1344 | Menteşe Bey |
| Orhan Gazi | c. 1281-1362 | Also known as Orhan Bey, second Ottoman Sultan, father of Murad I |
| Osman Gazi | c. 1258-1326 | Also known as Osman Bey, founder of the Ottoman Empire |
| | | |
| Parvillé, Léon | 19<sup>th</sup> c. | French architect, employed for the restoration of Bursa monuments destroyed in the earthquake of 1855 |
| Postinpuş Baba | 14<sup>th</sup> c. | Heterodox religious man of Khorasan |
| | | |
| Saruhan Bey | ?-1345 | Founder of Saruhan Emirate |
| Savcı Bey | 14<sup>th</sup> c. | Son of Sultan Murad I |
| Şehinşah | 1461-1511 | Son of Bayezid II |
| Selim I | 1467-1520 | Ottoman Sultan (1512-20) also known as Yavuz Selim, father of Süleyman the Magnificent |
| | | |
| Şemseddin | 15<sup>th</sup> c. | Kadı of Bursa |
| Sheikh Bedreddin | 1359-1419 | Ottoman minister of justice and education - rebel |
| | | |
| Sinaneddin Yusuf Paşa | ?-? | Beylerbeyi of Rumelia |
| Sitti Hatun | 1435-1486 | Wife of Mehmed II and daughter of Süleyman, from Dulkadir Emirate in southeast Anatolia |
| | | |
| Şücaeddin İlyas Bey | ?-1421 | MenteşeBey |
| Süleyman Çelebi | ?-1411 | Son of Bayezid I |
| Süleyman I | 1495-1566 | Ottoman Sultan (1520-66) also known as Süleyman the Lawgiver or Süleyman the Magnificent |
| | | |
| Süleyman Paşa | 1316-1360 | Son of Orhan Gazi |
| Süleyman Şah | ?-? | Son of Mehmed of Aydın Emirate |
| Sultan Abdullah | ?-1481 | Son of Bayezid II |
| Sultan Mustafa | 1451-1474 | Son of Mehmed II, brother of Cem Sultan |
| | | |
| Sultan Şah Hatun | ?-? | Sister of Mehmed, son of Aydın |
| | | |
| Taceddin the Kurd | 14<sup>th</sup> c. | *Müderris* |
| Tacü'n-nisa or Taj al-Nisa Hatun | 15<sup>th</sup> c. | Wife of Murad II first, then of İshak Paşa |

| amerlane | 1336-1405 | Timur Lenk: Mongol Conqueror of Asia |
| heodora | c. 500-548 | Byzantine Empress (527-48), wife of Justinian I |
| orlak Kemal | 14th c. -1416-19 | rebel |
| akup Bey | ?-after 1483 | commander of Mehmed II and teacher of Cem Sultan |
| akup Çelebi | ?-1389 | Son of Murad I, brother of Bayezid I |
| avukluoğlu (Yoğurtluoğlu) Mehmed Bey | 15<sup>th</sup> c. | A local potentate at Tire |

# FURTHER READING

AKURGAL, E., *The Art and Architecture of Turkey*, Oxford, 1980.

ALDERSON, A. D., *The Structure of the Ottoman Dynasty*, Oxford, 1956.

ANHEGGER, R., *Beiträge zur frühosmanischen Baugeschichte*, İstanbul, 1953.

ARIK, O., *Turkish Art and Architecture*, Ankara, 1985.

ASLANAPA, O., *Türkische Fliesen und Keramik in Anatolien*, İstanbul, 1965.

ASLANAPA, O., *Turkish Art and Architecture*, London, 1971.

ASLANAPA, O., *İznik Tile Kiln Excavations Part I*, Istanbul, 2000.

ATASOY, N.; RABY, J., *Iznik, The Pottery of Ottoman Turkey*, London, 1994.

BABİNGER, F., *Mehmet the Conqueror and His Time* (tr. From German by R. Manheim), Princeton, 1978.

BRANDENBURG, D., *Die Madrasa, Ursprung, Entwicklung, Ausbreitung und künsterische Gestaltung der Islamischen Moschee-Hochschule*, Graz, 1978.

CAHEN, Cl., Pre-Ottoman Turkey, New York, 1968.

CAHEN, Cl., *La Turquie pré-Ottomane*, 1988.

CARSWELL, J., *Iznik Pottery*, London, 1998.

ÇAĞMAN, F.; ATASOY, N., *Turkish Miniature Painting*, Istanbul, 1974.

DEMİRALP, Y., *Erken Dönem Osmanlı Medreseleri (1300-1500)*, Ankara, 1999.

DEMİRİZ, Y., *Osmanlı Mimarisinde Süsleme I (Erken Devir 1300-1453)*, Istanbul, 1973.

EVLİYA EFENDİ (EVLİYA ÇELEBİ), *Narrative of Travels in Europe, Asia and Africa in the 17th Century* (tr. By J. Von Hammer-Purgstall), 3 vols. London, 1834, 1846 & 1850.

DERMAN, U., *The Art of Calligraphy in the Islamic Heritage*, Istanbul, 1998.

FRISHMAN, M.; KHAN, H., *The Mosque, History, Architectural Development and Regional Diversity*, London, 1997.

GABRIEL, A., *Une Capitale Turque, Brousse (Bursa)*, Paris, 1958.

GIBBONS, H. A., *The Foundations of the Ottoman Empire*, Oxford, 1916.

GOODWİN, G., *A History Ottoman Architecture*, London, 1971.

GOODWİN, G., *The Janissaries*, London, 1994.

GOODWİN, G., *A Guide Edirne*, Istanbul, 1995.

HAMMER-PURGSTALL, Von, *Histoire de l'Empi Ottoman* (tr. From German by J.J. Hellert), 1 vols. Paris, 1835-43.

HİLLENBRAND, R., *Islam Architecture*, Edinburgh 1994.

IBN BATTUTA, *Travels in Asi and Africa 1325-54* (tr. An selected by H.A.R. Gibb London, 1983.

IMBER, C., *The Ottoma Empire, 1300-1481*, 1990

İNALCIK, O.E. -Pitche D., *An Historical Geograph of the Ottoman Empire 1972.

İNALCIK, H., *The Ottoma Empire, The Classical Ag 1300-1600*, London, 1973

İNALCIK, H., *An Econom and Social History of th Ottoman Empire, 1300-160C 2 vols., Cambridge, 1994

JANSSENS, H. F., *I. Battou ta, 'Le Voyageur de l'Islam 1304-63*, 1948.

RITOVOULOS, M., *The History of Mehmet the Conqueror* (tr. By C. T. Riggs), Princeton, 1954.

KURAN, A., *The Mosque in Early Ottoman Architecture*, Chicago, 1968.

KURAN, A.; SÖZEN, M., *Anadolu Medreseleri*, 2 vols., 1969-1972.

KÜHNEL, E., *Die Moschee*, Graz, 1974.

LEMERLE, P., *L'Emirat d'Aydın*, Paris, 1957.

LEVEY, M., *The World of Ottoman Art*, London, 1975.

ÖNEY, G., *Turkish Tile Art*, Istanbul, 1976.

ÖNEY, G., *Anadolu Selçuklu Mimarisinde Süsleme ve El Sanatları*, Ankara, 1978.

ÖNEY, G., *Beylikler Devri Sanatı XIV-XV Yüzyıl (1300-1453)*, Ankara, 1989.

OTTODORN, K., *Das Islamische Iznik*, Berlin, 1941.

ÖZEL, M., ed., *Traditional Turkish Arts*, Istanbul, 1992.

PETERSEN, A., *Dictionary of Islamic Architecture*, London, 1996.

REİNDL, H., *Männer um Bayezid. Eine Prosopographische Studie über die Epoche Sultan Bayezids II (1481-1512)*, 1985.

RESTLE, M., *Istanbul - Bursa, Edirne, İznik*, 1976.

SÖNMEZ, Z., *Başlangıçtan 16. yy'a Kadar Anadolu Türk-İslam Mimarisinde Sanatçılar*, Ankara, 1989.

TAESCHNER, F., *Zünfte und Bruderschaften in Islam*, 1979.

UZUNÇARŞILI, İ. H., *Anadolu Beylikleri*, Ankara, 1998.

ÜNAL, R. H., ed., *Birgi (Tarihi, Tarihi Coğrafyası ve Türk Dönemi Anıtları)*, 2001.

ÜNSAL, B., *Turkish Islamic Architecture in Seljuk and Ottoman Times 1071-1923*, London, 1959.

WİTTEK, P., *Das Fürstentum Mentesche*, 1934.

WİTTEK, P., *The Rise of the Ottoman Empire*, 1938.

WULZİNGER, K.; WİTTEK, P.; SARRE, F., *Das Islamische Milet*, Berlin, 1935.

YETKİN, S. K., *L'architecture Turque en Turquie*, Paris, 1962.

YETKİN, S. K.; ÖZGÜÇ, T., et al, *Turkish Architecture*, Ankara, 1965.

YETKİN, Ş., *Historical Turkish Carpets*, İstanbul, 1981.

ZACHARİADOU, E.A., *Trade and Crusade, Venetian Crete and the Emirates of Menteshe and Aydın (1300-1415)*, Venice, 1983.

# AUTHORS

## Gönül Öney

Gönül Öney graduated from the Faculty of Languages, History and Geography at the University of Ankara in 1955. She joined the academic staff of the same university in 1957. After getting her Ph.D. in History of Art in 1961, she became assistant professor in 1967. She was awarded full professorship in 1972 and she served as professor in the History of Art Department from 1972 to1981.

After 1981, Professor Öney continued her academic career in Ege University in Izmir. She was named Dean of the Faculty of Letters in 1982 and served in that capacity until 199 when she became Deputy Rector of Ege University, a position that she presently holds.

Professor Öney specializes in Turkish-Islamic art and architecture. Her publications include numerous articles and books published abroad in English or German.

She is a member of the "Group of Specialists on Heritage Education" of the Council of Europe and ICOMOS.

## Rahmi H. Ünal

Born in 1937, Professor. Ünal graduated from the Faculty of Letters at Istanbul University in 1959. He joined the academic staff in the History of Art Department of Atatürk University in Erzurum as assistant in 1961. He went to France as a scholar in 1963 to continue his studies in the History of Turkish-Islamic Architectural History. After receiving his Ph.D. from the Faculty of Letters of Sorbonne University, he returned to his previous position at Atatürk University in 1965. He became Associate Professor in 1968 and Full Professor in 1976. Since 1978 he has been Professor of the Faculty of Letters, Ege University. He has written various books and articles on Turkish History and Turkish-Islamic Architectural History. He is currently Head of the History of Art Department.

## Aydoğan Demir

A Lecturer in History, he was born in İzmir in 1938. He graduated from the History Department of the Faculty of Letters at İstanbul University in 1960. He worked as a teacher in Salihli High School from 1960 until 1963 and between 1963 and 1980 he taught in the Institute of Education. He has been working as lecturer in History in Ege University, Faculty of Letters, History and History of Art Departments since 1980. He has published several articles on Ottoman archive documents and on Ottoman tombstones.

## İnci Kuyulu

Born in 1957, she graduated from Hacettepe University, Social and Administrative Sciences Faculty, Department of History of Art in 1980. She received her M.A. degree in 1982 and Ph.D. in 1989. She has since been serving as an assistant professor at the History of Art Department of the Faculty of Letters, Ege University. Her work has been published widely on Turkish and Islamic Art and Architectural Decoration.

## Lale Bulut

Born in 1960, she graduated from Ankara University, Faculty of Languages, History and Geography, Department of History of Art in 1983. She received her M.A. degree in 1987 and Ph.D. in 1991. She has since been serving as an assistant professor at the History of Art and Archaeology Department of the Faculty of Letters, Ege University. Her work has been reproduced in various publications on Turkish Minor Arts.

## Yekta Demiralp

Born in 1959, he graduated from the Faculty of Languages, History and Geography of the University of Ankara, Department of History of Art in 1980. He worked as an art history teacher in Samsun from1981 to1984. He received his M.A. degree in 1990 and Ph.D. in 1997. He is currently serving as an assistant professor at the History of Art Department of the Faculty of Letters, Ege University. He has been involved in various publications on the History of Turkish and Islamic Art and Architecture.

## Şakir Çakmak

Born in 1964, he graduated from Ege University Faculty of Letters, Department of Archaeology and Art History in 1986. He received his M.A. degree in 1991 and his Ph.D. in 1998. He is now a research assistant at the Faculty of Letters, Ege University. He has been involved in various publications on Turkish-Islamic Art and Architectural History.

## Ertan Daş

Born in 1963, he graduated from Ege University, Faculty of Letters, Archaeology and History of Art Department in 1986. He received his M.A. degree in 1998. He is a research assistant in the same department. He is also a professional photographer and is responsible for the photography in this volume.

# ISLAMIC ART IN THE MEDITERRANEAN

This International cycle of Museum With No Frontiers Exhibitions permits the discovery of secrets in Islamic Art, its history, construction techniques and religious inspiration.

## Portugal

IN THE LANDS OF THE ENCHANTED MOORISH MAIDEN: Islamic Art in Portugal. Eight centuries after Christians reconquered their lands from the Muslims, towns of the ancient "Gharb al-Andalus" (western Andalusia) have preserved the Legend of the beautiful enchanted Moorish maiden whose spell was broken by a Christian prince; the artistic route of Muslim presence in Portugal also expresses, through a subtle interdependence between constructive techniques and decorative programs, popular regional architecture. The exhibition gives the visitor a clear view of five centuries of Islamic civilisation (the Caliphate, Mozarabic, Almohade and Mudejar Periods). From Coimbra in the confines of the Algarve, palaces, Christianised mosques, fortifications and cities all of which affirm the splendour of past glories.

## Turkey

EARLY OTTOMAN ART: The Legacy of the Emirates.
Highlighting this exhibition are the works and monuments most representative of the finest period of western Anatolia, the cultural and artistic bridge between European and Asian civilisations. In the 14th and 15th centuries, the transition to a Turkish-Islamic society led artists of the Turkish Emirate to elaborate on a brilliant artistic union culminating in Ottoman art.

## Morocco

ANDALUSIAN MOROCCO: A Discovery in Living Art.
From the beginning of the 8th century, Islamic Moroccans looked beyond the Pillars of Hercules (Gibraltar) and settled in the Iberian Peninsula. From then on, both shores shared the same destiny. From continual cultural, social and commercial exchange animating this extreme of the Maghreb, for more than seven centuries, sprang one of the most brilliant facets of Muslim civilisation. Authentic Hispano-Maghreb art left its stamp not only on resplendent, monumental architecture, but also in the characteristics of the cities and traditions of extreme refinement. The exhibition reflects the historic and social wealth of the Andalusian civilisation in Morocco.

## Tunisia

IFRIQIYA: Thirteen Centuries of Art and Architecture in Tunisia.
Since the 9th century, without breaking with traditions inherited from the Berbers, Carthaginians, Romans and Byzantines, Ifriqiya was able to assimilate and reinterpret influences from Mesopotamia, through Syria and Egypt, and from al-Andalus. This is a unique form of syncretism, of which numerous vestiges prevail even today in Tunisia, from the majestic residences of the Muslim sovereigns in the capital to the architectonic rigor of the "Ibadism of Jerba". The visitor is invited to look at existing *ribats*, mosques, *medinas*, *zawiyas* and *gurfas* (large rooms containing bedroom suites) to witness their imprint on a land abounding with history.

**Spain I**- Andalusia, Aragon, Castilla La Mancha, Castille and Leon, Extremadura, outskirts of Madrid.
MUDEJAR ART: Islamic Aaesthetics in Christian Art.
The art of the Mudejars (Muslim population remaining in Andalusia after the Reconquest) has an unquestionably unique place among all expressions of Islamic art. It deals with the visible manifestation of a splendidly cultured cohabitation with comprehension with a unique understanding between two civilisations that, in spite of their political and religious antagonism, lived a fructiferous artistic romance. Applying schemes, although rigorously Islamic, the Masters of Works and Mudejar artisans, famous for their outstanding knowledge in the art of construction, erected for the newly arrived Christians innumerable palaces, convents and churches. The selected works, chosen for their variety and abundance, testify to the exuberant vitality of Mudejar art.

## Jordan
THE UMAYYADS: The Rise of Islamic Art.
Following the Arab-Muslim conquest of the Middle East, the seat of the Umayyad Dynasty (661-750) was moved to Damascus, where the new capital inherited a cultural and artistic tradition dating back to the Aramaean and Hellenistic Periods. Umayyad culture benefited by this move from the frontier between Persia and Mesopotamia and between the countries of the Mediterranean world. The position was favourable for the emergence of an innovating artistic language, in which the subtle mixture of Hellenistic, Roman, Byzantine and Persian influences, produced architectural order and decorative originality. Through the diversity of the works presented, the exhibition also offers the opportunity to reflect on the Iconoclast phenomena.

## Egypt
MAMLUK ART: The Splendour and Magic of the Sultans.
Under Mamluk domination (1249-1517), Egypt became a prosperous commercial route-crossing centre. Great riches came to the country. Cairo was one of the most powerful, secure and stable cities of the Mediterranean basin. Scholars from all over the world came to settle there, attracting their followers and students. Mamluk architecture and decorative art displays the vitality of commerce, the intellectual energy and the military and religious force of this period. Characterised by elegant and vigorous simplicity, the purity of lines is similar to modern models. The works selected between Cairo, Rosetta, Alexandria and Fua represent the height of Mamluk Art.

## Palestinian Authority
PILGRIMAGE, SCIENCES AND SUFISM: Islamic Art in the West Bank and Gaza.
During the reigns of the Ayyubid, Mamluk and Ottoman Dynasties, numerous pilgrims, from all over the Muslim world came to Palestine. This dynamic tide of religious fervour gave a decisive impulse to the development of *Sufi* thought, through the *zawiyas* and *ribats*, which multiplied all over the country. Various study centres welcomed the most distinguished scholars. In this way, they obtained considerable prestige and conditions became favourable for the expansion of refined art, which conserves its power to fascinate, even today. The monuments and Islamic architecture

proposed for the exhibition clearly reflect these great dimensions of pilgrimages, study and sufism.

## Israel
SHARING THE SACRED: The Secular and Religious Life of Three Civilisations.
The singularity of the Holy Land, where even in case of conflict, always knew how to maintain cultural exchange between the three religions of the Old Testament are here, brought to light in a magnificent way through the Islamic trail. From the arrival of the Muslims in the 7th century during the era of the Crusades, vestiges and architectural monuments display cultural continuity, mixed with manifestations of originality integrating the heritages of the Romans, Byzantines and successive Muslim dynasties.

## Italy - Sicily
ARAB-NORMAN ART: Islamic Culture in Medieval Sicily.
An Island in the middle of the Mediterranean, Sicily is a land of encounter, where various cultures have coincided and adjusted mutually, reaching a new harmony. Unique in the European panorama, Arab-Norman architecture, relatively speaking, is different from that found in the Islamic world. The exhibition presents it from the standpoint of its uniqueness and provides some codes for interpretation permitting better identification. An attentive visitor will better appreciate the admirable fusion of elements, originating from Byzantine, Arab and Norman cultural spheres, employed in this art, which is as original as it is refined.

## Algeria
WATER AND ARCHITECTURE OF THE DESERT: The Mzab Pentapolis.
More than 1000 years ago, 600 km south of Algeria, the Capital, a structured urban nucleus was founded, which with time and the enormous tenacity of its inhabitants, became the present Mzab. The Ibadites settled there in the beginning of the 9th century when it was an inhospitable, extremely arid desert region. Between 1012-1353 they constructed five cities with a sophisticated irrigation system. Inspired by a rigorous philosophy rejecting ostentation and superficiality, Ibadite architecture produced authentic masterpieces of such pureness and so functional in nature that it inspired masters like Le Corbusier. The exhibition permits one to discover the exemplary management of space and water through the history of the Pentapolis.

## Spain II - Catalonia
ISLAM IN CATALONIA: Bisagra Culture in the Border Region.
As a product of the expansion of Carolingian countries toward Islamic Andalusian territories, Catalonia was born on a frontier, in an area where mutual fertilisation of two cultures became evident. The innumerable castles and towers located on the fringes of bordering Islamic territories witnessed not only the conflictive nature of the residents, cultural interchange and reciprocal influences, traces of which are patent in the architecture, gardens and decoration, and also in linguistics and the toponymy and even some popular traditions today. The proposed trail underlines these particulars and shows examples of neo-Arabian architecture such as those produced by the Catalan architect Antonio Gaudi, a renowned architect of the 20th century.